Active Ageing?

Perspectives from Europe on a vaunted topic

Critical Studies
in Socio-Cultural Diversity

Editor-in-Chief: Dr Sara Ashencaen Crabtree

Current and future titles in the same series

Practice Research in Nordic Social Work:
Knowledge production in transition
Edgar Marthinsen and Ilse Julkunen

Rainforest Asylum
The enduring legacy of colonial psychiatric care in Malaysia
Sara Ashencaen Crabtree

Men and Masculinities in Europe (2nd edition)
Keith Pringle, Jeff Hearn, Harry Ferguson,Dimitar Kambourov,
Voldemar Kolga, Emmi Lattu, Ursula Müller, Marie Nordberg, Irina
Novikova,Elzbieta Oleksy, Joanna Rydzewska (Editors)

Diversity and the processes of marginalisation and otherness:
Giving voice to hidden themes
Sara Ashencaen Crabtree (Editor)

The Cup, The Gun and The Crescent:
Social welfare and civil unrest in Muslim societies
Sara Ashencaen Crabtree, Jonathan Parker & Azlinda Azman

For better or worse:
Marriage and family in Sarawak
Hew Cheng Sim (Editor

Active Ageing?
Perspectives from Europe on a vaunted topic

Edited by
María Luisa Gómez Jiménez
& Jonathan Parker

Whiting & Birch
MMXIV

© Whiting & Birch Ltd 2014
Published by Whiting & Birch Ltd,
Forest Hill, London SE23 3HZ

ISBN : 9781861771339

Printed in England and the United States by Lightning Source

Contents

I

Active Ageing?
Perspectives from Europe
on a vaunted topic

Jonathan Parker and María Luisa Gómez Jiménez

Introduction

The year 2012, was designated the European Year of Active Ageing. This book results from a weeklong symposium, held at the University of Málaga in 2012, comprising academics and students from seven European countries exploring and critically analysing the concept of active ageing. The symposium celebrated the contribution that older people make to our societies, whilst being somewhat cautious of over-emphasing the 'active ageing' label and reducing it to a 'Pollyannaish' platitude.

Seminars, workshops and lectures explored, discussed and problematized the concept of active ageing from a range of sociological, psychological, nursing, therapeutic and social work perspectives. The aim of the symposium was to enrich the debate on central social issues connected with older people's needs, keeping in mind that solutions for social problems only result when there is a real felt awareness of the needs and possibilities that our diverse social systems can offer. How individual older people as social actors engage with the world, with each other across the generations, and how cultures, at a micro and macro-level, and psychologies influence these interactions highlights difference and challenges prescriptive panaceas. Yet heterogeneity amongst older people offers opportunities to value different approaches and ways of living and shows us a wider range of preparing for our ageing population and changing world.

In the context of on-going recession and socio-fiscal crisis throughout Europe, addressing the complexities of ageing, and the contemporary European emphasis on active ageing in particular, demands interdisciplinary responses, drawing together different actors, varied and contrasting perspectives and research on the topic of (active) ageing. The concept sometimes belies understanding the issues and caring for today's older people, whilst offering promise to younger generations. This book pulls together key elements of the symposium and interlinks strands of cross-European collaboration that will assist the development of future thought and practice.

Background

The book is timely in addressing issues that stretch across disciplines from medicine, to social care, from environmental design to housing, from politics and economics to philosophy. Ageing affects us all, even if unfortunately some of us do not ourselves age long. Our societies are ageing, we age as individuals and our needs increase in terms of consumption and care, although the rates and levels of need are not, in themselves, a problem of ageing.

In order to prepare for the social, economic and political challenges that are and will arise from individual and population ageing, governments, NGOs and policy makers are struggling to determine novel ways in which we can address new adaptations of Malthus' identification of geometric population increase versus an arithmetical resource increase, and, most fortunately, adding a more humane moral tone to the debate.

In 2002, the World Health Organization developed a policy framework intended to inform discussion and the formulation of global action plans to promote healthy and active ageing at their World Assembly in Madrid, Spain. It is, therefore, fitting that this book should stem from another conference in Spain a decade later.

The World Health Organization (2002) defined active ageing as:

Active ageing is the process of optimizing opportunities for health, participation and security in order to enhance quality of life as people age.

Active ageing applies to both individuals and population groups. It allows people to realize their potential for physical, social, and mental well being throughout the life course and to participate in society according to their needs, desires and capacities, while providing them with adequate protection, security and care when they require assistance. (p. 12)

This definition was interpreted widely. To be active was not taken to relate solely to physical activity but to all types of participation in social, economic, cultural and spiritual activities even with declining energy, health and capability. Whilst identifying the importance of independence this was contextualized, recognizing the social aspects of being human and so emphasized interdependence and autonomy.

The European Year of Active Ageing stressed solidarity between generations as key to securing a future in which people could age well. There were, owing to the challenges faced in late modern society as well as the result of the stranglehold that neoliberal ideologies have on the Western world, economic considerations underpinning this focus. The hitherto untapped economic potential and the possibility of a continuing workforce could be marshaled to confront production and consumption demands, perhaps under the banner of enhancing dignity and worth.

The different approaches that could be taken to the concept of active ageing are likely to reflect different ways of seeing the same thing, all sharing some truths and yet all undergirded by covert ideologies. It is hoped that our symposium and the resulting book offers some illumination of these ideologies so we can take a measured and informed perspective, choosing what we value and why we value it, whilst exploring respectful and dignified ways of negotiating our ageing societies.

A note on language and terminology

Both UK English and US English are used within this volume, as both are commonly used English variants throughout Europe. A variety of terms for older people are also employed reflecting the particular approach of authors. These include elder, senior, and elderly person. Where possible we have chosen to avoid the homogenizing adjective 'the elderly', otherwise we have stayed with author preference.

Structure of the book

The book comprises twelve core chapters from seven European countries. Chapters consider diverse issues broadly relating to active ageing when considering the World Health Organization definition above. Firstly, chapters two to seven examine some of the theoretical and conceptual issues we use to understand ageing in late modern society. These chapters reflect the importance of integrated approaches that do not privilege one theoretical conception above others but help to illuminate different aspects of what ageing means to individuals, families, communities, policy-makers and academics, and politicians. From a theoretical basis, there is an exploration of macro and micro-practice issues in working with older people and ageing issues in society. The chapters recognize the contribution that students can make to the future of human service practice with older people and in relation to our ageing populations and societies. The examples used are wide and varied but not presented as exhaustive; rather they will act as examples of positive contributions to ageing, even when physical and cognitive frailty looms large.

Following this more theoretical excursus, but nonetheless conceptual and informed by theory, chapters eight to twelve offer insights informing and informed by daily practices in social work, therapies, nursing and housing, showing how an emphasis on active ageing, in the round, can help to address some of the needs that arise for the oldest old and for those made vulnerable in society. The concluding chapter explores a core change in the religious make-up of Europe that will impact on our understanding of and approaches to ageing in contemporary European society, Islam and active ageing. This is taken as a concluding chapter because of its pivotal importance in our societies and because of the almost hidden nature of the debate.

The book will be of interest to academics in social and behavioral sciences, and practitioners from social work, housing, psychology, nursing and health care professions as well as policy-makers. No standardized format has been used within the chapters, allowing authors to present their work in the manner felt best to them and also an ideological commitment to diverse knowledges. This reflects a deliberate choice reflecting the variety of presentations, discussions and explorations that took place over the symposium International Week in Málaga in April 2012, and hopefully capturing the particular approaches taken whether from an academic, student or from a practice perspective.

Following our introduction to the original symposium, the concepts we cover under the banner of 'active ageing' guides the structure and outline of the book, and we delineate a two-part structure to the work in which theoretical approaches and practice reflections forge the two sides of the coin we hope to offer to the reader.

Part 1 Theoretical approaches to active ageing: public policies and social issues

The first six chapters explore a variety of theoretical and conceptual approaches to active ageing. There should be a degree of disagreement and edginess to these chapters. Academic debate seeks and articulates 'truths' but moreover relentlessly seeks to overthrow those same 'truths' for more refined versions. It recognises the illusory and contextualised aspect of these truths.

In chapter 2, Jonathan Parker and Sara Ashencaen Crabtree seek to problematize the concept of active ageing through a theoretical journey into the sociologies of ageing. The use of these theories in social work practice is explored.

In their chapter they argue that the application of sociological theories often presents great challenges to practitioners in many fields of human practice, particular social work. Sometimes the explicit use of theories is actively avoided in social work with many practitioners protesting that they do not see their relevance because, they claim, social work is a practical job. Others simply position theories as college-based rites of passage to which, once completed, they do not need to, nor should, return. Parker and Ashencaen Crabtree argue that some social workers espouse an anti-intellectualism that fails to understand that all practice is based upon an understanding of the world whether that be local, at a personal level, an agency adopted and tacit approach, a procedural or legislatively prescribed model, rather than a more formal, recognised method of practising social work. However, their argument is that if social workers are to practise effectively they must develop understanding grounded in knowledge and theories of what might be happening in the situations in which they find themselves.

The chapter introduces the context of contemporary social work practice with older adults following which the practical relevance of social gerontological theories. The use and development of active ageing approaches is critiqued in politico-economic terms and problematised within human service delivery, demanding revision in social work in culturally nuanced and individualised ways.

Gabriele Schäfer take forward similar issues but from a different perspective in chapter 3 and address psychological theories of successful ageing. Schäfer states that many countries across the world are experiencing increasingly ageing populations. These countries range from those with western cultures such as America and the members of the European Union to those with eastern cultures such as Japan. There is growing concern about the various impacts that ageing populations are having in these countries.

The problem is highly complex as Schäfer points out. For example, an ageing population can be a burden on the health care system but there are also positive effects of ageing. Studies have shown that even late in life, potential exists for physical, mental, and social development. Also, the economic demands on older people are many and a simple reduction in numbers causes a wide range of problems.

Schäfer's chapter explores a number of psychological theories of successful ageing and considers factors such as gender, cultural heritage and migration.

In chapter 4, *Ageing in Developing Countries: Challenges and Solutions* Urtė Lina Orlova and Egle Sumskiene from Lithunia reflect further on the unique challenges of ageing populations. As they state, population ageing at the level we now see is unprecedented, a process without parallel in the history of humanity. Alongside this, the pace of population ageing is faster and the numbers greater in developing countries than in developed countries. Whilst the percentages of older persons are significantly greater in the more developed regions, the number of older people is increasingly in the less developed regions leading to deep social, economic, political and health-based challenges. From the middle of the 20th century, the number of people aged 60 or older increased globally by an average of 8 million persons every year. Of this increase, 66 percent occurred in the less developed regions and 34 percent in the more developed regions. As a result, the proportion of the world's population over 60 living in the less developed regions rose from slightly over half (54 per cent) in 1950 to 62 per cent in the year 2000. By 2050, nearly four fifths of the world's older population will be living in the less developed regions (UN 2009). The economic challenge is clear given that currently, older people and their young dependents make up a substantial and growing proportion of the poor in developing countries and, of course, these people are least able to escape chronic poverty in the contemporary neoliberal world. Older people are also more likely to have chronic illnesses and diseases, they face severe constraints to gain and income upon which to survive. The survival of children and older people in times of crisis is strongly linked. Alongside this, in the context of the HIV and AIDS pandemic, older people are paradoxically put into care situations. They are now responsible for care of an estimated 60% of orphans and vulnerable children (UNICEF 2003).

The fast ageing of populations around the world is presenting challenges for developed and developing countries. Orlova and Sumskiene indicate that these include (WHO 2011):

+ strains on pension and social security systems;
+ increasing demand for health care;
+ bigger need for trained-health workforce in gerontology;
+ increasing demand for long-term care, particularly in dealing with dementia;
+ the raising of pervasive ageism that denies older people the rights and opportunities available for other adults.

They explore how some of these challenges can be counteracted by implementing the World Health Organization measures (WHO 2011):

+ Ensuring that older population have a basic level of financial security
+ Developing age-friendly environments
+ Availability and accessibility of effective health care
+ Maintaining social patterns that influence the well-being of older adults

María Luisa Gómez Jiménez discusses *Housing for Seniors: an overview of policies and challenges for an active aging in place in Spain* in chapter 5. In her chapter Gómez Jiménez describes the main public policies regarding seniors and how public law can influence the strategies develop specially regarding the provision of proper housing for seniors. Her analysis of the public issues connects with the economic crisis, and the distribution of jurisdictions and legislative capabilities that allow for a better approach in terms of the challenges that public authorities face when promoting active ageing.

Gómez Jiménez discusses the Spanish housing market, in the aftermath of the burst of the housing bubble. The orientation of new models of occupancy and facing new family models are a reality which contrast with the typology of housing provision for seniors (not just assisted living facilities but special housing adapted to their needs.) This in contrast with an 'active ageing in place' trend which will demand in the future the definition of a new affordability for the new 'seniors housing zoning',

In chapter 6 Cornelia Kricheldorff explores the concept of 'geragogy', an integrated model of learning for older people designed to enhance and expand possibilities for integration and social participation.

Postmodern life means to live in an atmosphere of continuous change, fast paced with rapid development and movement. Ageing, in this context, is seen as part of a process of individualization and faded traditionalism, which means that constantly continued adaptation to the nuances of contemporary life is necessary. As a result, Kricheldorff purports that older people are forced to keep their connections with culture, economics and their environment by learning so they must also keep up their educational abilities. Using the underlying concepts of risk society, she states that because of the changes in society and social environments, older people are required to continue their efforts in learning and taking over responsibility for their own circumstances of life, for instance, by analyzing their conceptions of life and planning new strategies. In this sense, education contributes to ensuring integration into society by enabling older people to equal participation. Therefore educational gerontology has the strategic key-task to design the collective aging-process in the sense of a development which offers a richer and more human quality of life. This concerns also the building and renewal of identity, and the development of meaningful roles and tasks that make a life in social solidarity and relatedness possible. Kricheldorff believes that geragogy has emphasized the central importance of educational gerontology since its inception and represents a clear means of facilitating active ageing amongst the current old in society.

Jaap Olthof, in chapter 7, considers Europe's ageing, which, as statistics indicate, has happened rapidly, from the perspective of the Netherlands. He describes how after an era of astonishing growth in the world's population, we are seeing currently on a global level a delaying demographic growth. Compared to global figures, the Netherlands is inhabited by a relatively young population nevertheless, perhaps building on global fears of ageing and the negative conceptions it has raised, Dutch politics claim ageing to be a 'societal disease' and we find their statements often flavoured by a pejorative approach towards ageing. These negative images of ageing emphasise the limits for social security, health and welfare and an inevitable change of social solidarity which is envisaged in a redesign of the social welfare state after decades of economic liberalization. In the context of the rise of globalisation and neoliberal market philosophies, Olthop states that, since the 1980s, the Dutch have transformed their universalistic welfare state into a neo-liberal welfare state model and zero in on maximum efficiency and cutting down costs.

Part 2 Community, social and health practices with older people

Part 1 explored the theoretical and conceptual underpinnings recognising the malleability of these, and the second part of the book applies some of these concepts in ways developed to help and assist vulnerable people to age well. We know social and human service practices will change that the evidence upon which practices are based is contextualised in history and society, dependant on political and economic conditions and will develop over time. However, our application of practices assists in those developments, hopefully making the former more appropriate for those receiving them.

In the next contribution, chapter 8, Jonathan Parker describes a small scale group project developing and delivering reminiscence work with people with dementia and undertaken by social work students as part of their practice learning experiences. The potential for enhancing the student learning experience and additional benefits for staff and group participants are explored and the limitations of the study critiqued. Findings indicated that students and staff gain mutual benefits from such projects which also have the potential to create possibilities for the enhancement of service delivery. The project stemmed from a desire and objective to ensure the sustainability of reminiscence work as part of an earlier cross-European comparison of the use of volunteers in working with people with dementia. However, sustainability issues require careful planning and thought. The study highlights the need for the participation of all stakeholders, especially those who are marginalised, in developing and undertaking groupwork.

In chapter 9, Lenka Maťhová and Zuzana Staffová describe the development of *Canistherapy in Nursing Homes in the Czech Republic. They define* canistherapy as a method of rehabilitation that has its own specific place in the panoply of comprehensive rehabilitation care for older people who are vulnerable and especially those experiencing some degree of cognitive decline or dementia. According to Maťhová and Staffová canistherapy improves the physiological, psychological and social lives of clients whilst having a positive effect overall on the quality of life of older people in nursing homes. Maťhová and Staffová argue that professional implementation of canistherapy, which includes careful planning and training for canistherapeutic teams, is the basic requirement for accepting this approach as an effective and successful therapy.

Katrien Meireman and Elke Plovie rehearse again the rise in older people throughout Europe, stating that when we take a close look at European societies, it is clear that the proportion of older people in societies is increasing. In 2060, 30% of the EU-population will be older than 65 years old, what that means is that one out of three persons of the 517 million estimated people in Europe will be 65 years or older. Writing about the Belgian context, Meireman and Plovie state that in 1920 only 10% of the Belgian population was older than 65 years, whilst it is now almost one in five. By 2060 this will have risen again to one out of four.

Meireman and Plovie identify several challenges in the changing demographic of Belgium; especially, how do we organize social concerns such as housing and care? Which roles can older people take in society and how should we support them in that? How can we manage government spending on pensions and health care? Their chapter considers these questions in the context of the 2012 European year of active ageing and solidarity between generations. They begin their discussion from a competence perspective on older people, with an emphasis on enjoying life and living independently.

In chapter 11 Andrea Piflsfestorge explores the use of biographical methods drawing on a particular nursing care/social work approach developed in Austria: the Böhm concept. Exploring the biographical method, Piflsfestorge used a case study of the *Haus St. Elisabeth,* a retirement home run by Caritas St. Pölten/Austria.

She describes the theory and method of Böhm's work and how it has been used in teaching students to use it in their learning. Piflsfestorge locates this in the context of active ageing and as a positive method to share.

María Luisa Gómez Jiménez, in chapter 12, examines Spanish public policies and practices for older people and sets them within the context of the European initiatives on active ageing. Gómez Jiménez explores both local and regional public bodies and paints a picture of complexity in contemporary Spain.

The chapter describes the practices of Spanish Town Halls and Regional Government developed to promote active ageing. She offers some cases examples from the Town Hall of Málaga and the Junta de Andalusia as a means of exemplifying the present situation and offering some alternatives.

In our final contribution, Ashencaen Crabtree and Parker illuminate religiously informed values and practice values; in addition to considering types of professional intervention that complement the generalized characteristics of Muslim elders. This is a topic that is infrequently broached or dealt with and yet the growing number of Muslim elders demands that we seek appropriate responses in the social and health care professions.

This chapter discusses some of the cultural disjunctures inherent in contemporary European society, and sets the scene for an understanding of Islam, the needs of Muslim elders and their families and their cherished values, ensuring the corporate and familial are not lost in our atomized society.

The book is offered as a disparate collection of narratives, theoretical and practical that offer perspectives on an important aspect of our current social life, ageing. The book offers ways forward but does so in a way that seeks resonances with the reader rather than promoting prescribed ways of engaging our diverse public. This we believe is the right way to move forward, especially when the promotion of active ageing represents such a diverse, multi-faceted and individualized concept.

The book leaves us with a range of questions. Active and healthy ageing starts not as we become older people or seniors in our society but when we are born, or even before conception. How should societies assist and support us in our health and active ageing? How much of our liberty should we offer to policy-makers, practitioners and governments to protect our health? Questions of individual versus corporate responsibilities abound and perhaps represent core questions that need to be tackled as we move forward.

2

Problematising active ageing: A theoretical excursus into the sociology of ageing for social work practice

Jonathan Parker & Sara Ashencaen Crabtree

Introduction

Active ageing represents a socio-political concept of the moment. As with many such concepts, policy and practices often overtake rigorous critique or evaluation and intelligent well-meaning people attach themselves to a bandwagon that reflects a political, philosophical or value-position but does not always derive from well thought through and tested analysis – theoretical or practical. Sociologists have, at times, allied themselves with ideas and thoughts that construct binary distinctions, allied with Manichean-type value positions (see Ashencaen Crabtree and Parker in this volume) and tribal positions that require us to stand back and reflect, which is what we intend to do in this chapter.

In respect of social work, the explicit use of theories is sometimes actively avoided, with social workers protesting that they do not see their relevance in what they claim are 'commonsense' and practically applied acts aimed at the rather elusive, contested and political concept 'making a difference'. This reflects an anti-intellectualism that pervades much public service work. It is something that fails to acknowledge that all social work practice – good or bad - must be based upon particular understandings of the world at personal, social or political levels, whether using procedural or legislatively prescribed models, or more formal, recognised methods of practising social work (Parker and Bradley, 2010; Parker, 2012). Social work with older people has not been a priority of policy-makers, workforce planners and academics. As such, a further block exists in developing the theoretical base as fully as other areas of practice.

Despite this anti-theoretical perspective, social workers need theories and models to guide their actions and to provide explanatory frameworks that make effective interventions possible if they are to make a positive difference in people's lives. In doing so, they contribute to ethical, evidence-based and accountable practice (McDonald, 2010).

This chapter will introduce the context of contemporary social work practice with older adults following which the practical relevance of social gerontological theories will be explored at micro, mezzo and macro levels as an example of the many ways in which theories impact on contemporary practice. The use and development of active ageing approaches will be critiqued in politico-economic terms and problematised within human service delivery, demanding revision in social work in culturally nuanced and individualised ways.

The term 'ageing' is contested and its arbitrariness can itself problematise ageing. Ageing is performed differently according to historical, political and socio-economic conditions. So, the older person in the UK may be markedly different chronologically from the older person in Laos, Cambodia, Vietnam. However, from an experiential perspective, it is certain that the older we get, we have increased health and social care needs and, concomitantly, we also tend to use more services, although this may be significantly concentrated into the latter parts of our lives, notably end of life. In respect of social work with older people, a varied range of other social divisions and categories impact on the ageing experience – gender, sexuality, ethnicity, religion, health, geographical location, social support, living arrangements and so forth. Given this complex context, it is clear that a robust understanding of theory, at a range of levels, is important (Wilson et al., 2008).

The relevance of theory

Theories are especially relevant to social work practice as they provide frameworks for understanding the complex and fluid situations of people who use services. They also have the potential to inform and improve practice by suggesting what could be done in specific situations (Trevithick, 2005; Parker, 2007a; 2008; Parker and Bradley, 2010). The concept of theory is explanatory and predictive, and may be defined at three levels, all of which are important in working with and understanding older people:

+ Grand theories (macro-level) theories that seek to establish global explanations, such as Marxism which could be used to understand some of the ways in which economically unproductive older people are marginalised in late-Capitalist societies)

+ Mid-range (mezzo-level) theories, which concern particular phenomena such as bereavement and loss, cycles of disadvantage, attachment, moral panics and so on. As ageing is associated, sometimes erroneously, with health concerns, economic disadvantage, bereavement amongst other social states, theoretical understanding at this level is important for social workers to negotiate through these.

+ Lower level or micro-theories (which articulate specific approaches to practice; 'how to do' theories); the theories or approaches that social workers often tend to see as most relevant but sometimes become enslaved to not seeing other level theories as offering different and sometimes alternative perspectives (Parker, 2012).

What is important to remember, of course, is that the lens through which we understand and apply these theories are coloured and ground by socio-cultural nuances and received wisdom, they are not *a priori* statements of the world. As a result, the ways in which they are received by older people engaging with social work services are refracted by the lens of their local conditions as much as by a shared characteristic such as chronology, social need or health condition.

Demographic challenges

The dramatic global population increase and ageing is central to social work and social policy initiatives. Powell (2010) suggests that predictions indicate an annual net gain of people over 65 years in excess of 10 million. United Nations figures posit a more rapid increase in developing rather than developed countries, 140% compared with 51%, respectively, from 2006 to 2030 (Krug, 2002). Population Trends (2004) indicates that the actual number and percentage of older people, in the UK, in the older age brackets is also rising. For instance, in 2011 it is estimated that there are 4.7 million people over the age of 75 years, 7.7% of the population and 41% of the older population (those over retirement age), whereas in 2031 this is estimated to rise to 7.7 million over 75 years, 11.9% of the population and 50% of people of retirement age. There is great economic diversity amongst these people. For those people living alone and dependent on state benefits, 42% of their income is spent on housing, fuel and food costs, whereas the 56% of 65 years and over owner-occupiers with no mortgage own 80% of the UK's wealth.

Whilst populations are ageing across Europe, the rates of population growth are significantly increased in other parts of the world. Comparing the percentage projected increase between 2000 and 2030 indicates this in respect of Europe and Southeast Asia.

Table 1

Population ageing in selected countries in Southeast Asia and Europe

| | Proportion of population over 60yrs (%) | | | | Increase in older people (65+) 2000-2030 |
	1970	1980	1990	2006	
Singapore	5.7	7.2	8.4	13	372
Malaysia	5.5	5.7	5.8	7	277
Thailand	4.9	5.2	6.3	11	197
Germany	19.9	19.3	20.4	25	63
France	18.1	17.2	19.1	21	56
United Kingdom	18.7	20.1	21.1	21	54

Source: adapted from Arifin and Ananta (2009)

Changes in the world's demography have important ramifications for social work with older people across the world, and demand a reinterpretation of what social work is and what it can offer, whether that is community action in developing countries, policy development across the world, or the more individualised approaches of care management in developed nations (Fu and Hughes, 2009). The economic challenges for social expenditure, pensions, for the maintenance of the workforce and for population replenishment come to the fore as the balance tips in favour of older rather than younger groups (Bengtson and Lowenstein, 2004); as do the health needs arising from increased longevity, and the socio-emotional needs arising from increased family disruption and reconstitution and multiple losses (Wilson et al., 2008). Changes in migratory patterns also create specific needs and demands as immigrant communities age, and cultures evolve. If social workers are to respond to these trends they need to take account of the theoretical understandings available within the core underpinning discipline of sociology.

Gerontological theories of ageing

Gerontology concerns the study of ageing across the lifespan although it is most often associated with older age. This in itself is important, as it locates the older person within a social and cultural context in which the dynamics of ageing are played out, and considers the needs of older people holistically alongside neonates, children, young people, young and older adults. If social workers keep this in mind they are more likely to avoid the risks of separating one group for special treatment on the basis of an arbitrary social division.

Gerontology, as a life-course discipline, therefore, recognises a diverse range of approaches to the concept of ageing. These are sometimes conflictual, and are often politicised by social and personal constructions made within the context of the theorist and student (McDonald, 2010). As Phillips et al. (2006) state, gerontological theory concerns the study of ageing from biological, psychological and sociological perspectives. In social work it is the theories from sociology, social policy and psychology that predominate but history, anthropology and economics are also significant. Hendricks and Powell (2009) argue that theory and theorising are central to erecting the scaffolding on which to drape conceptual and perceptual understandings of ageing since theories move beyond empirical observations of the 'what' to relational understandings of the 'why'. In a similar vein, Putney et al. (2005) suggest that social gerontology may be a model for promoting sociological theory as a social and civic good, something that is central to social work practice, that indicates how theories have their place in enhancing the lives of older people. The local conceptions of theory are important to remember here. Indigenous social work practices will construct theoretical approaches that share traits at times as more distant relatives than close kin (see Ling, 2004; 2007).

Within the literature, social gerontological theories are often described in chronological fashion perhaps reflecting an instrumental and somewhat naïve approach to lifecourse, although Putney et al. (2005) suggests also there was a move from the 'grand narratives' of functionalist disengagement theories to more individuated approaches. For instance, Bengtson et al. (1997) separates the linear chronology into a series of ages or shifts in thinking. However, these models can also be conceptualised in more traditional theoretical terms as macro, mezzo, and micro level theories (Penhale and Parker, 2008), or structural, professional and interpersonal approaches (Lymbery, 2005). This allows us to avoid the pitfalls of privileging a progressive discourse that not only suggests theories are improving in their explanatory power but also dismisses the value of previous theorising. A consideration of theory by level permits viewing by explanatory breadth, and critically to consider theories that others may reject simply for being out of fashion or themselves 'old'. Powell and Hendricks (2009), analysing critical social gerontological theories, recognise four core themes which interweave the macro, mezzo and micro explanatory levels. Economic and political theories influence the global world and policy assumptions and developments, but theories also recognise the impact of power imbalances and how groups are theorised according to reproductive capacities, youthfulness and currently privileged aspects productivity. This leads, for instance, to gender inequalities at all levels including age. Individual approaches to ageing have become atomised and subject to understanding through 'masks' reflecting the disjunctures between external appearances and internal subjectivities as seen within cosmetic surgery, bio-technologies and lifestyle choices. Indeed, technologies of cosmeticisation allow for the continual recreation of the self within developed and economically prosperous contexts, whilst increased surveillance (Foucault, 1977) through assistive technologies alters the nature of the experience of social care (see Parker, 2005) in which personal identities and self-worth are diminished.

Biomedical approaches to ageing

Biological and medical approaches to ageing in developed countries have credence in the increased longevity people enjoy and advances in reducing infant and maternal mortality, leading to a reduction in the birth rate and, subsequently, monumental changes in demography as seen earlier. In the Western world, theories of ageing from bio-medical perspectives also reflect anxieties concerning individual mortality and its association with the physical and overt processes of ageing. The study of biological ageing can be further separated into specific areas such as cellular ageing, genetic and evolutionary theories, stochastic theories that concern the build up of physical, environmental and life-style insults over time (Sauvain-Dugerdil et al., 2006).

In social work circles there has been an almost universal rejection of a purely bio-medical approach to ageing, partly because of a tendency to associate the older person solely with physical and mental decline, 'biological reductionism' (Biggs, 1993), and partly because of a 'tribal identity' preference amongst social workers for social models. There are problems, however, in rejecting biological perspectives because of a misplaced emphasis on and uncritical acceptance of social models. The experiences and problems associated with disease, illness and physical decline in old age should not be minimised or dismissed. Also, there are clear social work needs arising from these situations. For instance, the older person who falls at night may not only be at risk of injury and broken bones but may risk losing the ability to cook, shop or even remain in their own home, therefore demanding an integrated, rather than tribal response from services, that is centred around the person's needs. Biological, decremental decline approaches to ageing are not necessarily the predominant ones for social workers who would not wish to define older people simply in terms of illness and disease categories. There is a need, however, to have a sound understanding of bio-physiological changes, such as age-related sensory change, and indeed expected psychological changes such as in cognitive processes, in order to distinguish between those aspects of ageing that one may expect and those that require further investigation and/or assistance, which might include social work.

Sociological approaches to ageing

Sociological perspectives on ageing at the macro-level have also focused on decline and loss. Cumming and Henry (1961) focused on the functional tasks of disengagement from active (political and economic) social life as a preparation for the new generation and for the older person's inevitable decline and, ultimately, death. This approach failed to consider the politico-economic ramifications of the thesis, but saw the process as helping to preserve a functional social consensus and transition of social power (McDonald, 2010). A cultural critique was also missed by uncritically accepting the models developed within Western societies that were influenced by atomised, fragmented societies and the developing assumed economic hegemony and its imperatives. They also ignored the social and cultural imperatives of traditional societies making the (false) assumption that person-centred rather than community-focused approaches are necessarily preferred within civil society (Jared, 2013). However, simply because these theories have fallen out of vogue does not mean they can easily be ignored. Social workers may often fall into the trap of privileging those theories and models of understanding that are assumed to be in the ascendance without engaging with them critically or searching out the many nuanced variations and contradictions found in the messier worlds of practice. For instance, one may find a number of older people who actively seek to disengage from many prior roles and functions within their families and communities, but this may be a rational, individually and socially-determined choice. Whilst acknowledging some degree of socio-political influence on such disengagement and withdrawal, social workers would also understand this to be wider than the simple adoption of a system of normative social belief.

Role and activity theories also derive from mid-twentieth century functionalist sociologies and focus on those roles and behaviours associated with specific ages. These theories are most closely associated with Havighurst and Albrecht (1953) and Lemon et al. (1972). The focus on roles, stages and distinct changes and a shifting of power across generations was consonant with sociological theory at the time and reflected an understanding of society that could be associated with the eu-functionality of social systems; the maintenance of good order, preservation of functioning and competence, and also with individualised concepts of 'successful ageing' which discount social and cultural diversity and, whilst assumed to be universal, tended to privilege the settings in which they developed. However, these approaches, termed by Bengtson et al. (1997) as first generation gerontological theories, still have relevance for social workers if they are understood as 'seeing through a glass, darkly' (1 Corinthians 13 v. 11); they do not show the full picture. These functionalist theories, however, underpin the operations of policy-makers throughout the Western world (Johns, 2010), and elsewhere, e.g. Southeast Asia (Arifin and Ananta, 2009). Ageing has been conceptualised as a time of decline and increasing need, even burden, by policy planners, health and social care professions and the general public. Negotiating the policy and legislative landscape requires engagement with these ideas, some of which may be considered antithetical to, or at least to sit in tension with, social work and its espoused values (although we must accept these too are not absolute but are culturally bound and interpreted). Although driven by concepts of 'burden' and the pathologisation of older people and their experiences (see Parker, 2005; Phillips et al., 2006), there is another side to the functionalist approach which is to understand how the component parts of society works together as a whole and how it continues to function. All social workers have a role in ensuring the good functioning of society and its maintenance (Davies, 1998). This is especially the case in the UK since the majority of qualified practitioners work for local government and other employers who fulfil statutory obligations for the state. So, we cannot dismiss this group of theories simply on the basis of political preference or 'anti-oppressive' sensitivities. Bearing in mind the context of ageing, the importance of societal functioning and community cohesion as we strive to tackle some of the challenges of ageing, it is interesting to consider how social workers may be instrumental in driving forward the 'active ageing' agenda currently championed.

Towards active ageing

Active ageing approaches, in part, represent macro-economic theories which underpin many of the social and health policies that drive social work and welfare across the world. However, the ways in which these are operationalised within the structures of social work organisations or in bespoke plans for individuals favour mezzo and micro level actions, and are often understood in terms of individual leisure or health behaviours (see Bowling, 2008). The term was introduced by the World Health Organization in the 1990s (WHO, 2002), and can be defined as:

> ... the process of enhancing the quality of life of older persons by optimising the opportunities for their health, participation, and self-fulfilment. (Ananta and Arifin, 2009, p. 25)

The concept of active ageing as a means of encouraging participation in social, political and economic life has global attraction (Cloos et al., 2010; Du and Yang, 2010; Ervik et al., 2006; Perek-Bialas et al., 2008; Piekkola, 2006). Contemporary theories of active ageing, have been employed in Southeast Asia to address the economic imperatives associated with an increasing ageing population (Ananta and Arifin, 2009), whilst recognising that making people happier and healthier through active ageing represents an end in itself. In Indonesia, Rahardjo et al. (2009) explored the concept of active ageing positively in a context in which there are few opportunities for older people but a growing economic need as the country ages. The need for active ageing policies is also evident in high income countries. Gultiano and Agustin (2009) identify the intergenerational imperatives of active ageing in the Philippines, recognising that focusing on the education, career choice, health and reproductive behaviour of younger women is likely to promote healthier, active lifestyles that will continue into old age. Active ageing needs to be considered in the context in which ageing is a mediator in the ways in which resources and services are allocated or denied (Mayhew, 2005; Ney, 2005), and in relation to other social variables such as gender (Lie et al., 2009; Venn and Arber, 2011). A focus on active ageing policies is likely to have positive economic consequences and allow countries to target need and social work resources more effectively.

The ways in which these approaches are understood, with their focus on macro-economics played out in the lives of individuals, indicates a need for clarity. For social workers, these theories are important in considering future services and resource allocation and call for an understanding of localised, nuanced approaches at the micro-level which address the individual's experiences of ageing. The confluence of these two – the macro social and economic imperatives of the World Health Organisation and Governments and concern for the individual in this world – represent an important site for social work practice. Individual social work is possible in this context because of the global emphasis on ageing as a challenge for political, economic and social life and the needs that arise, but individual change and behaviour is also likely to influence these global-structural models. There is a need to consider the interaction of the global and individual emphases and to model the mutual construction of new ways of addressing issues that impact on the local and global environments. Social workers are part of this construction.

The emphasis placed on economic, as well as social, productivity in active ageing (OECD, 1998) is, perhaps, indicative of the global spread of neoliberal market ideologies, although the World Health Organisation also emphasises quality of life issues (WHO, 2002). Walker (2009) is mindful that the concept allows a range of policy initiatives to be hidden within it, recognising the difference between European emphases on health, participation and well-being and a more US discourse that privileges economic productivity. Moving from the dependency discourse created by older people's association with the Welfare State has been important in developing the active ageing discourse. Whilst Walker laments that this still needs reflecting in the outworkings of the EU policy process, it may also be said that the same is necessary within social work practice.

An important critique to functionalist approaches, however, has come from critical gerontologists who challenge the existing structural frameworks, policy directions and social institutions constructed around ageing. This has led to the development of theories of the political economy of ageing and feminist gerontologies amongst others. Hendricks and Powell (2009, pp. 6-7) recognise that 'scholarly progress occurs ... within the penumbra of certified professional knowledge' and that critical social gerontology provides new ways of understanding the relations between personal identity and structures.

Also, associated with active ageing are the more radical political economy approaches, associated predominantly in the UK with Phillipson's (1982) social constructionist approach and with Estes and colleagues' (2001) 'ageing enterprise' in the US. Putney et al. (2010) highlight that these more radical approaches hark back to functionalist roots and age stratification theories which seek to identify the similarities and differences between age cohorts and through history, considering the interdependence of age cohorts and social structures (see Parsons, 1942). However, it is the neo-Marxist, conflict theory roots of this approach that are most commonly identified, understanding the dialectical relationship between older people and capitalism as creating the socio-political problems associated with ageing. Political economy theories draw attention to the ways in which politico-economic forces in society, and indeed globally, act to determine the allocation of social resources to ageing groups on the basis of that social division especially. Older people, it is claimed, represent a drain on resources and do not contribute to them and, therefore, inequalities and problem focused social policies result by those in power who privilege economic productivity (Phillipson and Smith, 2005). It is important for social workers approaching ageing through this lens to consider how older people fare differently according to education, employment, welfare and health policies; how these are influenced by and influence economic trends, and how social structures impact on and construct predominantly negative perceptions of ageing (Bytheway, 1995). This can provide social workers with alternative understandings of the experiences of older people and develop challenges to uncritical acceptance of (potentially) organisationally-preferred functionalist gerontologies. The homogenisation of older people within the political economy macro-theory is more subtly nuanced, however, with different experiences according to the levels of economic, cultural, social and individual capital that older people enjoy (Gilleard and Higgs, 2005). McDonald (2010) draws our attention to the differential experiences of older people across a range of social categories and divisions and shaped by history, demography, geography and so forth.

Subjectivities and biographies

From the 1970s, a 'second generation' of social gerontological theories evolved (Bengtson et al, 1997) that focused more on subjectivities and micro-level understandings. These included exchange theories across generations and considering individual resources and capital building on Homans' (1961) rational choice theory and theories deriving from symbolic interactionism (Mead, 1967). With theoretical refinement, a further generation of social gerontology has developed, much of which relates to the subjectivities that inform late modernity in Western nations (Giddens, 1991).

Socio-cultural ideologies, identity theories and life course and biographical approaches represent sociological theories that often intersect with psychological approaches, although Powell and Hendricks (2009) recognise the interplay between theories of human agency, including narrative and biography, and global-structural theories. These are also theories with which social workers, in the West especially, will be familiar in other forms or applications. Indeed, Giddens' (1991) 'reflexive project of the self' is not dissimilar to much thinking in contemporary Western social work which focuses on the life course development of the self in relation to biographies, history, experiences and contexts (Hockey and James, 2003). The self as a project can adapt to or mask the socio-political debilitations of ageing (Ogg, 2003; Biggs, 1999). To an increasing extent, global ageing selves are experienced and re-created in a rapidly changing set of socio-political and economic conditions. In the UK, this can be seen in recent White Papers and policy papers focusing on independence, choice and the individual. Phillips et al. (2006) state that biographical approaches, in fact, bring together gerontological and social work theory because they capture the sum of older people's experiences within their historically developing ecological contexts. This considers uniqueness, connectedness, continuities and discontinuities of individuals and their perceptions of the world. This has important implications for social work assessments and interventions, and should the worlds of those with whom social workers practise be inclusive of others it demands such a recognition within that practice. This can disquiet and challenge accepted notions of confidentiality and individualised focus whilst respecting the central person involved. For instance, the world of an older person engaged in an assessment of need with a social worker may locate themselves within a circle or group and assume that this will be fully taken into account in the assessment, whilst the social worker, bound by confidentiality, may be unable to engage fully with those others so important to the individual. The tension for social work may be the emphasis on principle over and above a person's needs? As the global and local converge social workers need to learn and adapt to diverse situations that start with the biography in context, whilst recognising the influences around and on that person. Biographical approaches have much merit but should we ignore their cultural boundedness, and concomitantly diminish community and corporate responsibilities, we risk imposing a particular set of practices towards ageing in society or alienating many groups. This presents a series of dangers in an increasingly mobile cultural and social world.

Biographical and narrative approaches, however, have been developed in exciting ways by Gubrium and Holstein (2003) who see the ways in which history and biography converge to construct meanings, and look at ageing in the context of the lived experience of those who are classed as or consider themselves to be old(er). These theories draw on broader theoretical developments from symbolic interactionism, phenomenology and ethnomethodology focusing on the subjectivities of individual social actors. The importance of these theories is perhaps immediately clear to social workers who come into contact with the lived experiences of people in diverse situations, with diverse histories on a daily basis (Parker, 2005; 2007b), and who assess these contexts and may intervene using life story and reminiscence-based approaches.

In Summary

Sociological theories permeate social work practice in all areas, including working with older adults. In this chapter we have focused on social gerontological theories, especially as they connect with the concept of active ageing, but we recognise these represent only one set of theories important to social workers and advise cultural sensitivity and caution in applying theories to the performance of social work so that they are used to enhance not diminish the lives of individuals, their families and communities. Integrating this emphasis with social work education and research may become increasingly important as the challenges of an ageing world deepen. Currently, gerontological social work is active in the US in respect of social work curricula (Curl et al. 2010; Eun-Kyong et al., 2006; Fenster et al., 2010; Nelson-Becker, 2011; Rowan et al., 2011) and in respect of social work research (Mehrota et al. (2009). Elsewhere this focus is less evident. In the UK, Chambers (2004) considers the importance of introducing critical gerontological theory into the curriculum as a means of understanding and responding to the challenges of ageing for women. Women are over-represented in health and social care and in proportions over all to men. Alongside this is a recognition that ageism and sexism combine. For Chambers, critical social gerontology offers a useful model to begin to address these issues.

Theories from social gerontology range from the global, macro-level to those focusing on the individual. These are central to social work practice at all levels. For example, social policies determine welfare provision in response to questions of ageing, mezzo-level theories help us to understand the particular situations older people find themselves in, and micro-level theories set out how social workers may practice with individuals, their families and communities. It is time to re-claim the theoretical and intellectual traditions central to providing appropriate social work to older people.

Note

An earlier version of this paper was recently published as Jonathan Parker 2012. 'Landscapes and portraits: using multiple lenses to inform social work theories of old age.' In Martin Davies (ed.) *Social Work with Adults: Policy to Practice*, Basingstoke: Palgrave Macmillan, pp. 285-299

References

Ainsworth, M. D. S., Blehar, M. C., Walters, E. and Wall, S. (1978) *Patterns of Attachment: A psychological study of the strange situation*. Hillsdale, NJ: Erlbaum.

Alzheimer's Disease International (2009) *World Alzheimer Report*, London: Alzheimer's Disease International.

Ananta, A. and Arifin, E. N. (2009) Older persons in Southeast Asia: From liability to asset, in E. N. Arifin and A. Ananta, (eds) *Older Persons in Southeast Asia: An emerging asset*, Singapore: ISEAS, pp. 3-46.

Arifin, E. N. and Ananta, A. (eds) (2009) *Older Persons in Southeast Asia: An emerging asset*, Singapore: ISEAS.

Bengtson, V., Burgess, E. and Parrott, T. (1997) Theory, explanation and a third generation of theoretical development in social gerontology. *Journal of Gerontology, Series B, Psychological and Social Sciences*. 52, 2, S72-S88.

Bengtson, V. and Lowenstein, A. (eds) (2004) *Global Aging and Challenges to Families*. New York: De Gruyter.

Biggs, S. (1993) *Understanding Ageing*. Buckingham: Open University Press.

Biggs, S. (1999) *The Mature Imagination: Dynamics of identity in midlife and beyond*. Buckingham: Open University Press.

Bowling, A. (2008) Enhancing later life: How do older people perceive active ageing? *Aging and Mental Health*, 12, 3, 293-301.

Bytheway, B. (1995) *Ageism*. Buckingham: Open University Press.

Cabinet Office (nd) *Big Society*, http://www.cabinetoffice.gov.uk/content/big-society-overview, accessed February 2011.

Chambers, P. (2004) The case for critical gerontology in social work education and older women, *Social Work Education*, 23, 6, 745-758.

Chief Secretary to the Treasury (2003) *Every Child Matters*, CM 5860, Norwich: HMSO.

Cloos, P., Allen, C., Alvarado, B., Zunzunegui, M, Simeon, D. and Eldemire-Shearer, D. (2010) 'Active ageing': a qualitative study in six Caribbean countries, *Ageing and Society*, 30, 1, 79-101.

Coulshed, V. and Orme, J. (2006) *Social Work Practice: An introduction*, 4th edition, Basingstoke: Macmillan.

Cumming, E. and Henry, W. (1961) *Growing Old: The process of disengagement*, Basic Books: New York.

Curl, A., Tompkins, C., Rosen, A. and Zlotnik, J. (2010) A case study of professional change: The impact of the National Gerontological Social Work Survey, *Gerontology and Geriatrics Education*, 31, 3, 256-273.

Department of Health (2007) *Putting People First: A shared vision ad commitment to the transformation of adult social care*, http://www.dh.gov.uk/en/Publicationsandstatistics/Publications/PublicationsPolicyAndGuidance/DH_081118, accessed December 2010.

Department of Health (2011) *Living Well with Dementia: a National Dementia Strategy – good practice compendium*, http://www.dh.gov.uk/en/Publicationsandstatistics/Publications/PublicationsPolicyAndGuidance/DH_123476, accessed February 2011.

Du, P. and Yang, H. (2010) China's population ageing and active ageing, *China Journal of Social Work*, 3, 2/3, 139-152.

Ervik, R., Helgoy, I. and Christensen, D. (2006) Ideas and policies on active ageing in Norway and the UK, *International Social Science Journal*. 58, 571-584.

Eun-Kyoung, L., Collins, P., Mahoney, K., McInnis-Dittrich, K. and Boucher, E. (2006) Enhancing social work practice with older adults: The role of infusing gerontology content into the Master of Social Work Foundation curriculum, *Education Gerontology*. 32, 9, 737-756.

Estes, C. and Associates (2001) *Social Policy and Aging*. Thousand Oaks: Sage.

Fenster, J., Zodikoff, B., Rozario, P. and Joyce, P. (2010) Implementing a Gero-infused curriculum in advanced-level MSW course in Health, Mental Health and Substance Abuse: An evaluation, *Journal of Gerontological Social Work*. 53, 7, 641-653.

Foucault, M. (1977) *Discipline and Punish: The birth of the prison*, London, Penguin.

Fu, T. and Hughes, R. (2009) *Ageing in East Asia: Challenges and policies for the Twenty-first Century*, Abingdon: Routledge.

Giddens, A. (1991) *Modernity and Self-identity Self and Society in the Late Modern*

Age, Cambridge: Polity.

Gilleard, C. and Higgs, P. (2005) *Contexts of Ageing: Class, cohort and community.* Cambridge: Polity Press.

Gubrium, J. and Holstein, J.A. (eds) (2003) *Ways of Aging*, London: Wiley.

Gultiano, S. A. and Agustin, S. S. (2009) Work, income, and expenditure: Elderly and near-elderly women in Metro Cebu, Philippines, in E. N. Arifin and A. Ananta, (eds) *Older Persons in Southeast Asia: An emerging asset*, Singapore: ISEAS, pp. 218-243.

Havighurst, R. and Albrecht, R. (1953) *Older People*, London: Longman.

Hendricks, J. and Powell, J. L. (2009) Theorizing in social gerontology: the *raison d'être, International Journal of Sociology and Social Policy*, 29, 1/2, 5-14.

Hockey, J. and James, A. (2003) *Social Identities across the Life Course*, Basingstoke: Palgrave.

Homans, G. C. (1961) *Social Behavior: Its elementary forms.* New York: Harcourt Brace Jovanovich.

Johns, R. (2010) *Social Work, Social Policy and Older People*, Exeter: Learning Matters.

Kitwood, T. (1997) *Dementia Reconsidered: The person comes first.* Buckingham: Open University Press.

Krug, E.G. (2002) *World Report on Violence and Health.* Geneva: World Health Organization.

Lemon, B. W., Bengtson, V. L. and Peterson, J. A. (1972) An exploration of the activity theory of aging, *Journal of Gerontology.* 27, 511-523.

Lie, M., Baines, S. and Wheelock, J. (2009) Citizenship, volunteering and active ageing, *Social Policy and Administration*, 43, 7, 702-718.

Lymbery, M. 2005) *Social Work with Older People: Context, policy and practice.* London: Sage.

Marshall, M. and Tibbs, M-A. (2006) *Social Work and People with dementia: Partnerships, practice and persistence.* Bristol: BASW/Policy Press.

Mayhew, L. (2005) Active ageing in the UK: Issues, barriers, policy directions, *Innovation: The European Journal of Social Sciences*, 18, 4, 455-477.

McDonald, A. (2010) *Social Work with Older People*, Cambridge: Polity Press.

Mead, G.H. (1967) *Mind, Self and Society from the standpoint of a social behaviourist*, Chicago: University of Chicago Press.

Mehrota, C. M., Townsend, A. and Berkman, B. (2009) Enhancing research capacity in gerontological social work, *Educational Gerontology.* 35, 146-163.

Miesen, B. and Jones, G. M. M. (eds) (1997) *Care Giving in Dementia: Research and applications.* London: Routledge.

Nelson-Becker, H. (2011) Advancing an aging-prepared community: Models and lessons from training initiatives in gerontological social work, *Journal of Religion, Spirituality and Aging*, 23, 1/2, 92-113.

Ney, S. (2005) Active ageing policy in Europe: between path dependency and path departure, *Ageing International*, 30, 4, 323-342.

OECD (1998) *Maintaining Prosperity in and Ageing Society.* Paris: OECD.

Ogg, J. (2003) *Living Alone in Later Life*, London: Institute of Community Studies.

Parker, J. (2001) Interrogating person-centred dementia care in social work and social care practice. *Journal of Social Work.* 1,3, 329-45.

Parker, J. (2005) Constructing Dementia and Dementia Care: Daily practices in a day care. *Journal of Social Work* 5, 3, 261-278.

Parker, J. (2007a) The process of Social Work: Assessment, planning, intervention and review, in M. Lymbery and K. Postle (eds) *Social Work. A Companion to Learning*, London, Sage.

Parker, J. (2007b) Constructing dementia and dementia care: disadvantage and daily practices in a care setting. In P. Burke and J. Parker (eds) *Social Work and Disadvantage*. London: Jessica Kingsley Publishers.

Parker, J. (2008) Assessment, Planning, Intervention and Review In M. Davies (ed) *The Encyclopaedia of Social Work*. Oxford: Blackwell.

Parker, J. and Bradley, G. (2010) *Social Work Practice: Assessment, planning, intervention and review*, 3rd edition, Exeter: Learning Matters.

Parsons, T. (1942) Age and sex in the social structure of the United States, *American Sociological Review*, 7, 604-616.

Penhale, B. and Parker, J. (2008) *Working with Vulnerable Adults*, London: Routledge.

Perek-Bialas, J., Ruzik, A. and Vidovicova, L. (2008) Active ageing policies in the Czech Republic and Poland, *International Social Science Journal*. 60, 559-570.

Phillips, J., Ray, M. and Marshall, M. (2006) *Social Work with Older People*. 4th edition. Basingstoke: Palgrave.

Phillipson, C. (1982) *Capitalism and the Construction of Old Age*. London: Macmillan.

Phillipson, C. and Smith, A. (2005) *Extending Working Life: A review of the research literature, Department for Work and Pensions, Research report No. 299*, http://research.dwp.gov.uk/asd/asd5/rports2005-2006/rrep299.pdf accessed February 2011.

Piekkola, H. (2006) Nordic policies on active ageing in the labour market and some European comparisons, *International Social Science Journal*. 58, 545-557.

Population Trends (2004) http://www.statistics.gov.uk/statbase/product.asp?vlnk=6303, accessed November 2010.

Powell, J. L. (2010) The power of global aging, *Ageing International*. 35, 1, 1-14.

Powell, J. L. and Hendricks, J. (2009) The sociological construction of ageing: lessons for theorising, *International Journal of Sociology and Social Policy*, 29, 1/2, 84-94.

Putney, N. M., Alley, D. E. and Bengtson, V. L. (2005) Social gerontology as public sociology in action, *The American Sociologist.* 36, 4, 88-104.

Rahardjo, T. B. W., Hartono, T., Dewi, V. P., Hogervorst, E. and Arifin, A. (2009) Facing the geriatric wave in Indonesia: Financial conditions and social support, in E. N. Arifin and A. Ananta, (eds) *Older Persons in Southeast Asia: An emerging asset*, Singapore: ISEAS, pp. 270-298.

Rowan, N., Faul, A., Birkenmaier, J. and Damron-Rodriguez, J. (2011) Social work knowledge of community-based services for older adults: An educational model for social work students, *Journal of Gerontological Social Work.* 54, 2, 189-202.

Sauvain-Dugerdil, C., Leridon, H. and Mascie-Taylor, N. (eds) (2006) *Human Clocks: The bio-cultural meanings of age*, Bern: Peter Lang AG.

Seebohm Report (1968) *Report of the Committee on Local Authority and Allied Personal Social Services*, London: HMSO.

Smith, J. (2002) Preface in Department of Health, *Requirements for the Training of Social Workers*, London, Department of Health.

Trevithick, P. (2005) *Social Work Skills: A practice handbook*, 2nd edition, Buckingham: Open University Press.

Venn, S. and Arber, S. (2011) Day-time sleep and active ageing in later life, *Ageing and Society*, 31, 2, 197-216.

Walker, A. (2009) Commentary; The emergence and application of active aging in Europe, *Journal of Aging and Social Policy*, 21, 1, 75-93.

WHO (2002) *Active Ageing: A policy framework*. Geneva: World Health Organization.

Wilson, K., Ruch, G., Lymbery, M. and Cooper, A. (2008) *Social Work: An introduction to contemporary practice*, London: Longman.

3
Theories of successful psychological aging: A critical perspective

Gabriele Schäfer

Introduction

In this chapter, psychosocial theories of successful aging such as the continuity theory, the competence and environmental press theory, the Selection, Optimization and Compensation (SOC model), and the activity and disengagement theory will be analysed. Following this will be a presentation of individual factors that impact on the aging process such as behavioral health and physical fitness, optimal cognitive functioning, emotional and motivational (affect, control, and coping) optimal regulation, and high social functioning. Individual and sociocultural aspects of aging are interconnected and the ways individual factors unfold in the aging process depend on sociocultural factors such as the economic development of a country, socioeconomic status, ethnicity, poverty, and education levels. It is argued that psychological theories of successful aging do not take all the relevant individual and sociocultural factors into account and tend to generalise across cultures.

Understanding how people grow old requires knowledge about physiological changes, psychological processes and sociocultural conditions in a given society and culture. Aging is both a collective and individual process and it involves many variations in cognitive functioning, physical changes, and mental health. The aging process of each individual unfolds in a particular culture and society which in turn shapes social and psychological experiences. According to Walker (2010) Western Europe and Japan are the world's oldest regions. They will share demographic aging trends over the next 20 years which result from falling death rates, decreases in disease and disability and increased longevity. He claims that the sheer scale of the demographic changes which are still taking place have not been widely grasped. The EU presented a mid-range projection which shows that by

2050 the proportion aged 65 and over will have risen by 77 % (Economic Policy Committee, 2005). These are remarkable changes and families, communities, states and the EU will increasingly feel the impact of these developments.

Walker (2010) posits that following World War II there was a common stereotype in Europe of older people as passive recipients of pensions and social assistance. Such discourses echoed ideas of passivity and dependency. Since 1970 these discourses have started to change. The transition from a mainly passive to a more active political orientation among old people was encouraged by policy makers at local and national levels. Current discourses now embrace ideas of 'successful aging' (Fisher, 2002) or 'active aging' (see Walker, 2010; WHO, 2002). Both of these concepts are used here interchangeably.

The World Health Organization (WHO) (2002, p. 12) defines active aging as

... the process of optimizing opportunities for health, participation and security in order to enhance well-being and quality of life as people age ...

This process is dependent on a number of aspects such as a set of macro environmental, economic, social, health and social services, personal (genetic, psychological and behavioral) factors. This broad definition includes both personal and social factors which are important in the understanding of successful or active aging.

The new paradigm in the field of aging research reflects a positive view (see Gergen & Gergen, 2001, Fries, 1989). This demonstrates how ideas about aging are influenced by societal and cultural constructions which then in turn can give rise to different perceptions about older people and different policies for older people.

Finally the mere concept of 'age', the process of aging, or the individual differences in how a given person, in a given society, ages are, to some extent, sociocultural phenomena. (Fernandez-Ballesteros, 2008, p. 4)

He concludes that the process of aging cannot be reduced to either biomedical or sociocultural conditions.

I am interested whether ideas of active aging or successful aging are mirrored in psychological theory and what kind of studies support or reject these relatively new discourses.

Theories of psychosocial successful aging

Bowling (2007) states that the literature on successful aging reveals a wide range of different definitions, which reflect a theoretical, academic or scientific bias. Biomedical researchers seem to emphasise physical and health functioning whereas psychologists concentrate on subjective areas like life satisfaction or well-being. In contrast social scientists are more interested in socioeconomic conditions such as social participation, as key criteria for successful aging. Successful aging is certainly a complex multidimensional construct and should be seen through many different disciplinary and interdisciplinary lenses. Fernandez-Ballesteros (2008, p. 58) defines positive aging as 'the life course adaptation process for arriving at an optimal physical (including health), psychological (optimal cognition and emotion-motivation regulation), and social functioning in old age.'

Since it is not possible to present all the relevant biological, psychological and sociocultural aspects of successful aging there will be a focus on psychological theories on successful aging. This is followed by a discussion of whether these theories reflect the actual sociocultural realities in modern societies.

Continuity theory

According to Atchley (1989), continuity theory is based on the view that aging people tend to cope with day to day life by using familiar strategies. These strategies are grounded in past experiences and help to maintain and preserve both internal and external structures. He claims that the degree of continuity falls into one of three general categories: too little, too much, and optimal. If people experience too little continuity they feel that life is too unpredictable. Too much continuity can create a feeling of boredom and stagnation because there is not enough change to make life interesting. The best strategy involves an optimal sense of continuity that provides enough change for life to be experienced as interesting but not to be overwhelmed by unpredictable change. Continuity can be experienced on an internal or external level. Atchley explains that internal continuity refers to a remembered inner past, for example, experiences, temperament, talents and skills which relate to one's personal identity. Internal continuity provides feelings of self-esteem, ego integrity and competence whereas external continuity relates to past physical and social environments, role relationships and activities. One can develop feelings of external continuity when one moves in familiar environments or with familiar people such as family. Atchley emphasizes that maintaining both internal and external continuity is very important for successful adaptation in later life. Internal discontinuity such as experiences of dementia can destabilise one's personal identity. External discontinuity can be caused by the loss of one's familiar environment that typically happens when one has to move into a retirement home. This can negatively affect ones' social identity. Therefore, it is important to monitor a person's internal and external continuity.

Competence and environmental press

In order to understand psychosocial aging it is necessary to focus on the relationship between the individual and the environment (Wahl, 2001). The competence-environmental press approach is a theory that incorporates elements of the biopsychosocial model into the person-environment relation (Wahl, 2001).

Competence is the upper limit of an individual's ability to function in five areas: physical health, sensory-perceptual skills, motor skills, cognitive skills, and ego strength. According to Kail and Cavanaugh (2007) these domains are seen as underlying all other abilities. They reflect the biological and psychological forces.

Environmental press refers to the physical, interpersonal, or social demands that people are confronted with through the environment. Physical demands include having to go grocery shopping in a busy city. Interpersonal demands include having to adjust to different kinds of people. Social demands refer to traditions or laws that place certain norms on people. Competence and environmental press change when people age and reflect life-cycle factors. If a person has low competence too many environmental demands can result in maladaptive behaviors and negative affect. On the other hand too few demands on a person with high competence can also result in negative effects (see Kail & Cavanaugh, 2007). According to Kail and Cavanaugh (2007, p.580) 'aging is more than an equation, as the best fit must be determined on an individual basis.'

How do individuals cope with particular combinations of environmental press (such as adjusting to a new flat) and competence (such as the beginning of dementia)? According to Lawton (1989) and Nahemow (2000) they respond in two ways: Firstly, they may choose to develop new behaviors in order to meet new needs or desires and secondly they may allow the situation to determine the options they have which means they exert very little control.

Kail and Cavanaugh (2007) state that this model has considerable research support. This is because it accounts for the reasons why people choose the activities they do (Lawton, 1982), move to a particular form of housing (Lawton, 1982) or exert a degree of control over their lives (Langer & Rodin, 1976). I agree with Kail and Cavanaugh (2007) that there is merit to the view that aging is a complex interaction between a person's competence level and environmental press which is mediated by choice. This approach can be applied to a variety of real-world situations.

The SOC Model

Baltes and Baltes (1990b) propose a theoretical framework that has received empirical support. According to them three mechanisms regulate the adaptive aging process: selection, optimization, and compensation.

Selection is a universal mechanism that exists through the life cycle. In the case that individual resources are declining, selection is very important and serves as an adaptive mechanism. Baltes and Baltes distinguish two kinds of selection: elective and loss-based selection. Elective selection refers to the required balance between his/her needs and desires and the available resources. Loss-based selection occurs when the person's competencies are decreasing or are impaired and his/her demands or preferences need to be adjusted to a new situation. Adjusting personal needs to social environments is seen as essential for successful aging.

Optimisation refers to individual growth and development with respect to accumulating knowledge, skills or virtue throughout the life span. The choice of which skills are best suited to an individual depends on the social and cultural context. An example of optimization is practicing scales when one is starting to play the piano. In most cases one has a choice from a range of different methods of optimisation.

Compensation is a process for counteracting losses and declines. The process of activating or finding alternative means is called compensation. For instance, in old age a possibility to optimise existing skills may mean to still play the piano although one's hands might be stiffer and one has to play more slowly because of the lack of flexibility.

Jopp and Smith (2006) conceptualise the SOC model as a coping mechanism or life-management strategy that has protective functions which are determinants for active aging and well-being. This model has been tested by a number of researchers in a variety of settings that range from long-term care to older worker contexts (Abraham & Hansson, 1995; Rothermund & Brandstadter, 2003). Lehr (2007), however, criticizes a model that encourages a possibly premature selection of activities, that is motivated by the aging process. She also questions whether a model that is oriented towards 'objective indicators' and neglects 'subjective indicators' such as the contentment and subjective well-being, encompasses sufficient conditions to adequately measure and define successful aging.

Disengagement theory and activity theory

The disengagement theory of aging states that 'aging is an inevitable, mutual withdrawal or disengagement, resulting in decreased interaction between the aging person and others in the social system he belongs to' (Cummings & Henry, 1961, p. 227). This approach claims that it is both natural and acceptable for older adults to withdraw from society (EbersolE, 2005, p. 108). This withdrawal from society supposedly leads to feelings of freedom for older people because it releases them from having to obey norms in a social context (Damianopoulos, 1961). Havighurst (1963) and Havighurst, Neugarten and Tobin (1964) then relativise this theory by pointing out that individual components contribute to successful aging. Depending on individual character and personality structure some people are happy to withdraw from society whereas others prefer to remain integrated and active in a social environment.

The activity theory proposes that successful aging happens when older adults stay active and maintain social interactions (Lehr, 2007). It was developed by Robert J. Havighurst in 1961. The theory assumes a positive relationship between life satisfaction and activity. In 1964, Bernice Neugarten asserted that satisfaction in old age depended on active maintenance of personal relationships and endeavors (Bengtson & Putney, 2009). The activity theory asserts that as people age, they start to lose the identity they had in work or in family life (see Havighurst, 1961). However, those who continue to participate in activities and interact socially have a higher quality of life and tend to live longer and experience better health. This is due to the enhancement of the self through still being actively involved in life. Lemon et al. (1972) found a confirmation of their hypothesis that activity in different social roles has a positive effect on self-image of older people. According to them, a positive self-image is an important condition for life contentment and successful aging.

The activity theory can be criticised because it overlooks inequalities in health and economics, which affect the ability of older people to engage in such activities. It also does not take into account that some people do not desire to maintain social contacts or engage in new challenges, but nevertheless feel contentment and satisfaction with their lives. Lehr (2007) states that both the activity theory and the disengagement theory have research support depending on concrete roles and the specific personality of the person.

In summary, the psychological theories that have been presented all tend to focus on a concept of aging that has developed in modern societies. They tend to be universal and lack a discussion of the actual sociocultural and socioeconomic conditions such as poverty, illness, marginalisation of migrants (especially older migrants) and isolation in modern societies that certainly have an impact on aging. These theories also tend to be monocultural and do not take into account how migrants or native indigenous people experience the aging process. In the following part a discussion of individual factors (e.g. stopping smoking and heavy drinking, adapting to a healthy diet) and sociocultural factors of aging (for example, good public policies through pension systems and access to good health care) will be presented.

Individual factors and aging

Fernandez-Ballesteros (2008) suggests a multidimensional-multilevel approach to active aging. He suggests four domains in which psychological and behavioral conditions are organised:

1. behavioral health and physical fitness,
2. optimal cognitive functioning,
3. emotional and motivational (affect, control, and coping) optimal regulation, and
4. high social functioning.

For him, positive aging can be defined as the life course adaptation process for arriving at an optimal physical, psychological and social functioning in older age. Since aging is strongly associated with what people do, there is strong research support for the importance of developing and maintaining physical health in the process of aging.

According to Kail and Cavanaugh (2007) biological theories of aging claim that aging is caused by the body's system wearing out because the processes within the cells develop harmful substances or the cells deteriorate over the course of time. This means that endurance, hearing, vision and a sense of smell decline with age. Death is genetically programmed. There is a higher risk of cardiovascular disease, shortness of breath, increased risk of chronic obstructive pulmonary disorder, sleep disturbances and cancer in old age. The body's metabolism affects how people age and both the intake of calories and stress have an impact on the process of aging. Health risks are affected by lifestyle. Exacerbating this is the fact that overall death rates from diseases have declined in recent decades.

Bortz (1982) collected evidence that showed that physical activity could be considered a key factor for active aging. Apart from physical activity, a balanced Mediterranean type of diet (Renaud et al., 1995), not smoking (Fernandez-Ballesteros, 2008) and moderated drinking (WHO, 2002, p. 25) also constitute well known successful aging habits. Even when these are habits are developed in later life they still have a positive effect.

Optimal cognitive functioning

There is also strong evidence that cognitive functioning has an important impact on the aging process. According to Fernandez-Ballesteros (2008) the most important threat people feel when approaching old age is a decline of cognitive functioning, or worse, to become mentally impaired or demented. Working memory typically declines with age (Zacks et al., 2000).

> Working memory involves the processes and structures involved in holding information in mind and simultaneously using it to solve a problem, make a decision, perform some function, or learn some new information. (Kail & Cavanaugh, 2007, p. 558)

They explain that working memory has a small capacity and deals with information that is used right now, serving as a kind of blackboard. It is important to keep this information active and they point out a good way of doing this is rehearsing.

On easy tasks, younger and older people have only few differences, whereas, on difficult tasks younger people do better (Fernandez-Ballesteros, 2008). Age differences on semantic memory tasks are typically absent (Bäckman et al., 2001). Fernandez-Ballesteros (2008) emphasises that during the past decade research on cognitive functioning showed that:

1. Distal factors stem from both the socialisation process (education attainment, family SES, and childhood cognition) and the current environment, e.g. lifelong education or social condition.
2. Aerobic training that reaches from moderate to high fitness training has a positive effect on brain function. Physical exercise seems to be an important protective factor against the development of dementia and cognitive impairment.
3. There is broad cognitive plasticity and also reverse capacity throughout the life cycle and that includes old age.
4. There is evidence that daily cognitive activity and social or leisure activity have a positive effect in cognitive functioning. They seem to work as protective factors for cognitive impairment.

On top of that long-term cognitive intervention programs improve cognitive functioning in healthy elder people.

These research outcomes show that effective training and good interventions can certainly optimise cognitive functioning. However, whether people are motivated to maintain high cognitive functioning is also connected with good emotional and motivational functioning.

Emotional and motivational functioning

Generally, subjective well-being is a positive evaluation of one's life that is associated with positive feelings (Kail & Cavanaugh, 2007). Ryff and Essex (1991) explain that well-being in older age is related to self-acceptance, the positive relationships to other people, autonomy, control of the environment and having a goal in life. According to these authors it is necessary to constantly realise one's potential so that one can remain open to new experiences. Through this process one can experience new levels of self-competence. If a person was hindered in developing these qualities, then the type of personality develops that is stagnant. There is a body of academic literature on health, that claims positive emotions (and that includes positive thinking as well as positive attitudes) are psychological states that are correlated with longevity and a healthy life (Leventhal & Patrick-Miller, 2000; Mayne, 2001). Cavenaugh (1996) found that research shows that what adults believe about their memory ability is related to how well they perform. It may perhaps be the case that changing your beliefs about memory aging may help you to develop compensatory strategies that might help to compensate these changes. Thankfully, new research shows that positive emotions can be trained. Seligman, Steen, Park and Perterson (2005) have developed interventions for promoting positive emotions, positive thinking, and optimism. This is a breakthrough since it is also known that the opposite can be created through negative emotions. Negative emotional conditions such as depression, feelings of loneliness and pessimism are psychological conditions that are strongly associated with mortality, illness, suicide and dementia in old age (Pennix et al., 1998; Peterson, Seligman & Vaillant, 1988, Stek et al., 2005). Carstensen et al. (2000) state that until recently, emotional development was not studied in adulthood because it was automatically assumed that emotional functioning paralleled biological and cognitive functioning in adulthood and old age, namely becoming dysregulated and rigid in old age. Kail and Cavanaugh (2007, p.565) point out that only 'a minority of older adults have mental health problems, and most such problems respond to therapy.' Contrary to popular belief, the rate of severe depression declines from young adulthood to old age (Gatz, 2000; Qualls, 1999). This research outcome also holds cross-culturally (Chou & Chi, 2005). Older adults also demonstrate, as compared to younger individuals, an increase in emotional complexity and heterogeneity (e.g. Carstensen et al., 2000). In comparison with younger and middle age people, older people reported less negative emotional experience and greater emotional control. Age is associated with more differential experience (Carstensen et al., 2000). Furthermore, elder adults report better self-regulation than younger adults (e.g. Gross et al., 1997). Having a more articulate emotional system might be perceived as an important characteristic for successful aging.

Although usually people experience many stresses and losses throughout their life-span, there are only minor changes throughout old age with respect to happiness, well-being, and life satisfaction (Fernandez-Ballesteros, 1996). Coping with stress successfully seems an essential factor for successful aging. Indeed successful aging can be considered as a coping process. Aspinwall and Shelley (1997) propose proactive coping as the process through which people anticipate or detect potential stressors and are able to act in advance to prevent the effects or to mute their possible impact. Proactive coping has five steps:

1. Resource accumulation,
2. Recognition of potential stressors,
3. Initial appraisal,
4. Preliminary coping efforts, and
5. Elicitation and use of feedback concerning initial efforts.

Taking into account that aging is a process with numerous stressors, and considering the importance of successful aging, proactive coping seems a valuable concept. Fernandez-Ballesteros et al. (1988) report that, in several samples of people older than 65, that death of partner, retirement, chronic illness and subsequent disability, and financial difficulties are the most frequently named life stressors. Lazarus (2003) points out that from negative life experiences some individuals are able to extract positive psychological growth after they were able to cope in grieving over major loss. This usually comes after a considerable psychological struggle. There is both research about the loss of one partner through death (e.g. Tedeschi & Calhoun, 2004) and about divorce (King et al., 2004) that shows that even these difficult events can create potential growth. Good coping strategies are self-regulated processes that help to adapt or overcome biological, environmental and social stressors. It is comforting that research has shown that positive emotions can be trained.

Social functioning and social participation

It is widely supported in the literature that social interaction is an important factor for successful and healthy aging. Social functioning is associated with longevity, survival, physical and mental health, good cognitive functioning, and general life-satisfaction and well-being (see Antonucci et al., 2002; Fernandez-Ballesteros, 2008). Social participation and social engagement are crucial aspects of well-being throughout the life-span. Social interactions within the family, friendship circles, or (paid or unpaid) work environments, help the individual to maintain optimal emotional and cognitive functioning. With respect to family relationships, sibling relationships become more important with age and the ties between sisters are the strongest (Schmeeckle et al., 1998, cited in Kail and Cavanaugh, 2007). Kail and Cavanaugh (2007) explain that long-term marriages tend to be happy until one partner becomes seriously ill. This is because there is a slower potential for marital conflict and at the same time greater potential for pleasure (Connidis, 2001). However eventually all older marriages will end because one partner will die. Most people experience this as the most traumatic event that will ever happen to them. Widowhood is more likely to occur in old age (Martin-Matthews, 1999). Mostly both widow and widower will suffer a financial loss but widows often suffer more from difficult financial circumstances (see McGarry & Schoeni, 2005). Apart from marriage and other family relationships, friends play an important role in old age. According to Rawlins (2004) patterns of friendships among older adults are quite similar to those among young adults. Older women tend to have more numerous and more intimate friendships than older men do. Fernandez-Ballesteros (2008, p. 128) concludes that: 'There is broad empirical evidence that social activity is associated with survival, longevity, morbidity as well as with optimal cognitive and emotional functioning.'

The third-fourth age distinction

Baltes and Smith (2003) distinguish between the third and the fourth age. The third age is perceived as the 'good news' whereas the fourth age was seen as the 'bad news'. The 'good' age relates to the young old (ages 60-80) and the fourth age as the oldest-old (over age 80). The young old have:

+ Increased life expectancy, with more people living longer lives and aging successfully.
+ Substantial potential for mental and physical fitness, with improvements occurring with each generation.
+ Evidence of emotional and cognitive reserves.
+ High levels of personal and emotional well-being.
+ Effective strategies to cope with the gains and losses of later life.

The oldest-old experience:

+ Increases in the negative effects of chronic stress
+ Substantial losses in cognitive functioning and the ability to learn.
+ High prevalence of dementia (50% in people over age 90), multiple chronic conditions and frailty.
+ Difficulties with the quality of life and with dying with dignity.

This distinction seems useful as an analytical tool when one considers successful physical, cognitive and emotional aging and considering future implications on policy development in aging societies. Theories of successful or active aging need to take into account up to what age it is likely that old people are able to maintain good physical, cognitive and emotional functioning.

Sociocultural factors and aging

The 1996 U.N. Population Database (cited in Kail and Cavanaugh, 2007, p.542) shows that the current range of how long populations of different countries live, extends from 38 years in Sierra Leone to 80 years in Japan. This considerable divergence in life expectancy reflects the vast differences in genetic, sociocultural and economic conditions such as health care and levels of disease across both developing and industrialised nations. Biological theories of aging pose that aging consists of constantly declining functions and changes in extra-cellular structures that are accompanied with an increasing proneness to illness which eventually leads to the death of the organism (Schachtschnabel, 2004, p. 4). However, as seen above there is a dramatic difference in longevity in different countries which indicates that life expectancy is, to a degree, socially constructed. Biomedical advances and medical measures such as cancer screening, better treatment of hypertension, diabetes, coronary artery disease, and arthritis are sources of morbidity compression. Unfortunately, many countries are excluded from these advances and discourses of 'active aging' or 'successful aging' can seem somewhat cynical, given the world-wide differences in medical, economic, education and environmental conditions.

Until the 1970s, a generally negative view of old people was reinforced by their exclusion from the political and policy making systems of most European countries (Walker, 2010). These social constructions also operated to reinforce negative stereotypes of older people which in turn posed stereotype treats to older people. This negative tide in public discourses on aging began to turn in the 1970s in Europe because of underlying macroeconomic shifts and the rise of neo-liberalism. Since then a political shift has taken place and the new policy label that is attached to the new policy discourse is 'active aging' (Walker, 2010). So far there is no comprehensive approach to aging within the EU. The EU needs to agree and also implement a wide range of social and economic strategies in order to create social and political change. It is necessary to develop a fresh approach that shift active aging discourses from their dominant productivist focus on employment and neoliberalism to a more comprehensive participatory focus.

The economic impact of the demographic change will include much higher pensions costs and increases in health care costs in all Western countries. It is well known in the academic literature that socioeconomic development is strongly related to life expectancy at both the national and the individual levels (e.g. Nicholson et al., 2005; Kail & Cavanaugh, 2007; Falk et al., 2011). Education attainment and lifelong learning play an important role in the aging process. According to Kubzansky, Berkmann and Seemann (1998), low levels of education are associated with poor health conditions and low psychological functioning. People with higher education have a lower mortality as well as morbidity risk than people with low educational attainments (Lampert & Mielck, 2008, cited in Bertermann, 2010, S. 621). People with lower educational attainments experience difficult work conditions such as hard physical labor, shift work, monotonous work processes, high pressure at work and little opportunity to exert influence into one's work environment (Lampert & Mielck, 2008, cited in Bertermann, 2010, p. 621). On top of that people with higher education and a higher professional standing attribute more meaning to a healthy lifestyle. They tend to smoke less, partake of a healthier diet and are physically more active than people with a lower socioeconomic status (Knesebeck, 2008). People with higher education also take better care of their health by participating in regular health checks, developing more health related knowledge, are better able to communicate with medical staff and recover better from the effect of illnesses (Hernes, 2009).

The impact of social class on longevity is caused by reduced access by poor elderly to goods and services, especially medical care. This characterises most ethnic minorities in the United States, the poor and many older adults (National Center for Health Statistics, 2004a). Socially disadvantaged older people experience an earlier onset of multiple diseases and they are more affected in their functional capacity than average older people of their age group (Rautio et al., 2005). In the United States most of financially disadvantaged older people have no health insurance and many are unable to pay for a healthy lifestyle. Kail and Cavanaugh (2007) give as an example that lead poisoning from old water pipes, air pollution, and poor drinking water are major problems in large urban areas, but many old people cannot afford to move.

Immigrant status also affects people's health in the States. One reason for this is that they may have problems communicating with family members or professionals because they may not be fluent in English (Usita & Blieszner, 2002). Language and cultural differences need to be considered in performing medical examinations with immigrants. Members of different ethnic groups may vary considerably in how comfortable they are in allowing strangers (e.g. physicians) to examine them (Bysma, Ostendorf & Hofer, 2002). On top of that cultural differences can result is mislabeling or misdiagnosing problems (McConotha, Stoller & Oboudiat, 2001).

The health status of immigrants and U.S.-born older adults show that even when socioeconomic status is controlled, immigrants show poorer health than U.S.-born individuals with the same background (e.g. Angel, Buckley & Sakamoto, 2001). African Americans' average life expectancy at birth is roughly 6 years lower for men and 5 years lower for women than that of European Americans (National Center for Health Statistics, 2004b). By the age of 65 the average life expectancy for African Americans is only about 2 years less for both men and women Americans (National Center for Health Statistics, 2004b). A reason for that might be that they do not have the same access to good quality care as European Americans. Gonzalez, Haan and Hinton (2001) also report that higher rates of depression are found among older Mexican Americans who are at least acculturated. This may indicate that language and other barriers affect both physical and mental health. The prevalence of frailty is also higher within the African American population. The percentage of people needing assistance show that African Americans have the highest rate with 25%, followed by Latino Americans (21%), Asian Americans (19%) and European Americans (15%) (AgingStats.gov., 2004).

In Germany, Falk et al. (2011) found in their empirical study that the situation is also problematic for older migrants because of numerous barriers such as a loss of family cohesion, poverty, lack of knowledge about health insurance and general system of health care, their children having school problems, worries about educational possibilities for their children, generational conflicts, value conflicts and marginalisation in society. They also mention that people in the health system have the stereotype that families look after the elderly migrants which is not necessarily the case. In 2004, 84,6% of Turkish migrants over 65 had no professional training and 56,9% did not have a formal school education (Özcan & Seifert, 2004). Hahn (2011) also emphasises the lack of a formal education and the lack of the German language as problems older migrants face in Germany. Inability to speak German means communication with doctors, hospitals, health care services and community representatives becomes very difficult for older migrants.

Concluding thoughts

Psychological theories of successful aging are useful because they provide a theoretical framework that has inspired research into the complex process of aging. However, I would caution against using these theories uncritically and applying them to all cultures and societies. These theories tend to be universal and monocultural. 'Successful aging' or 'active aging' are concepts that have developed as a response to aging societies in a climate of neoliberal politics in the United States and Europe.

When one discusses successful or active aging it is necessary to differentiate between the third and fourth age. While it is likely one will successfully age through the 65-80 year phase this becomes more difficult from 80 years onwards. The continuity theory stresses that maintaining both internal and external continuity is very important for successful adaptation in later life. However, it is much more likely that people over 80 will lose their spouses, experience health problems and have to shift into hospitals, retirement homes and hospices. This experience of internal discontinuity can potentially destabilise a person's sense of personal identity. Through such traumatic experiences, a process, that previously could have been considered as successful aging can easily transform into resignation and depression. I would argue that to a degree successful aging is age-dependent. The SOC model can also be criticized. If a person suffers from a debilitating chronic disease, poverty or isolation it will be more difficult to successfully select strategies to counteract losses and declines. As has been stated above, the activity theory can be criticised because it has a potential to overlook inequalities in economics and health that can create barriers to the ability for older people to age successfully. This theory also ignores the fact that some older people do not wish for social interactions or to experience new challenges but nevertheless feel contentment and satisfaction with their lives. With respect to the disengagement theory depending on individual character and personality structure, some people are happy to withdraw from society. However, others prefer to remain active. Both the activity theory and disengagement theory have research support (Lehr, 2007). It depends on specific roles and the personality of an individual whether old age is connected with activity or disengagement. Therefore, this theory also cannot be applied universally across culture. A theory that encompasses both individual competence as well as the environment is the competence-environmental press approach. This theory has considerable research support because it accounts for the reasons why people choose the activities they do (Lawton, 1982), move to a particular form of housing (Lawton, 1982) or exert a degree of control over their lives (Langer & Rodin, 1976). There is indeed merit to the view that aging is a complex interaction between a person's competence level and environmental press which is mediated by choice. This approach can be applied to a variety of real-world situations.

Apart from the competence-environmental press approach psychological theories of successful aging do not sufficiently take into account that aging is an individual as well as collective process that depends on genetic factors, and cognitive, emotional and social functioning. Aging is strongly associated with what people do and empirical evidence shows how important it is to maintain physical health in the process of aging. As we have seen, health related behaviors are strongly related to socioeconomic background and educational attainment. Therefore it is necessary to take one's status in a particular culture into account when one tries to conceptualise successful or active aging. The aging process of each individual unfolds in a particular culture and society which then in turn influences social and psychological experiences. To what degree an aging person can fully participate in society is dependent on many factors such as socioeconomic status, ethnicity, poverty, wealth, and educational attainment. There is a need for more psychological research into the area of successful aging in a number of different cultures and societies.

References

Abraham, J.D. & Hansson, R.O. (1995). Successful aging at work: An applied study of selection, organization, optimization, and compensation through impression management. *Journal of Gerentology: Psychological Sciences*, 50 B, 94-103.

AgingStats.gov. (2004). *Older Americans 2004: Key indicators of well-being.* Retrieved Augsut 7, 2005, from http://www.agingstats.gov/chartbook2004/default.htm

Angel, J.L., Buckley, C.J. & Sakamoto, A. (2001). Duration or disadvantage? Exploring nativity, ethnicity, and health in midlife. *Journal of Gerontology: Social Sciences*, 56B, 272-284.

Antonucci, T., Okorodudu, C. & Akiyama, H. (2002). Well-being among older adults on different continents. *Social Issues*, 58, 617-627.

Aspinwall, L.G. & Shelley, T.E. (1997). A stitch in time: Self-regulation and proactive aging. *Psychological Bulletin*, 121, 417-436.

Atchley, R.C. (1989). A continuity theory of normal aging. *The Gerontologist*, 29, 183-190.

Bäckman, L., Small, B.J. & Wahlin, A. (2001). Aging and memory: Cognitive and biological processes. In J.E. Birren & K.W. Schaie (Eds.), *Handbook of the psychology of aging* (5th ed., pp. 349-377). San Diego, CA: Academic Press.

Baltes, P.B. & Smith, P. (2003). New frontiers in the future of aging: From successful aging of the young old to the dilemmas of the fourth age. *Journal* of Gerontology: *Psychological Sciences*, 49, 123-135.

Baltes, P. B., & Baltes, M. M. (1990). Psychological perspectives on successful aging: The model of selective optimization with compensation. In P. B. Baltes & M. M. Baltes (Eds.), *Successful aging: Perspectives from the behavioral sciences* (pp. 1–34). New York: Cambridge University Press.

Bertermann, B. (2010). Aktives Altern und Bildung. In G. Nägele, (Ed.), *Soziale Lebenslaufpolitik: Sozialpolitik und Sozialstaat* (pp. 619-636). Wiesbaden: Verlag für Sozialwissenschaften.

Bowling, A. (2007). Aspiration for older age in the 21st century: What is successful aging? *International Journal of Aging and Human Development*, 64, 263-297.

Bengtson, V.L. & Putney, N. (2009). *Handbook of theories of aging*. Springer Publishing Company.

Bortz, W.M. (1982). Disuse and aging. *Journal of American Medical Association*, 248, 1203-1208.

Bylsma, F.W., Ostendorf, C.A. & Hofer, J.P. (2002). Challenges in providing neuropsychological and psychological services in Guam and the Commonwealth of the Northern Marianas Islands (CNMI). In F.R. Ferraro (Ed.), *Minority and cross-cultural aspects of neuropsychological assessment: Studies on neuropsychology, development and cognition* (pp. 145-157). Bristol: Swets & Zeitlinger.

Carstensen, L.L., Mayr, U., Pasupathi, M. & Nesselroade, J.R. (2000). Emotional experiences in everyday life across the adult life span. *Journal of Personality and Social Psychology*, 79, 644-655.

Cavenaugh, J.C. (1996). Memory of self-efficacy as a key to understanding cognitive aging. In F. Blanchard-Fields & T.M. Hess (Eds.), *Perspective on cognitive changes in adulthood and aging* (pp. 488-507). New York: McGraw Hill.

Chou, K.L. Chi, I. (2005). Prevalence and correlates of depression in Chinese oldest-old. *International Journal of Geriatric Psychiatry*, 20, 41-50.

Connidis, I.A. (2001). *Family ties and aging*. Thousand Oaks, CA: Sage.

Cross, J.J., Carstensen, L.L., Pasupathi, M., Tsai, J., Gotestam, C. & Hsu, A. (1997). Emotion and aging: Experience, expression, and control. *Psychology and Aging*, 12, 290-299.

Cumming, E. & Henry, E. W. (1961). *Growing Old*. New York: Basic.

Damianopoulos, E. (1961). A formal statement of disengagement theory. In E. Cumming & W.E. Henry (Eds.), *Growing old – the process of disengagement* (pp. 210-218). New York: Basic Books Inc.

Ebersole, P. (2005). *Gerontological nursing and healthy aging*. Elsevier Health Sciences.

Economic Policy Committee (2005). *The Impact of Aging on Public Expenditure*. Brussels, European Commission.

Falk, K., Heusinger, J., Kammerer, K., Khan-Zvornicanin, M., Kümpers, S.

& Zander, M. (2011). *Arm, alt, pflegebedürftig: Selbstbestimmungs- und Teilhabechancen im benachbarten Quartier.* Berlin: edition sigma.

Fisher, B.J. (2002). Successful aging and life satisfaction: A pilot study for conceptual clarification. *International Journal of Aging and Human Development,* 41: 239-250.

Fernandez-Ballesteros, R., Diaz, P., Izal, M. & Hernandez, J.M. (1988). Conflict situations in elderly people. *Psychological Reports,* 63, 171-176.

Fernandez-Ballesteros, R. (2008). *Active aging: The contribution of psychology.* Göttingen: Hogefe & Huber Publishers.

Fries, J.E. (1989). *Aging well.* Reading, MA: Addison-Wesley.

Gatz, M. (2000). Variations on depression later in life. In S.H. Qualls & N. Abeles (Eds.), *Psychology and the aging revolution* (pp. 239-254). Washington, DC: American Psychological Association.

Gergen, M. & Gergen, K. (2001). Positive aging: New images for a new age. *Age International,* 27, 1-10.

Gonzales, H.M., Haan, M.N. & Hinton, L. (2001). Acculturation and the prevalence of depression in older Mexican Americans: Baseline results of the Sacramento Area Latino Study on Aging. *Journal of the American Geriatrics Society,* 49, 948-953.

Hahn, K. (2011). *Alter, Migration und Soziale Arbeit: Zur Bedeutung von Ethnizität in Beratungsgesprächen der Altenhilfe.* Bielefeld: Theorie Bilden, Transcript Verlag.

Havighurst, R. J. (1961). 'Successful aging'. *The Gerontologist* 1: 8–13.

Havighurst, R. J. (1963). Successful aging. In C. Tibbits & W. Donahue (Eds.), *Process of aging* (299-320). New York: Williams.

Havighurst, R. J., Neugarten, B. L. & Tobin, S. (1964). Disengagement and patterns of aging. *The Gerentologist,* 4, 24.

Hernes, G. (2009). Education and Health Prevention. In U.M. Staudinger & H. Heidemeier (Eds.), *Altern in Deutschland* (Vol. 2) Altern, Bildung und lebenslanges Lernen (Nova Acta Leopoldina, 100 (364). Stuttgart: Wissenschaftliche Verlagsgesellschaft.

Kail, R.V. & Cavanaugh, J.C. (2007). *Human Development. A Life-Span View.* Australia: Thomson Wadsworth.

Langer, E.J. & Rodin, J. (1976). The effects of choice and enhanced personal responsibility for the aged: A field experiment in an institutional setting. *Journal of Personality and Social Psychology,* 34, 191-198.

Lawton, M.P. (1982). Competence, environmental press, and the adaptation of old people. In M.P. Lawton & P.G. Windley, & T.O. Byerts (Eds.), *Aging and the environment. Theoretical approaches* (pp. 33-59). New York: Springer.

Lawton, M.P. (1989) Environmental proactivity in older people. In V.L. Bengtson & K.W. Schaie (Eds.), *The course of later life: Research and reflections* (pp. 15-23).

New York: Springer.

Lampert, T. & Mielck, A. (2008). Gesundheit und soziale Ungleichheit. Eine Herausforderung für Forschung und Politik. GGW, 8 (2), 2-16.

Lazarus, R.S. (2003). The Lazarus Manifiesto for positive psychology and psychology general. *Psychological Inquiry*, 14, 172-189.

Lehr, U. (2007). *Psychologie des Alterns*. Wiebelsheim: Quelle & Meyer Verlag.

Lemon, B.W., Bengtson, , V.L. & Peterson, J. A. (1972). An exploration of the activity theory of aging: Types and life satisfaction among immovers to a retirement community. *Journal of Gerontology*, 27, 511-523.

Leventhal, H. & Patrick-Miller, L. (2000). Emotions and physical illness: Causes and indicators of vulnerability. In M. Lewis & J.M. Havilands-Jones (Eds.), *Handbook of emotions* (2nd ed., pp. 523-537). New York: Guilford.

Jopp, D., & Smith, J. (2006). Resources and life-management strategies as determinants of successful aging: On the protective effect of selection, optimization, and compensation. *Psychology and Aging*, 21, 253–265.

King, L., Baker, A., Burton, C. & Velazquez, L. (2004). *Change, happiness, and maturity: Narrative accounts of the good things in life*. Paper presented at the American Psychological Association, Honolulu, August.

Knesebeck, O. (2008). Soziale Ungleichheit, Gesundheit und Krankheit im Alter. In A. Kuhlmey & D. Schaeffer (Eds.), *Alter, Gesundheit und Krankheit* (pp. 120-130). Bern: Verlag Hans Huber

Kubzansky, L.D., Berkman, L.F., Glass, T.A. & Seeman, T.E. (1998). Is educational attainment associated with shared determinants of health in the elderly? Findings from MacAthur studies of successful aging. *Psychosomatic Medicine*, 60, 578-585.

Martin-Matthews, A. (1999). Widowhood: Dominant renditions, changing demographics, and variable meaning. In S.M. Neysmith (Ed.), *Critical issues for future social work practice with aging persons* (pp. 27-46). New York: Columbia University Press.

Mayne, T.J. (2001). Emotions and health. In T.J. Mayne & G.A. Bonnanno (Eds.), *Emotions, current issues and future directions* (pp. 361-397). New York: Guilford.

McConotha, J.T., Stoller, P. & Oboudiat, F. (2001). Reflections of older Iranian women: Adopting to life in the United States. *Journal of Aging Studies*, 15, 369-381.

McGarry, K. & Schoeni, R. (2005). Widow(er) poverty and out-of-pocket medical expenditure near the end of life. *Journal of Gerontology: Social Sciences*, 60, 160-168.

Nahemow, L. (2000). The ecology theory of aging: Powell Lawton's legacy. In R.L. Rubinstein & M. Moss (Eds.), *The many dimensions of aging* (pp. 22-40). New York: Springer.

National Center for Health Statistics, (2004a). *Health, United States 2004. With chartbook on trends in the health of Americans.* Retrieved July, 17, 2005, from http://www.cdc.gov/nchs/data/hus/hus04.pdf

National Center for Health Statistics, (2004b). *Older Americans 2004: Key indicators of well-being.* Retrieved July, 17, 2005, from http://www.agingstats. gov./chartbook2004/defautlt.htm.

Nicholson, A., Bobak, M. M., Michael, R.R. & Marmot, M. (2005). Socio-economic influences on self-rated health in Russian men and women – a life course approach. *Social Science and Medicine,* 61, 2345-2354.

Öczan, V. & Seifert, W. (2004). *Lebenslage älterer Migrantinnen und Migranten in Deutschland.* Expertise im Auftrag der Sachverständigenkommission „5. Altenbericht der Bundesregierung'. Berlin.

Pennix, B.W., Guralink, J.M., Feruci, L. Simonsick, E.M., Deeg, D.J.H. & Wallance, R.B. (1998). Depressive symptoms and physical decline in community-dwelling older persons. *Journal of American Medical Association,* 279, 1720-1726.

Peterson, C., Seligman, M.E. & Vaillant, G.E. (1988). Pessimistic explanatory style is a risk factor for physical illness. A thirty five year longitudinal study. *Journal of Personality and Social Psychology,* 55, 23-27.

Rawlins, W.K. (2004). Friendship in later life. In J.F. Nussbaum & J. Coupland (Eds.) *Handbook of communication and aging research* (2nd. ed., pp. 273-299). Mahwah, NJ: Erlbaum.

Rautio, N., Heikkinen, E. & Ebrahim, S. (2005). Socio-economic position and is relationship to physical capacity among elderly people living in Jyväskylä, Finland: Five- and Ten-year follow up studies. *Social Sciences and Medicine,* 60, 2405-2416.

Rothermund, K. & Brandstadter, J. (2003). Coping with deficits and losses in later life: From compensatory action to accommodation. *Psychology of Aging,* 18, 896-905.

Ryff, C.D. & Essex, M.J. (1991). Psychological well-being in adulthood and old age: descriptive markers and explanatory processes. *Annual Review of Gerontology and Geriatrics,* 11, 144-171.

Schachtschnabel, D.O. (2004). Humanbiologie des Alterns. In A. Kruse & M. Martin (Eds.), *Enzyklopädie der Gerontologie* (pp. 167-181). Bern: Huber.

Schmeeckle, M., Giarusso, R. & Wang, Q. (1998, November). *When being a brother or sister is important to one's identity: Life stage and gender differences.* Paper presented at the annual meeting of the Gerontological Society, Philadelphia.

Seligman, M.E.P., Steen, T.A., Park, N. & Peterson, C. (2005). Positive psychology progress: Empirical validation of interventions. *American Psychologist,* 60, 410-421.

Steck, M.L., Vinkers, D.J., Gussekloo, J., Beekman, A.T.Fr., van der Mast, R.C.

& Westendorp, R.G.J. (2005). Is depression in old age fatal when people feel lonely? American *Journal of Psychiatry*, 162, 178-180.

Tedeschi, R.G. & Calhoun, L.G. (2004). Posttraumatic growth: Conceptual foundations and empirical evidence. *Psychological Inquiry*, 15, 1-18.

Usita, P.M. & Blieszner, R. (2002). Immigrant family strengths: Meeting communication challenges. *Journal of Family Issues*, 23, 266-286.

Walker, A. (2010). The emergence and application of active aging in Europe. In: G. Nägele, (Ed.), *Soziale Lebenslaufpolitik: Sozialpolitik und Sozialstaat* (pp. 585-602). Wiesbaden: Verlag für Sozialwissenschaften.

WHO (2002). *Active aging. A policy framework*. Geneva: Author.

Zacks, R.T., Hasher, L. & Li, K. Z. H. (2000). Human memory. In F.I.M. Craik & T.A. Salthouse (Eds.), *Handbook of aging and cognition*. (2nd ed.). Mahwah, NJ: Erlbaum.

4
Changing self identity of elderly people: The case of Lithuania

Urtė Lina Orlova and Egle Sumskiene

Highly developed systems of medical and social services have led to constantly increasing expectations of longevity and high quality of life among elderly European Union residents. The main objective of the research reported in this chapter is to analyse the concept of 'good life' in old age, identity construction processes and social roles in old age and the relationship dynamics between social workers and dependant older people. The chapter reports a qualitative research study based on concepts of constructive social work and grounded theory conducted in 2011-2012 in rural and urban areas of Lithuania.

Research data show that helping professions are important in dealing with the processes of ageing. However, while medical doctors hold visible positions of authority, social workers often remain invisible actors in the network of helping professions. Dependant older people actively participate in the construction of their self-identity. The ways in which identity is constructed in later years of life is changing due to a range of factors, but it is influenced by external factors such as emigration of younger generations. Elderly people (especially those who live in residential care homes) experience particular issues in self-identity construction. One of the most interesting aspects we have found is the re-creation of the romantic self.

The authors believe that practising social workers who are aware of the processes involved in self-identity management, quality of life and the factors which influence it, can improve the well-being of older people.

Introduction

Europe celebrated 2012 as The Year for Active Ageing and Solidarity between Generations and declared positively the increasing life expectancy of its citizens. Highly developed systems of medical and social services have led to constantly increasing expectations among older people both to live longer and enjoy a high quality of life. The main topic of this chapter concerns the quality of life of the dependant older people who use social service and have contacts with social workers in their everyday lives. The participants of this research are dependant older people (age from 70 to 92 at the time of interviews) who live independently in private (or family-owned) homes or in residential care homes in both rural or urban areas of Lithuania. The main objective of the research was to analyse:

1. identity construction processes and social roles in old age
2. relationship dynamics process between social workers and dependant elderly people
3. concept of 'good of life' in old age

This research is one of only a few research projects in Lithuania which focus on life quality. The authors have applied a constructivist grounded theory approach (Charmaz, 2010).

Results and discussion

The results of the research are presented in accordance with a constructivist grounded theory framework. First, the initial research questions are discussed, and second, the sensitising concepts and general disciplinary perspectives are presented. Subsequently, there follows an overview of the data collection process, and finally important aspects of research results are presented.[1]

Lithuanian society is ageing and elderly people are becoming one of the main social work client groups. The process is affected by emigration from the country and lower birth rates within it. It is important to note that life expectancy has not changed dramatically over the years. Also there is a clear difference of 11 years between female and male life expectancy in Lithuanian society, with women enjoying the greater longevity. Older people (those over 65) who become dependant have two possibilities to maintain their quality of life: (1) to stay in their private homes and receive social services at home provided by formal or informal care givers, or (2) to enter a residential care home. The two possible scenarios have significant implications for the self-identity of the older people themselves. There are important changes in their social networks as well.

The self-identity of older people is co-created by those people self-defining as older and their significant others. There are important actors in older people's social networks. These comprise persons who have direct every day contacts with the older people; persons who contact via electronic devices (usually the younger generation (e.g., children, grandchildren); 'ephemeral people' (e.g. *first love*); and representatives of helping professions (medical doctors and social workers). Older people who start living in residential care homes have to embrace new relations with friends and neighbours.

Dependant older people have contacts with two helping professions predominantly, medical professionals and social workers. There are big differences in how older people react to those two types of helper. Medical profesionals are usually mentioned positively, with respect and thankfulness. On the other hand, social workers are often invisible and are mentioned only rarely in the interviews.

Main statements from the research

1. Lithuanian society is ageing. Therefore, it is important to understand the increasing role of social and medical services for older people.
2. Helping professions (in particular medical doctors and social workers) are important in addressing some of the processes of ageing, but those two professions enjoy different statuses from the point of view of older people themselves. Medical doctors hold visible positions of authority while social workers are invisible actors in their networks.
3. Dependant older people actively participate in the construction of their self-identity. Their social networks are changing, and they are influenced by external factors such as the emigration of younger generations.
4. Older people (especially those living in residential care homes) experience specific dimensions of self-identity. One the most interesting aspects is re-creation of the romantic self.

Ageing Lithuanian society

Social work promotes social change, harmony, social cohesion and empowerment of people. Based on bodies of knowledge and a unique set of principles and values social work engages people and structures to address life's challenges and to enhance well-being. Well-being is one of the main dimensions for social work practionioners. Older people are one of the most significant groups of social work service users whose quality of life highly depends on social workers.

The European Union's population is getting progressively older. According to the Eurostat 2012 bulletin, this has resulted from a significant and continuous increase in life expectancy from birth combined with low fertility rates and the entry into retirement of the post-World War II baby-boom generation (Eurostat, 2012: 40). The same tendency is being observed in Lithuanian society.

A short overview of the factors of ageing in Lithuanian society is important to understand the increasing role of social and medical services for elderly people. At the beginning of 2011, the Lithuanian population amounted to 3, 244, 601 persons (Statistics Lithuania, 2012). There are three main reasons why Lithuanian society is ageing, first of which is the decreasing birth rate[1]. Since 1990, fertility has been rapidly and steadily declining in Lithuania, reaching a level far below that required for population replacement (Stankuniene, Jasilioniene, 2008). According to statistical research before the 1990s the total fertility rate (TFR) of Lithuania stood close to a level sufficient to ensure population replacement, i.e. it was close to 2.0. However, the TFR varied from 1.24 to 1.27 throughout the period from 2002 to 2005, whereas in 2011 it reached 1.76 (Statistics Lithuania, 2012).

Second comes the number of deaths in young age. Statistics from the World Health Organization (2011) indicate that Lithuania is on top when it comes to suicides with 61.3 men and 10.4 women per 100,000 inhabitants deciding to end their lives amounting to 34.1 suicide per 100,000 inhabitants per annum. Teenagers and middle-aged men represent the most risk prone groups. In 2009, suicides among 15-19 year olds per 100,000 of the age group population equalled to 15.1 (compared to a low of 2 in Spain). The death rate from suicide in Lithuania was approximately three times the EU average while the rates in Hungary (21.7) were around double the average. Also, Romania (2009) at 14, Lithuania, Greece, Poland, Latvia, Cyprus and Belgium (2006) had the highest death rates (10 or more deaths per 100 000 inhabitants) resulting from transport accidents in 2010 (Eurostat September, 2012).

Thirdly, there is the emigration of young people. After Lithuania joined the European Union emigration became a big problem in the country. The majority of emigrants are young people (age 20 – 29) - according to data from the Lithuanian Statistical Department, 40.5% of all emigrants in 2010. In numerical terms, that amounts to 33,600. What makes matters worse is the data indicating that 60% of young people wish to emigrate (Public Policies, 2012).

The three aforementioned factors – low fertility rates, younger age mortality, and increased emigration - are important trends in Lithuanian society for comparison with those in the West European countries where life expectancy is increasing due to lower birth rates and longer life span.

Table 1
Life expectancy in Lithuania. (Statistics Lithuania, 2011)

Year	Total				Urban		Rural
	Female	Male	Female	Male	Female	Male	
2000	77.5	66.8	78.2	68.0	76.1	64.6	
2005	77.4	65.4	78.3	66.8	75.9	62.9	
2006	77.1	65.3	77.8	66.4	75.7	63.5	
2007	77.2	64.9	77.9	66.0	76.1	62.9	
2008	77.6	66.3	78.4	67.5	76.3	64.1	
2009	78.6	67.5	79.4	68.5	77.2	65.9	
2010	78.8	68.0	79.5	69.1	77.5	66.0	

There is an obvious difference (11 years) in female and male life expectancy in Lithuania. However, as we can see, life expectancy has not actually changed dramatically over the years, (Table 1). According to the Eurostat data (March 2011) for the European Union as a whole, life expectancy at birth averaged 82.2 years for women and 76.1 for men during the period from 2006 to 2008. The biggest gaps in life expectancy at birth between women and men were recorded for the Baltic States where women could expect to live between 11.1 (Lithuania) and 10.2 (Latvia) years longer than men.

Comparison of life expectancy of older people in Lithuania and the United Kingdom shows different patterns. Life expectancy in the UK is clearly continuing to increase, driven mainly by the ongoing postponement of deaths from the degenerative diseases. According to Howse (2006) the fall in mortality rates at older ages has in fact accelerated in recent years with average annual rates of improvement in mortality in the UK in 1998-2002 in the age group of 70-79 males increasing by 3,7% and for female group of 60-69 by 3,1%.

According to *The Statistics Lithuania 2012*, during 2010 more that 11,200 elderly people received social services (assistance at home or 'social care money') and 3,700 elderly people lived in 100 residential care homes established by state, municipalities or church-based organizations (see Table 2).

Table 2
Elderly people (Lithuania) Statistics Lithuania, 2012

	2010	2011
Total population	3,329,000	3,244,600
Aged over 65	534,401	535,769
Aged over 65 living in care homes	3,700	3,663
Receiving social services at home	11,258	n.d.

According to *The Statistics Lithuania 2012*, during 2010 more that 11,200 elderly people received social services (assistance at home or 'social care money') and 3,700 elderly people lived in 100 residential care homes established by state, municipalities or church-based organizations (see Table 2).

Methodology: Constructivist grounded theory

Grounded theory is probably the most popular research method used by qualitative researchers in the social sciences. While the methodology originated in sociology (Glaser & Strauss, 1967) it has been applied to numerous disciplines since. Researchers outside of sociology have remodelled – adopted and adapted – the methodology to fit their own disciplines. The study by McCallin (2012) identifies three main versions created by (1) Glaser (1992); (2) Strauss & Corbin (2008); (3) Charmaz (2006).

Charmaz (2006) suggested a model of grounded theory akin to a constructivist version of grounded theory. Important and valuable aspects of this approach include:

+ The argument that there are multiple realities in the world and generalisations are partial, conditional and situated in time and space;
+ Co-constructing data with participants and recognising the subjectivity that influences their lives is in keeping with a participatory researcher's value system;
+ Presenting an abstract account of an experience is the pivotal point (in classical grounded theory conceptualisation and the idea of finding a core category is the main goal). The participants' narratives are important. Rich, accurately detailed descriptions are considered to be most important and meaningful;
+ Themes, not concepts and categories, are attractive.

Figure 1.
Model of grounded theory methodology by Charmaz, 2006.

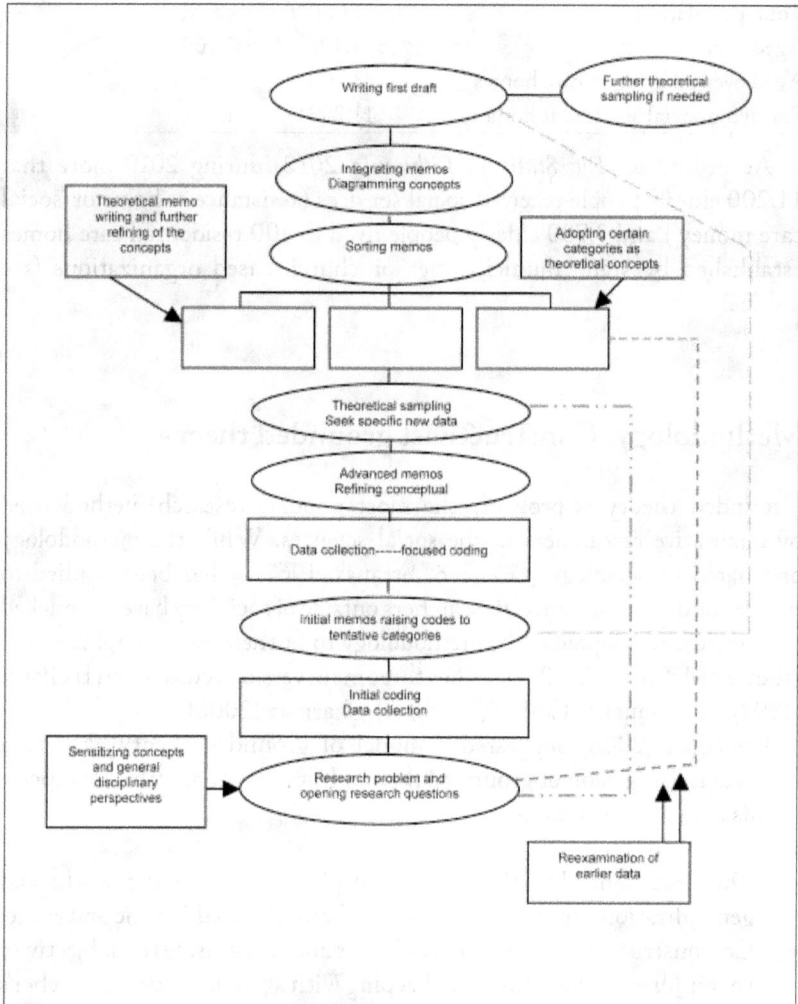

Constructive social work

Sensitising concepts that influence the process of this type of grounded theory research come from the perspectives of constructive social work. The seminal work behind this theoretical perspective is found in Parton and O'Byrne (2000).

According to Parton and O'Byrne (2000), the main points in this social work theory for practice are:

1. constructive social work argues that social work is as much, if not more, an art than science and proceeds on the basis that practice is better characterised as a practical-moral activity rather than rational-technical;
2. the constructive social work approach is affirmative and reflexive and focuses on dialogue, listening to and talking to the other;
3. the focus is narrative and different stories;
4. constructive social work emphasizes process; and
5. it is developing knowledge for practice.

Constructive social work uses a narrative mode of thought and seeks to gain credence in life like stories, and it is not interested in the general principles with wide application but rather in the local knowledge that is created. One can explain 'local' as being linked to the persons and circumstances within which they are produced and not claiming any wider application. Therefore, the life stories which are analysed accept uncertainty, complexity and flux.

Bruner (1986) analyses what he calls two components of narrative – the 'landscapes of actions' (which include events which are linked in the sequence over time) and the 'landscapes of consciousness' (which include interpretations, meanings, reflections on the events, thoughts, realisations and conclusions). Researchers usually can find gaps or contradictions in the life stories, which are an invitation to look for meaning deeper and further.

Developments in the concept of 'quality of life'

There is a rich variety of definitions of 'quality of life', each of them capturing specific aspects of the same social phenomenon. Rapley (2008) suggests a classical distinction in the conceptualising 'quality of life': objective well-being (e.g. *Human Development Index*) or subjective well-being (e.g. the index developed by the *Australian Centre of Quality of Life*) (Diener & Lucas, 1999; Diener, 2006). Health related 'quality of life' researchers provide one of the richest fields of theoretical discussion and empirical studies (Rapley, 2008). Also for more pragmatic needs there is available a more practical view of what quality of life comprises (Gilhooly, 2001). Most recent developments of definition of the concept are connected to cultural context and values or moral standards: hedonism as pleasure for one or eudaimonia as happiness for all (Gilhooly et al., 2005).

As cited in Noll, (2004: 6), the influence of moral values might be an answer to the question raised by Zapf (1986) who analyses the concept of quality of life as a multi-dimensional concept (Table 3). The most interesting are situations of 'adaptation' and 'dissonance'.

Table 3
Theoretical analysis of the concept 'life quality' Zapf (1986)
(as cited in Noll, 2004: 6)

	Subjective life conditions are good	Subjective life conditions are bad
Objective life conditions are good	Well-being	*Dissonance*
Objective life conditions are bad	*Adaptation*	Deprivation

In the 'adaptation' situation one can observe a 'paradox of satisfaction'. This scenario happens when a person finds himself or herself in an objectively poor situation, but nevertheless the subjective quality of life is evaluated positively. In a dissonant situation one can observe 'the dilema of dissatisfaction'. This scenario develops when objective quality of life is positive, but a person evaluates his or her subjective quality of life as negative.

Initial research questions

Our initial research questions were: (1) if old age is one of the realities of social life how it is constructed from the perspective of dependant older people themselves; and what are the layers of meaning of the concept within 'good life' in old age; (2) how one can describe the relationship between older persons and social workers, and what roles do social workers play in this interaction; (3) in terms of self-identity and social roles in old age, how do the roles of older people evolve and how do they develop?

Data collection

The data were collected during the period from June 2011 to March 2012 (Orlova, 2012). A sample of participants was identified consisting of 13 older people (3 men and 10 women) who could participate in the interviews, being in good physical health. Participants were born between 1920-1940 and had unique experience of political and cultural changes in society (from pre-WWII authoritarian regime to fifty years of Soviet occupation with communist rule and finally, to modern democracy in Lithuania as a member state of the European Union).

Participants were born in various ethnic regions of Lithuania and they belonged to different nationalities. Participants lived either in their own private homes or in residential care homes for elderly people. Half of the participants lived in urban areas and another half in rural areas of Lithuania. The interviews were semi-structured with a major focus placed on participants' life story narratives including some specific, but open-ended questions.

Research and interviews in natural settings require sensitive planning, which is worth the effort, especially when talking to older people about their personal experiences and life stories. Interviews were undertaken in the home environment of the participants where they could feel comfortable. This natural setting encouraged older people to speak about their experiences in a context that the researchers and respondents may not otherwise have considered (Leonard, Evans, & Armitage, 2010). Artifacts in the home environment provided additional non-verbal contextual information that was very useful for the interviews.

Identity in old age: Initial memos

Several categories which are being developed in the research will be discussed. The authors have chosen them because of their emotional and psychological importance to the elderly research participants.

Definition of old age

None of the participants were aware of the concept of 'social construction' or the idea that people could create social world and social order by themselves. But during the interviews most of them said clearly that older people define their 'elderliness' by themselves. Participants say that: 'old age is not only about the age or health status of the person. The person himself or herself creates his/her old age' (Elzbieta, 92).

The most obvious subjective criterion for 'old age' is the process of 'non-renewal'. At this point respondents gave a lot of of examples and explanations. For example, one respondent stated that a 'young person is like a foal who is happily gamboling in the meadows and an old person is like an old horse which stands quietly with the head down' and continued that old age can be said to occur when the 'person does not have power anymore' (Rita, 85). Old age could also be experienced as a tendency for stagnation.

Participants presented their opinions about different stages of human life as well (from an age focused perspective)

+ People around 25 are young and without experience: 'A young person is like young tree which can be easily bent by the wind, and so happens to the young people who have no experience, no taste of life' (Rita, 81);
+ By age of 35 person is still young but already understands everything and knows the taste of life from personal experience;
+ At the age of 50 there is golden point and beyond it physical beauty starts shrinking (as Elzbieta, 92) put it: 'It is the age when I made the last portrait photos of myself');
+ At 60 one still can be carefree and 'whistle around happily'. So, in general a human being is young until age of 70 (because person still can marry); but
+ When the age of 70 comes person usually feels 'body drop', pains in the body and suffers various illnesses;
+ Around age of 80 the real old age starts and person feels that something is really going on;
+ Age of 90 years and more is already a positive in itself: 'It is a reason for respect from others and being proud about yourself' (Nastute, 89).

Self identity and social network in old age

Most participants admitted that with age social contacts and relations become more limited, but their importance grows. Also, other significant changes in social networks occur. Two major reasons are (1) the emigration of younger generations and (2) coming to live in residential care homes which means that a lot of privacy is lost and person has to learn the rules of living in residential care, i.e., devising ways to maintain existing social relationships, enacting strategies to establish new ones and reframing subjective assessments of well-being in the face of new circumstances (Debra and Burge, 2012). Living in a residential care home also means that person will stay there until death as examples of people going back home are extremely rare. Statistical data also support this statement: according to the Department of Supervision of Social Services (2010, 2011) each year almost four hundred residents leave elderly residential care homes. Around 85% of them die, 5% choose another care institutions and only less than 10% (40 individuals) come back to the community.

There is a general feeling among participants that the 'circle of close people is shrinking' (Apolonija, 85), but still contains many visible and invisible actors because social networks have become increasingly important (Tang and Lee, 2011). Some of the actors in the network never could have existed in any time before the digital era (see Table 4 – '*Electronic people*'). Some of the actors appear only because they live in residential care homes (table No. 4 – '*Boys' 'mafia' for breaking the rules of care homes*'). Street and Burge notice that new residents experience an entirely novel cast of institution-specific characters offering fresh relationship potential, and expanding social circles to include staff members, co-residents and even co-residents' visitors.

Scharlach (2009) argues the importance of the social network. According to him older people with more actual and potential sources of social support have better physical and psychological well-being and greater resilience in response to diseases and other life stressors. Cornwell (2011) suggests that while on average older people have smaller social networks than middle aged and younger adults, they also tend to be embedded in more supportive, stronger networks.

Research data identify the following three ways of maintaining networks:

1. active (calling, sending post cards)
2. passive (e.g. answering incoming phone calls)
3. pretending as if problem of empty network does not exist at all.

Helping professions

This chapter summarises the type of network actors according to their roles and influences. The term 'visibility' in the context of this research shows an actor's active, usually positive attitude towards elderly person (see Table 4 – *'Medical professionals'*). The invisible actors are those who do exist but the participants themselves do not begin talking about them during the interview. They may admit the existence of an invisible actor but would comment on it briefly and jump back or forward to more comfortable topic (see Table 4 – *'God'*). It is striking to notice the trend that such themes as religion, death and status of dependant person are almost avoided.

Table 4

Actors in the network of identity

Visible actors in the network of identity	*Invisible* actors in the network of identity
Neighbours in residential care home; People in the street; Virtual people (family members, relatives, friends and colleagues in photos); Electronic people (close relatives, friends, family members contacted via phone, Skype); Ephemeral people (*e.g.* people from long ago, first love); Friends (friends; ex-colleagues); Medical professionals; Non-professional helping people (neighbors, family members, volunteers); Boys' 'mafia' for breaking the rules of care home (e.g. for illegal use of alcohol); Girls' 'tea party' and 'self-support' group (elderly ladies meeting and spending time together while playing table games or just enjoying a cup of tea).	Social workers as professionals; in some cases they do exist, but most often only under their personal names (e.g. – Liuda; Margarita); Religious personalities usually from Catholic background. One can identify their presence by religious pictures on the wall, rosary near the bed, very short comments on religious practice, etc. The silence about religious life might be also inherited from the times of Soviet regime when this topic was kept as a very personal matter; Death. The natural process of death is often personalised approaching death as 'she'. This 'ephemeral lady' is the most invisible actor and she usually comes into life narrative via funny stories and anecdotes.

The role of a social worker is, we believe, very special. This invisibility of social worker as a dedicated professional might be due to several reasons. After discussing this topic with social workers working in residential care homes the authors formulated a 'raw' hypothesis based on the following presumptions: (1) there is negative connotation to receive social help or have status of dependant person, therefore the connection 'social worker – dependant person' is being hidden; (2) social work profession is relatively new in Lithuania (and other post-Soviet countries), lacking respect and recognition in the society, services provided by them are perceived as domestic, plain and usually taken for granted; (3) social workers in residential care homes (in Lithuanian case) are the ones who meet a person on his arrival to residential care home but they also are the last ones to part with the residents by arranging funeral details. Therefore, the 'social worker' topic may be avoided because of negative emotional reactions to natural and unavoidable process of death. Of course, the hypothesis presented here is to be investigated deeper and more precisely.

Romantic self in old age

While analysing interviews with the elderly participants living in residential care homes another major topic appeared, namely self-image with light romantic nuance. Most of the research participants are widowed and have lived with only one partner all their life. Elderly participants usually report that due to difficult living conditions in young age (especially those who returned back home to Lithuania from exile in Siberian labour camps) they had very limited space and time to develop romantic contacts with representatives of the opposite sex. Now, in their elderly years, they live in the residential care home. In the new living space this kind of relationship becomes possible. The romantic self is usually 'hidden', but not very well and can be sensed in many actions. Older people resort to great variety of actions to attract attention (see Table 5).

As a final note it is important to mention one of the most touching moment in narratives of life stories of the elderly participants to whom we spoke. The relationship between grandchildren and grandparents is extremely important. Even love stories of grandchildren (but not of their own children!) are experienced by the elderly people as very important. They describe the lives of their grandchildren in very vivid and vibrant manner. Rita (81) puts it this way: 'Oh, my grandson - he is such a good boy! When

Table 5
Romantic self of men and women

Women in action:	Men in action:
• saying 'Hi' to men; • making up hair; picking the right clothes; make-up; • striving to be beautiful when alive because 'she is 80, but still not old, because she is beautiful' (Rita, 81); • to be beautiful in death process; • demonstrating their material well-being; • talking about social capital which means to have grandchildren, family, friends.	• talking to women and visiting them in their rooms; • behaving as if having real love affair; • participating in the process of decision making in residential care home (Kazimieras,85); • 'polite' drinking (e.g. *aperitif* before starting conversation); • breaking the rules of care home; • demonstrating their material well-being; • talking about social capital (professional career in the past, job and grandchildren).

he was getting married I thought 'I have to live longer so I could meet my great grandchildren'. Now – and people are soooo greedy (*giggles*) – I want to live even longer. My great grand-daughter is now almost two years of age, and I want her to remember me. So, I have to live for at least two more years'.

As researchers, we believe that practising social workers who are conscious of the processes of self-identity management and social network creation by older people can contribute to the improvement of their well-being. We believe that this research will provide some useful insights for that purpose.

Conclusions

Our four key conclusions are:

1. Lithuanian society is ageing; therefore, it is important to understand the increasing role of social and medical services for the elderly people.
2. Helping professions (in particular, medical doctors and social workers) are important in the process of ageing, but those two professions have different statuses. Medical doctors hold visible position of authority while social workers are invisible actors in older people's networks.

3. Older people actively participate in the construction of their self-identity and social networks and maintaining contacts change.

4. Older people (especially those who live in residential care homes) experience special set of dimensions of self-identity. One of the most interesting aspects is the re-creation of the romantic self.

Note

1. Definition of birth rate: This entry gives the average annual number of births during a year per 1,000 persons in the population at midyear; also known as crude birth rate.

References

Bruner, E. (1986) Ethnography as narrative. In V. Turner & E. Bruner (Eds), *The Anthropology of Experience*, Chicago, IL: University of Illinois Press, pp. 139-155.

Charmaz, K. (2006) *Constructing Grounded Theory. A practical guide through Qualitative Analysis*, London: Sage.

Corbin, J. A., & Strauss, A. (2008) *Basics of Qualitative Research*, 3rd ed. Thousand Oaks, CA: Sage.

Cornwell, B. (2011) Age Trends in Daily Social Contact Patterns. *Research on Aging*, 33 (5), 598-631.

Department of Supervision of Social Services (2010, 2011). Retrieved November 12, 2012, from http://www.sppd.lt/lt/informacija/Statistika/

Diener, E. (2006) Guidelines for National Indicators of Subjective Well-Being and Ill-Being. *Applied Research in Quality of Life*. 1(2), 151-157.

Diener, E., and Lucas, R. (2000) Explaining differences in societal levels of happiness: relative standards, need, fulfillment, culture and evaluation theory. *Journal of Happiness Studies*, 1(2), 41–78.

Eurostat. European Statistics. Retrieved 15 November, 2012, from http://epp.eurostat.ec.europa.eu/statistics_explained/index.php/Population_change_at_regional_level

Gilhooly, M. (2001) *Transport and Ageing. Extending Quality of Life for Older People Via Public and Private Transport. Economic and Social Research Council.* Retrieved November 29, 2010 from http://bura.brunel.ac.uk/

bitstream/2438/1312/1/PDF%20ESRC%20Transport%20Final%20Report.
pdf

Gilhooly, M., Gilhooly, K., Bowling, A. (2005) Quality of Life: Meaning and
Measurement. In Walker, A. (Eds.) *Growing Older: Understanding quality of
life in old age*, Mc Graw-Hill: Open University Press, pp. 1-14.

Glaser, B. G. (1992) *Basics of Grounded Theory Analysis*. Mill Valley, CA: Sociology
Press.

Howse, K. (2006) *Increasing life expectancy and the compression of morbidity: a critical
review of the debate*. Working paper number 206. Oxford Institute of Ageing.

Juozeliūnienė, I., Kanapienienė, L.(2011) Šeimos žemėlapio metodas. *Sociologija.
Mintis ir veiksmas*, 2(29), 35-54.

Leonard, R., Evans, S., Armitage, L. (2010) *Care Networks Project Growing and
Maintaining Social Networks for Older People*. Retrieved 23 November, 2012,
from http://www.adhc.nsw.gov.au/__data/assets/file/0005/236498/11_
Care_Network_final_report_Oct_10_for_publication.pdf

McCallin, A. *Which Grounded Theory?* [electronic version] Retrieved 25 April,
2012 from http://www.groundedtheoryonline.com/what-is-grounded-
theory/classic-grounded-theory.

Noll, H.H. (2004) Social indicators and quality of life research: Background,
achievements and current trends. In Genov, N. (Eds.), *Advances in
sociological knowledge. Over half a century*, vol. 1. Wiesbaden: VS Verlag fuer
Sozialwissenschaften, pp 151-181.

Orlova, U.L. (2012) Initial memos on quality of life of elderly people. *VII
Krakowska Konferencja mlodych uczhonych. Krakow*, 291.

Parton, N., and O'Byrne, P. (2000) *Constructive Social work. Towards a new practice*,
Bainsgstoke: Palgrave.

Rapley, M. (2008) *Quality of life research: a critical introduction*, Los Angeles: SAGE,.

Public policies. Retrieved October 27, 2012, from http://www.public-policies.eu/
index.php/problem/Emigration-rate-in-Lithuania-among-young-people-is-
getting-higher_86

Scharlach, A. E. (2009) Creating aging-friendly communities. *Generations*, 33(2),
5–11.

Stankuniene, V., Jasilioniene, A. (2008) Lithuania: Fertility decline and its
determinants. In: Hoem, J. M. (Eds.), *Childbearing Trends and Policies in
Europe*. Retrieved November 14, 2012, from http://www.demographic-
research.org/special/7/

Statistics Lithuania (2012) Databases. Retrieved 10 June, 2012 from http://db1.
stat.gov.lt/statbank/default.asp?w=1024

Street, D. & Burge, S.W. (2012) Residential Context, Social Relationships, and
Subjective Well- Being. In *Assisted Living Research on Aging*, 34(3), 365-394.

Tang, F. & Lee, Y. (2011) Social Support Networks and Expectations for Aging in Place. *Research on Aging,* 33(4), 444-464.

Walker, A. (eds) (2005) *Growing older: understanding quality of life in old age,* Mc Graw-Hill: Open University Press.

World Health Organisation (2012) *Public Health Action for the Prevention of Suicide,* WHO.

5

Housing for seniors:

An overview of policies and challenges for an active ageing in place in Spain

María Luisa Gómez Jiménez

Introduction

This chapter will describe the main public policies regarding seniors and how public law can influence the strategies developed specially regarding the provision of proper housing for seniors.

The analysis of the public issues connected with the economic crisis, and the distribution of jurisdictions allow a better approach in terms of the challenges that public authorities face when promoting active ageing.

As for the housing market, in the aftermath of the 'burst' of the housing bubble, the orientation of new models of occupancy and the facing of new family models are a reality which contrast with the traditional typology of housing provision for seniors (not just assisted living facilities but special housing adapted to their needs.) This stands in conflict with an 'active ageing in place' trend which will demand in the future the definition of a new affordability for the new 'seniors housing zoning'.

Ageing society and economic crisis: The European context

The Scenario: European Year of Active Ageing

The demographic of ageing is focusing in recent years the attention of practitioners, academics and researchers[1]. The reason for that, is the huge impact which an aged population may have for policy-makers, and the distribution of resources, and therefore for the all society in general. The economic impact of this trend has been the theme of many studies, along the last years, and now when we are implementing measures to fight again the economic crisis, this factor plays a significant role in the way we can anticipate greater social problems[2].

The European Commission took an early part in the debate[3] connecting the main aspects involved in the examination of an ageing population and society; these include the provision of services, health care, long term-care, unemployment benefits, social inclusion and participation, and age discrimination. A testament to the seriousness with which such concerns were held was the declaration of 2012, as European Active Ageing year[4], introducing the notion of active ageing in the agenda of policy makers around Europe. In fact, public spending on health already accounts for 7.8% of GDP in the EU, and by 2060, public expenditure on acute health care and long-term care is expected to increase by 3 % of GDP predominantly as a result of the ageing population[5]. To face these challenges the EU Commission has enacted in 2011 a strategic implementation plan[6], which is focusing on actions in 3 pillars: prevention; screening and early diagnosis; care and cure; and active ageing and independent living. These plus the support towards horizon-scanning themes such as 'Thematic marketplace: Innovation for age friendly buildings, cities and environments'[7] with a definition of the specific action of 'Promoting innovation for age friendly and accessible buildings, cities and environments', motivates the need for an specific attention to the reality of our cities' landscapes and the proper definition of tools able to provide from the use of ITCs, the required accessibility for an ageing environment.

The first step which the EU Commission has undertaken, has been the creation of a partnership which is defined as a 'distinctive opportunity to help deliver on the policy objectives of the Europe 2020 flagships: the Innovation Union, Digital Agenda for Europe, New Skills for New Jobs and the European Platform against Poverty and Social Exclusion'.

The need of regulatory reforms

In the process of taking the right steps towards the objectives of the Plan the EU Commission needs to undertake some regulatory reforms. Especially, the official documents reflect the case for those regulatory barriers, which have proved to be an issue throughout the European Union. This is the case for the *European Data Protection Law*, including health data, or the patient's rights in cross borders care[8,] and the case for the innovative public procurement[9]. While these processes take place, the case for a national and regional policy definition and their adjustment to the European scenario implies the definition of their regulatory impact taking into account the mission and vision of the EU, so that the transit towards the reforms can be soft. The financial instruments of the European Union targeted to promote these steps will be define soon in the framework of the new European research programs – Horizon 2020[10].

The ways in which these regulations will be implemented in each country will take into account the previous state of art regarding the care of seniors and their capacity to become part of the solution and not part of the problem. This implies a new way of approaching the fact of an aged Europe, and means in practical terms the need to create tools for increasing not just the role of seniors in society but their integration in the productive and economic systems by involving their know-how and expertise in those societies which are supposed to provide them the required pensions, health and social services.

Definition of concepts like 'personal Autonomy' and 'Dependency'[11], and its connection with this provision of services, allowed a first approach to the topic of healthy ageing. Despite the effort to define a general framework to fight against age discrimination and to assure healthy ageing in the European Union, true it's that the results depends on the different national approaches, social and health-care systems[12].

The projection of healthy ageing in land planning and the lack of jurisdiction of EU law in defining zoning:

Land planning cannot ignore the transformation of our society and their increasing demand for adapted buildings where the removal of architectural barriers is a must. Land planning, and urban planning does not belong to the sphere of jurisdiction of the EU policy, notwithstanding the effort of the European union to define an environmental policy and to integrate the Social Services for seniors provision in the liberalization process enacted by the 'Bolkestein Directive.'[13] However, these issues are central to enacting healthy ageing policies throughout society.

The way in which the issue of *health care provision* is solved in each European country introduces also key elements for the definition of an expected result regarding the provision of health care in an increasingly demand-led scenario. Also, the professionalism of those who dedicate their lives to care for seniors, becomes a must when the job they develop is having a high impact in society overall. Lastly, the *role of ICT* in the provision of services and in the empowerment of patients[14] in the field, has created a unique opportunity to address new challenges by being able to connect technologies with needs providing suitable solutions for all. In this sense the European Commission has proposed a Decision on the Strategic Innovation Agenda of the European Institute of Innovation and Technology (EIT) for 2014-2020[15] identifying 'Innovation for healthy living and active ageing' as one of the priority themes for the EIT Knowledge and Innovation Communities (KICs) wave in 2014-2015.

All these elements taken together emphasize the role of public authorities and the significance of an adequate public policy able to create opportunities and to transform challenges into new chances of growing older positively. The building up of health care structures oriented to the provision of these services is a must in the near future because of the changing demography. Elements of the debate connect also with the urgency for public intervention in respect of older people and the definition of proper regulations to control the role of companies able to provide services, and for some to invest in tax-refundable activities with the idea of increasing their level of social corporate responsibility.

As for the distinction of public and private partnerships in the innovative agenda from the EU, it is clear that they need to interact in order to achieve the main goal of promoting better quality of life for seniors citizens[16].

Coming to the ground: The Spanish case

The European situation described above mentioned the huge interest of policy-makers in enacting a just and workable policy to promote active ageing throughout the whole of Europe. This contrasts with the possibilities of each country to provide a sustainable healthy ageing for all its citizens. In Spain, despite the fact of the different distribution of seniors in the Spanish geography the ageing process is of concern to sociologists, economists, lawyers and policy-makers[17].

These aspects, which are connected with the idea of active ageing, allowed policy makers to define in broad terms a variety of actions to pursue inside in the form of programs able to promote the activity of seniors. One of main issues, which have been taken into account so far, is the integration of ICT in the provision of active ageing. Thus, in the year 2012, the OPTICAE[18] project was presented in the framework of the CEAPAT-IMSERSO. The project was included in the working program of the Spanish contribution to the European year of active ageing, and it was mainly focused on presenting results regarding the need to develop the use of ICTs as a means of increasing business opportunities in the field of assisted technologies aimed at improving the quality of life of the ageing population.

The final report of the project summarizes the main actions and projects undertaken in the field of autonomy and seniors and divide the cases included in three main categories:

1. Solutions at home, to better improve the quality of life of seniors at home
2. Socio-health care provision with a specific orientation to seniors
3. Tools to increase participation of seniors in the society.

It is accepted that seniors wish to age in place. As for the Spanish situation, there is data to demonstrate the distance between the specific residences or facilities for seniors and their previous houses. This data is important because it reflects that Spanish seniors do not move very far away from the place they are used to living in if they move into accommodation for seniors. It is suggested that they want to keep former networks. It is not the concept of ageing in place which needs to be considered - which is a very strong trend in Europe – but also the effects that the existence of the same population – whilst growing older - may have in the revitalization and urbanization of cities.

In the following table, we can see the distances between the residence – as public facilities for seniors, as part of the public services - and the previous house. As we have pointed before, seniors represent a high percentage of those who own their homes. The figure shows that the location of the public facility is often near their previous house, and, if it is further away, it is located in the same neighbourhood or municipality. This reaffirms the strong tendency or wish to age in familiar places even if the seniors do not have the option to remain in their house, and they need to move to a residence.

Table 1
Distance between residence and public facilities

	%
Near	24.2
Far, but in the same neigbourhood or municipality	25.4
Far	32.9
Not far, not near	3.3
No answer	14.2

So, it is suggested that the policy for seniors developed in each country must take into consideration this trend to age in place and improve the stock of existing units to allow it to be adequate to seniors' needs. Elderly people generally reside in large, old homes, with some deficiencies in terms of facilities and equipment. Thus to assure independent living for seniors ageing in place housing policy needs to design new models of living. Two possibilities may be developed. The first is the need to adapt the building to the specific needs of seniors and removing, for instance, architectural barriers. The second is the provision of services at home (in-home or domiciliary care).

In both cases, however, the owner would be likely to be the senior, or his/her family as we have seen. So this does not entirely offer a model for public housing provision.

An accessible environment is the basis for ensuring independent living for people with reduced mobility. The built environment and the way it is or is not accessible, play an increasingly important role in people's standards of life and self development. It is an essential element in an active independence which enables all categories of citizens to contribute to society, and thus reduces the dependence of vulnerable people on public subsidies and services. In the context of an ageing population, paying attention to accessibility is an essential element of any policy aiming at promoting the independence of people as long as possible, thus reducing the need for publicly sponsored specific services, while responding to people's needs.

The European concept of accessibility in a spatial geographical sense remarks on these ideas saying: 'Built environments should enable all individuals to develop as persons. Thus, their design has to take into account the diversity of the population and need which, we all have to be independent. Therefore, built environments, including each of their elements and components, should be designed in a way that they enable everybody to access the different opportunities available: culture, space and buildings, communications, transport and services, economy, participation...'[19].

The concept of accessibility concerns the idea of in-home care services, which are another option used in Spain to provide services to seniors who decide to remain at home. In Spain the in-home care services can be defined as: 'An individualized program to prevent and to rehabilitate, in which you can get a range of services and professional and technical intervention consisting of personal in-home care of psychosocial, family, and environmental support, provided in the house of the elderly person who is dependent to a certain degree.'

The adaptation process of an existing stock of housing to accomplish this trend, however, demands the allocation of expensive and constrained economic resources, since in most cases seniors cannot afford to pay the adaptation- expenses on their own.

Because of this, National Housing Projects since 2006, assigned an allocation of resources to help the modification of housing for seniors. In this sense, the example of the Orden VIV/2784/2006, July 27, passed on September 12, 2006, which establishes a number of economic measures to assure that the frail elderly can adapt their homes to their needs. Nevertheless, as in the rest of the measures included in the Spanish Housing project the direction is not to create a new design of housing for seniors but to accommodate the existing stock of housing, and besides not give specific support to any kind of assisted, as an significant way of attending to seniors needs.

The projection for the new Housing project 2013 – 2016, which has been so far advertised points out that the main goal will be to remodeling and urban renewal and the housing projects connected to that[20]. The orientation of the new Housing Project which definition has not been concluded yet, needs to coordinate different provisions from regional government. The case for that has to do with the definition of Spain as a decentralized state[21].

The second important issue regarding 'ageing in place' is the provision of services required for seniors. One of the main characteristics of Spanish society regarding the care of their seniors at home, is the important role of the family in the caregiver system. In fact, the family is the main caregiver for seniors in Spain with sons and daughters acting as 'the informal caregivers'.

There is not an exact number of 'informal caregivers' that can be identified in Spain. The concept of the 'informal caregiver' includes not just the family, but also voluntary organizations that work together to support important public goals. Nevertheless the data shows that the number of persons needing specific care is growing year by year. According to this data more than 32% of Spanish seniors over 65 years old have a disability. This percentage falls to 5% when the rest of population is considered.

'Less money for doing more': seeking new opportunities and reshaping the Welfare State whereas housing for seniors is a must

The scenario described, must face a new situation as a consequence of the economic crisis. The way of tackling the current global financial crisis affecting the world resulting in austerity measures within the EU, has for Spain resulted in dramatic effects in terms of productivity and consumption. There is a potential need for economic rescue from the EU and a continuing crisis within the financial system, affecting in the direct way the confident of investors in the Spanish Banking systems, weaken the image and position of the country beyond the frontiers. Leaving apart the study of the causes of this economic crisis and the explanations which allow to understand why it is having a different impact in all countries, the case is that President of the Spanish Government had to undertake unpopular and risky measures to reduce deficit , by cutting expenses and reducing all kind of investments.

The case would have not been of much significance if the reductions had not affected a significant number of the Spanish population and sectors who experience the effects of the crisis personally. The economic rationality of reducing expenses, when it reaches the maximum projection produces just the opposite effect as expected, by reducing income and thereby expenditure, and increasing unemployment and the concomitant need for financial welfare assistance.

The shadows of the reduction measures in the different areas affect in a high proportion the normal development of social policies, since no social issue can be maintain at no cost. As a consequence of this, the national program of reforms which was sent already to the European Union is reshaping the Spanish Welfare state at a high speed, as never happened before since the introduction of the Spanish Constitution in 1978. This includes not just the lack of subsidies or financial support to address social issues but the design of a different structure reducing the number of public bodies able to provide health care- for seniors.

In this scenario, the hypothesis of promoting active 'ageing in place' by adapting the older person's home will only be affordable for those with enough economic resources. Support for a healthy and active ageing when the architectural barriers have not been removed when this was feasible creates a gap in provision for seniors based on income. The assurance of healthy ageing when this proceed will depends much on the will of those investing to make it possible in a more wider context able to overcome the effects of this economic crisis.

Notes

1   Víd. Gómez Jiménez, *Public Choices and Housing Opportunities for seniors citizens: Different scenarios in the United States of America and Spain in Chicago Kent Journal of International and comparative law, spring 2012.*

2   One interesting UK study, to do the comparison is the one carried out by DEMOS for WRVS, which compares the scenario for Sweden, Germany, and the Netherlands, readable in: http://www.wrvs.org.uk/Uploads/Documents/

Reports%20and%20Reviews/ageing_across_europe_may24_2012.pdf

3   Communication from the commission to the European Parliament and the council, Taking forward the Strategic Implementation Plan of the European Innovation Partnership on Active and Healthy Ageing, COM 2012 (83) final. DOCE, 29-2-2012.

4   Decision No 940/2011/EU of the European Parliament and of the Council of 14 September 2011 on the European Year for Active Ageing and Solidarity between Generations (2012)

5   Ageing Report 2009: http://ec.europa.eu/economy_finance/publications/publication14992_en.pdf

6   Strategic Implementation Plan – Strategic Part: http://ec.europa.eu/research/innovationunion/pdf/active-healthy-ageing/steering group/implementation_plan.pdf#view=fit&pagemode=none; Operational Part: http://ec.europa.eu/research/innovation-union/pdf/active-healthy-ageing/steeringgroup/operational_plan.pdf#view=fit&pagemode=none

7   Sic, Strategic Plan, ut Supra page 4.

8   As estated in the document regarding the Directive of European Parliament and of the Council 2011/24/EU of 93.2011 on the application of patients' rights in cross-border healthcare

9   Innovative public procurement means that the public sector takes on the role and risks of a lead customer, while improving the quality of its services and productivity. Proposal for a Directive of the European Parliament and of the Council on public procurement COM(2011) 896 final of 20.12.2011

10 Communication on Horizon 2020 - The Framework Programme for Research and Innovation. COM (2011) 808 final of 30.11.2011

11 The idea of lack of autonomy and the moment when an adult become a dependent persona arose the political debate in Spain in beginning of the nineties debate. Then the pass of the Act 39/96, to promote autonomy recognized the role of formal caregivers and defined the status of being 'a dependent person'. It's important to remember that the approach to the idea dependency, avoids any connection with the economic background of the person. True as it 's that one can be economically dependent on someone else, the recognition and the acknowledge of duties and freedoms the law was creating were targeted to those with lack of capacity to deal with their activities of daily living (from now on ADLS).

12 As can ben read in 'The Dependency Act – Some Notes Regarding the Interrelations between Housing and Social Services for Senior Citizens in Spain', in Social Vulnerability and Resilience in Europe, Budrich Verlag, 2013, in press.

13 'Bolkestein' Directive on Internal market, Directive 2006/123/EC has introduced significant changes in the definition of market of services with the

idea of increase the competitivity, and improving the market perfomance on the provision of services.

14　The way how to empower the patients open new challenges for public policy, true as it's that patients are the ones which deserves the best treatments and services. As the 'European Innovation Partnership on active and healthy ageing Consultation response' issued by the ESN European Social Network in UK in 26-1-2011: one of the main barriers for active Ageing is the insufficient involvement of 'end-users' (patients, older people, care professionals) in the development and deployment of new innovative solutions) .

15　COM(2011) 822 final of 30.11.2011

16　http://www.imsersomayores.csic.es/documentos/documentos/esn-consultation-01.pdf

17　We refers to some of these policies in chapter of this book.

18　Opportunities for firms regarding the implementation of ICTs in the process of gaining autonomy while ageing.

19　European Concept of Accessibility, 2003.

20　http://www.lamoncloa.gob.es/ServiciosdePrensa/NotasPrensa/MFOM/2012/121212-vivienda.htm

21　The Spanish Constitution declares: 1. All Spaniards have the same rights and obligations in any part of the territory of the State (section 139).

References

Communication from the commission to the European Parliament and the council, Taking forward the Strategic Implementation Plan of the European Innovation Partnership on Active and Healthy Ageing, COM 2012 (83) final, DOCE, 29-2-2012.

Frug, Gerald and Barron David, (2008) *City Bound. How States Stifle Urban Innovation.* New York: Cornell University Press.

Gómez Jiménez, (2012) Public Choices and Housing Opportunities for seniors citizens: Different scenarios in the United States of America and Spain, *Chicago Kent Journal of International and comparative law, spring.*

Encuesta Condiciones de Vida de las personas mayors (2004) Spain: Social Affairs Department IMSERSO.

Eur. Consult. Ass., (2003) Challenges of Social Policy in Europe's Ageing Societies, Doc. No. 1591.

Fainstein, Susan S. *The City Builders. Property Development in New York and London,* 1980- 2000. Second Edition. Revised. Kansas, 2001.

IMSERSO (2004): Seniors Living Conditions Enquiry Results. Madrid.

Promotion of Personal Autonomy and Care for Dependent Persons, Spanish Act 39/2006, Dec. 14, 2006, *available at* http://www.mepsyd.es/dctm/mepsyd/horizontales/prensa/documentos/2008/ley-dependencia.pdf?documentId=0901e72b80027756

Recommendation 1591: Challenges of Social Policy in Europe's Aging Societies 10 (2003), *available at* http://www.unece.org/pau/_docs/age/2007/AGE_2007_MiCA07_CntrRprtESPAdd5_e.pdf. [hereinafter *Recommendation 1591*].

6

Learning and education in later life in Germany: Development, trends and prospects

Cornelia Kricheldorff

The relationship between learning and education in later life

In German-language publications various terms are used to describe the field of learning and education in later life. On the one hand, terms such as 'learning in later life' (*Altersbildung*) 'learning throughout life' (*Lernen im Lebenslauf*), or 'lifelong learning' (*lebenslanges Lernen*) are employed, on the other hand expressions such as 'educational work with older people' (*Bildungsarbeit mit älteren Menschen*) or 'education in later life' are used. In terms of content, there is a close link to gerontology (*Gerontologie*) demonstrated by the increasing use of the term 'geragogy' (*Geragogik*), particularly in professional discourse, which mainly describes theory and implementation of education in later life from an educational point of view. However, the relevant literature has yet to come up with a consistent definition of the key terms 'learning' and 'education', sometimes used side by side and sometimes as synonyms. Some authors' definition of 'learning' corresponds to others' definition of 'education', creating a considerable lack of clarity and leading to overlap (Bubolz-Lutz et al 2010:14ff.).

However, there is clearly a general agreement that *learning* constitutes a basic human life process, allowing human beings to adapt to different and continuously changing conditions and situations in life, while at the same time facilitating an active approach to them. The ability to learn is also undeniably the general basis of education.

Education represents the constitutive element of institutionalised provision, forming the overall framework of the historically developed educational system (cf. Gukenbiehl 1998:86). From a functionalist point of view, education is seen as a tool of socialisation and integration in society as well as subjective social differentiation and distinction (cf. Barz 2006;

Gukenbiehl 1998:86). At the same time, education is understood as a value postulate, defined by historically changing models, education ideals and objectives (Gukenbiehl 1998:85; Kolland 2005:13). The definition of the 1960s German Educational Commission (*Deutscher Ausschuss für das Erziehungs- und Bildungswesen*) is still up-to-date; it defines as being educated any person who 'in his or her life continuously strives to understand themselves, society and the world in order to act according to the gained understanding' (*Deutscher Ausschuss für das Erziehungs- und Bildungswesen* 1960/61:404).

This understanding of education leads to very diverse approaches and application models of *education in later life*. It follows that education by far exceeds the offers provided by educational institutions for older and old people explicitly defined as such, including community colleges, third age academies, institutions run by the church and similar establishments (cf. Sommer et al 2004). In addition, places offering educational opportunities and settings for learning outside of educational institutions, which have their roots in everyday community life, are of particular interest. A very close link to the everyday life of older and old people is established and a much wider scope of possible educational needs can be addressed than in traditional educational establishments (Kricheldorff 2010).

Geragogy as theory and implementation of education in later life

Geragogy represents a very young scientific discipline and raises new questions regarding the specific needs and objectives of learning in later life. In turn it has been met with increased attention and much interest in gerontological and educational debates.

> Parallel to an overall increased focus on education in later life, geragogy has been receiving more and more recognition as the scientific discipline of education in later life, for and about later life and ageing – both within the framework of the increasingly diversified discipline of gerontology as well as on the part of political decision-makers. (Köster/Schramek 2005:232)

Debate in geragogical circles about an appropriate understanding of education in later life has been focussing strongly on the characteristics of education. Veelken (2003) for example names identity development and the discussion of old age-specific development issues within the framework of a specific historical culture and societal context and as the main task of education in later life. A holistic definition of education is introduced which is non-functionalist and therefore viable for all ages, including old age (Bubolz-Lutz 2000). Kade (2009) lists the following points as essential focus areas; skills for everyday life, action competence and social skills but also creative skills and competencies in a biographical context. The main concerns are self-reflexion, (self) feeling and (self) expression. Modernity theory has often identified the ability to reflect on one's biography and way of living as the mission of education. Reflecting on life's experiences as an important basis for a conscious construction of subsequent life stages includes making a decision on learning and life objectives for later life (cf. Kricheldorff 2005a, b). The development of new settings for learning and new forms of learning in very diverse practical fields of application is also a main concern of geragogy.

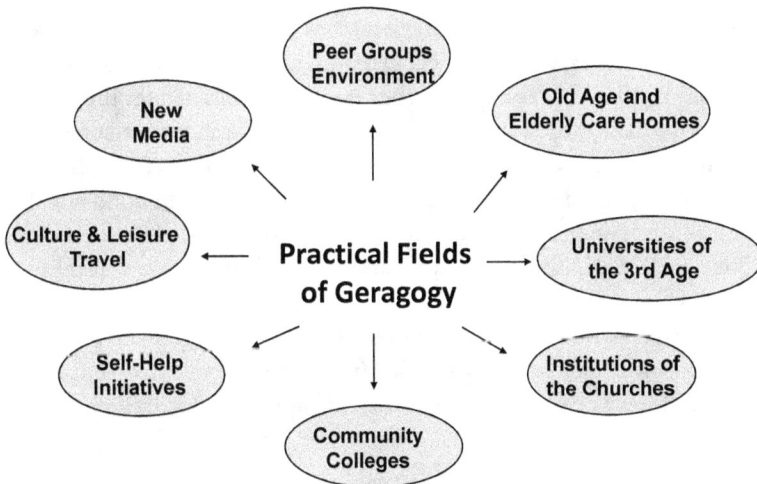

Figure 1: Practical Fields of Geragogy

Lines of development for education in later life and geragogy in Germany

Looking at the mission statements and concepts regarding education and learning in later life of the last 50 years highlights how, closely linked to the conventional view of age and ageing at the time, the lines of approach and the rationale behind geragogy as a discipline rooted in science have changed. It becomes apparent that at times theory and practical application have been and sometimes still are insufficiently linked. On the one hand it is maintained that the practical implementation of education in later life lags behind theoretical developments; on the other hand, it is argued that during the 1990s implementation, driven by older people themselves, was by far ahead of any theories.

The development of geragogy as a scientific discipline and its implementation can roughly be outlined in decades in order to highlight the respective changes in perspective. It needs to be taken into consideration that different frameworks and a lack of communication resulted in diverging developments in East and West Germany and in retrospect, differences can be noticed. Overall, an analysis of the history of education in later life shows the diverse changes which have occurred up until the present day (Bubolz-Lutz et al 2010:37ff.). Today even the term 'education in later life' is seen as too limiting. The more comprehensive term 'education focused on later life' is meant to underline a more open approach; education focused on later life is not only seen with the older generation as target group in mind but also as educational work on age-related topics throughout the entire life (cf Petzold & Bubolz 1976; Kade 1994). As a consequence, 'education in later life' and 'intergenerational learning' no longer contradict each other – older people experiencing learning amongst themselves (in age-homogeneous groups) and old and young people learning together (in age-heterogeneous groups) can be seen as different options of *one* educational approach focused on later life.

The 1960s: Practical implementation as organised socialising and 'the elderly' as conceptual target group

At the beginning of the 1960s the 'elderly' in West Germany are seen as a group on the edge of society lacking resources. Politics focuses on 'old-age poverty' as the key characteristic of old age: consequently state initiatives mainly concentrate on a system ensuring the financial security of older people.

At the same time, in the GDR an ambivalent relationship between the government and old people is starting to take shape; according to Olbertz and Prager (2000:127) older people are portrayed as 'veterans of the working sector' on the one hand, on the other hand the respect towards them sinks in line with their productivity. A generally broader level of education and qualification within society as a whole and a more open educational system prevent older people from being excluded; however they are not specifically addressed as a target group either. Nevertheless, lifelong learning is seen as the basis of finding satisfaction in ageing. Several providers offer educational opportunities accessible for older people; URANIA in the form of community colleges, the Free Association of German Trade Unions (*Freier Deutscher Gewerkschaftsbund*), the Culture Association of the GDR (*Kulturbund der DDR*) as well as the churches.

Educational opportunities specifically designed for older people in West Germany often take the form of organised socialising in supervised groups. The main providers are the churches as well as charities who aim for a few entertaining hours in the form of get-togethers for groups of older people. Some community colleges have started offering courses.

The 1970s: Compensatory, problem-oriented practical implementation and conceptual foundations for education in later life

The 1970s see more and more changes to the image of old age. Criticism of the conditions in society go hand in hand with a growing awareness of the social and societal character of age. The term 'equal opportunities' as the benchmark for living conditions is applied to the lives of older people as well. The findings show that the main reason for the more limited educational opportunities of older people lies in their continued 'disadvantaged' educational biography. This leads to methodical-didactic concepts critically analysing the so-called 'barriers to education' (in terms of biography, epochal blocking factors, fears of crossing a threshold). This is also the time of pioneering discoveries in psycho-gerontology; Lehr and Thomae's 1971 longitudinal study in Bonn proves for the first time that mental capacities do not dramatically decrease until the age of 80 (Lehr & Thomae 1987). Concepts for education in later life are now able draw arguments from an empirical basis when they had previously been rooted in the humanities, based namely on international findings in the French-speaking and English-speaking world. In this context, it becomes possible to develop the first concepts in 'geragogy', or 'gerontagogy' as some researchers dub the new discipline, in the German-speaking world. The lives of the participants are to be the basis for any educational work and therefore require a thorough critical examination to start with. According to this approach, education needs to assist older people in coping with their age and counteract disadvantages and deficiencies. Findings that the interest in education and the respective capacities are developed as early on as in childhood and youth lead to a call for continuous educational opportunities throughout the entire life aimed at contributing to a conscious, independent and healthy ageing process. Echoing these aims, concepts for education in later life focus on preventing the loss of capacities in old age, on coping with life's problems and development tasks as well as on gains in terms of the quality of life, on finding satisfaction in life and on discovering meaning to life.

The GDR equally experiences a review of the traditional image of old age – spurred by research conducted in the United States in the 1940s. This is reflected in the foundation of the so-called 'Veterans' Colleges' (*Veteranenkollegs*) at the Universities of Berlin, Leipzig and Halle.

The 1980s: Concept-oriented interventions and the 'tertiary socialisation approach

In the 1980s, members of the expert audience become increasingly aware of demographic changes. Against the backdrop of data indicating a growing proportion of older and old people, gerontology changes its approach and turns its back on a deficit-oriented concept of ageing. On the basis of psycho-gerontological research findings on the development potential of old people, gerontology devises a very optimistic view of old age with a particular focus on the competencies of older people. Intervention gerontology refers to the potential of older people in terms of activity and productivity and propagates a 'productivity of old age', employing very polarising views of age. A distinction is made between an active 'third' age and an inactive, more dependent 'fourth' age (Laslett 1995).

Based on the Competence Theory (Olbrich 1987), the practical implementation is characterised by an increase in opportunities for different target groups amongst older people, now called 'senior citizens'. In order to set it apart from health-related initiatives, education for senior citizens is now mainly defined as academic education, including higher education. Higher education establishments incorporate 'courses for seniors'. However, it is once again the older people with a strong foothold in education who profit from these opportunities. While several universities start offering courses for seniors the number of cultural opportunities and health training courses is also on the rise, in particular aimed at the 'younger old people'. The Tertiary Socialisation Approach by Veelken (1990) helps to advance the conceptual development of geragogy – allowing a sociological perspective on education in later life and education focused on later life and as such on its importance for each individual and society as a whole.

The 1990s: (Self) activation of older people and a change of concept to situation-based education

The 1990s see the rise of the image of the 'active old person' within society. As a result of this, the group of senior citizens is discovered as an 'economic factor'; this group is the fastest growing consumer group with an increased demand for services – from new technologies over travel opportunities for seniors to care provision.

At the same time, the Berlin Ageing Study (Berliner Altersstudie, Mayer & Baltes 1996 and 1999) obtains the first findings on very old people. Under the motto 'Old Age is Diverse' (*Alter hat viele Gesichter*) a gerontological school influenced by psychology outlines a differentiated view of old age based on empirical findings. The gerontologists Paul and Margret Baltes (1990) are able to demonstrate in their Selection, Optimisation and Compensation Theory on ageing (*Selektion, Optimierung und Kompensation* (SOK)) just how adaptable old people still can be when it comes to finding satisfaction and success in their specific situation. According to Baltes, by consciously choosing meaningful activities and roles (Selection) which in turn become more important and on which more attention is focused (Optimisation), people in later stages of life are still capable of compensating for losses suffered through ageing (Compensation). Essentially, the key point is the search for opportunities for each individual, allowing him or her to lead a self-actualising, if limited, life. This new conceptual model, which is however focussing on the preservation of behavioural patterns and attitudes and not accounting for the acquisition of new patterns and attitudes, becomes the gerontological key to a 'successful ageing process' and is reflected in the main objective for policies regarding senior citizens; the 'preservation of abilities allowing independent living'.

For the practical implementation in the field of education for older people this means a remarkably high uptake on training programmes promising the 'mastering' of old age with the help of memory and ability training, through continuous practice and an orientation on reality. Educational opportunities which encourage confrontation with the 'darker sides of old age' such as chronic diseases, personality changes, disorientation and dementia are less sought after and mainly taken up by people directly concerned. Reflecting their personal wish for an 'independent ageing' older people themselves start becoming more active – in terms of education as well as regarding services for older people in general. Providers no longer have a monopoly on offering education but older people themselves show initiative. Next to traditional educational opportunities, self-help group and initiatives founded by senior citizens themselves become increasingly important. Self-organised groups of older people are founded (self-help groups), aimed at working out a shared understanding of the situation as well as a plan for action, both in terms of the participants' personal situation and the conditions in society (cf. Klehm & Ziebach 1995). It is now the older people who, having achieved professional success, dedicate part of their retirement years to learning in a group. Education in later life becomes a means of fulfilling the desire to preserve self-determination in old age. Various providers and programmes discover the process of ageing itself as a topic. Inspired by the intention to learn how to age, the concept of an education focused on topics relating to later life emerges; the idea of a lifelong learning promising autonomy, mental and physical fitness and participation in society touches a nerve, in particular with many younger old people.

Geragogic concept development is characterised by differentiation. While the public focus (as well as public funding of research and development projects) towards the end of the 1990s is on 'young old people', scientists following a geragogic approach increasingly call for a critical analysis of this unilaterally positive view of old age. They initiate a 'realistic turnaround' towards a more differentiated view on the different situations and stages of old age. It is emphasised that politics should not only concentrate on educating the younger and agile old people and on creating culture and leisure initiatives. Specific measures should also encourage those people to participate in education who are no longer able to profit from public education due to health problems, disabilities and reduced mobility. Forms of education directly approaching people are tried out and researched (cf. Karl 1992), as well as forms of education within establishments offering services for old people and within the care sector. Parallel to these developments a *didactic turnaround in terms of concepts* can be witnessed as observations made in educational settings organised by old people themselves point to a reversed role allocation typical for the sector of education for older people. In seminar-like courses older people are not only active as learners but also as teachers, in the meaning to take an active role in the learning process.

German reunification reveals the different state of education for older people in the GDR compared to West Germany, structurally as well as in terms of the availability of opportunities; even today the image of the upkeep and preservation of productivity in old age, previously promoted by the government, still forms part of the self image of older and old people in the former East German states. This means that older people can be viewed as invariably interested in education and often as accustomed to education as well (Olbertz & Prager 2000:139).

The 2000s: Education focused on later life as intergenerational work and concepts aimed at inclusion and participation

The new millennium sees an intensification of the debate about demographic changes. In order to counterbalance horror scenarios of a 'battle of the generations' and a Welfare State which can no longer be financed, gerontology and politics develop a concept highlighting the potentials of old age (cf. Fifth Report on Ageing of the Federal Ministry for Family Affairs, Senior Citizens, Women and Youth 2006 - 5. *Altenbericht, BMFSFJ*, 2006). Older people who often leave the working sector as young as 50 are to be motivated and encouraged to discover their unexploited potential and to contribute to new fields of activity. Older people still active in the work sector are equally named as a target group for education; professional education is meant to strengthen their employability. However, the Fifth Report on Ageing does not only list points concerning the way older people lead their lives and preventative measures for old age as objectives – the integration and participation of older people in society is also to be promoted. In this context, intergenerational learning settings become increasingly popular. In order to create opportunities for old and young people to get into contact, 'multi-generational establishments' (Mehrgenerationenhäuser) are funded all over Germany, encouraging intergenerational dialogue and a mutual learning. In practical terms, educational provision introduces volunteering and active citizenship, prepares people for these settings and accompanies them. This encourages a 'new role for older people' – for example within the framework of the programme 'Practical Knowledge for Initiatives' (*Erfahrungswissen für Initiativen*). A specifically-designed educational programme is developed to train older people for their new responsibilities and roles in society.

Parallel to didactical developments in adult education, geragogical concepts also undergo fundamental changes: the main focus is no longer on teaching processes but on learning, and attempts are made to describe the learning process from the perspective of the learner. Constructivist concepts of learning are adapted; human beings are seen as self-determining systems not learning what is offered to them, but deciding independently what they are interested in (cf. Siebert 2006b). Today research focuses on learners and their inner self-determination processes as well as settings for learning. It is, for example, of interest how learning environments must be structured in order to motivate people to learn when they are older and to learn for old age. In addition, questions regarding institutions and communities/local authorities and their role in initiating learning processes related to old age as well as on how they can promote intergenerational dialogue ('Learning Regions') are of concern.

Debates on how to deal with demographic changes, in politics to start with and subsequently more and more frequently in scientific circles, in the first decade of the new millennium have highlighted the need for the development of a geragogic discipline with a more focused profile along these lines. On the one hand, it can be observed that while the subject matter is being addressed by many different parties, specific and previously developed geragogic approaches are not taken into consideration (e.g. education approaches for very old people). On the other hand, genuinely geragogic conclusions are drawn within the framework of external debates such as the economisation debate. An example is the discussion about a possible duty of older people to educate themselves, to remain healthy and to contribute to society with their potential (cf. Federal Ministry for Family Affairs, Senior Citizens, Women and Youth 2006; critical view Gösken, Köster & Kricheldorff 2007).

Informal settings for learning

By now various findings indicate that learning in later life also takes place outside of well-defined educational settings – a fact which has too long been neglected by the relevant experts. Everyday life, family and life's surroundings in general all give rise to diverse learning settings, which are often not instantly recognised as such. With the intention of obtaining specific knowledge and skills relevant for the specific individual or situation:

learners make use of diverse resources – magazines, friends, shop assistants, tradespeople, manuals, trial and error, but also (partially) institutionalised educational opportunities offered by building supplies stores, libraries or educational establishments – fully or in part; people stay away once they have found what they were looking for. The intention is less a certificate with an exchangeable value but the practical value or 'just because it's interesting'. Learners create a 'composition' using these different resources, designing their ways and methods of learning and deciding independently on content and objectives.' (Reischmann 2002:163).

Mainly older people with little access to traditional education establishments prefer this form of learning, which Reischmann calls *intentional-autodidactic, self-determined* learning. They prefer to use everyday resources in order to cope with new challenges and changes in their lives. Findsen (2006) at the University of Glasgow points out the same phenomenon. He lists three social institutions which constitute the main frameworks for non-formal and informal learning of older adults (which he defines as persons older than 55 years of age): family, church and the workplace. In this context, he also points to economic factors, the socio-demographic status, gender aspects and ethnic backgrounds which are relevant and have a determining role in which informal learning settings are preferred.

It is now generally accepted that a large part of the learning experience of older people takes place outside of education establishments. However, informal learning can also be distinguished in terms of the different forms and grades of reflexivity and the integration into institutions.

+ *The incidental,* en passant *learning,* which Reischmann (2004) calls 'Learning en Passant', is achieved mainly unconsciously and unplanned, triggered by learning stimuli, brought about by the meeting of a person or the coping with a new situation.
+ This can be distinguished from the *partially intentional learning* as part of activities which are not performed with the aim of learning as such, but which trigger or require learning. Examples would be a trip, attending a concert, a hobby or a new task which has been explicitly chosen. These situations are all characterised by the absence of a learning objective at the outset, although people can later often remember exactly what led to the acquisition of knowledge or a specific skill.
+ *Non-intentional* learning is characterised by external triggers or 'critical life events', which were neither planned nor expected, in connection with violent emotional reactions (e.g. shock, joy). The dealing and coping

with the situation constitutes the learning experience. The triggering situation can be identified and recalled (Reischmann 2004).

The EdAge Study (Tippelt et al 2009) examines these forms of informal learning in everyday settings. Figures demonstrate on the one hand how common informal learning in everyday situations is, making them an important learning setting. On the other hand, it becomes obvious that for roughly half or slightly more than half of the older population the internet (48%), volunteering (43%) and part-time jobs (54%) do not yet constitute settings for learning, while the respective other half profits significantly from these opportunities. These forms of informal learning emphasise direct responsibility and self-determination of the learner (cf. Siebert 2001:19f.). It can be questioned whether economic factors, the socio-demographic status, gender aspects and ethnic/cultural backgrounds as described by Findsen (2006) are the determining factors for this clear division amongst the respondents in users and non-users. No other informal learning setting included in the study showed such a significant difference. The EdAge Study fails to deliver a clear-cut answer. At the same time, figures indicate that learning achieved with the help of the internet or through volunteering is considered significantly less important than learning achieved through dialogue with family, partner and peers, i.e. the social network. Many different places, services and forms of media are used for informal learning, both for incidental, en passant learning and for partially intentional learning.

Against this backdrop, questions must be raised about whether the focus on older people's media skills really meets their needs and whether this is evidence of a cohort effect which will abate with future generations of older people or disappear altogether. Current figures for internet usage by older people point in this direction, indicating that 53.5% of people aged 50-69 had been using the internet occasionally, 51.6% within the previous four weeks and 35.8% the day before the survey. For people aged 70 and over only 15.9% had been online occasionally, 15.6% within the previous month and 10.2% the day before. Overall, the acceptance of new media among older people has significantly increased (Eimeren/Frees 2009:335).

> More and more older people are interested in modern information and communication technologies. This trend will become even more significant with future generations. (Gehrke 2008:14)

This opens up diverse potential areas for practical implementation, leaving aside traditional organisational structures, which have previously been neglected by education focused on later life. Paukens (2002) for example raises the question whether educational television of the 21st century ought to be limited to quiz shows and Meder (2002) sees the lack of informal education rather than informal learning as a problem in society.

Geragogy must therefore draw the consequence to put the concept of 'lifelong learning' on its agenda. This term encompasses:

+   Informal and self-organised learning,
+   Informal learning in formal settings and
+   Incidental learning or 'learning en passant'.

The main aim is to create opportunities and places for education which approach potential users directly in their everyday lives and in ways which meet their needs; these must enable a reflexivity going beyond traditional organisational structures, visibly linked to education. Otherwise informal settings for learning are in danger of 'becoming stunted' and turning into places of mere knowledge generation, with social and integrative aspects of education falling by the wayside. Education focussing on later life means more than the acquisition of knowledge and must therefore concentrate more on informal settings of learning.

Future developments of geragogy

The rapidly changing, knowledge-based society will turn the willingness and ability to learn and educate oneself into a basic requirement for future generations. This in turn necessitates the development of an integrated overarching education system, with the individual elements – nursery schools/child care and schools, professional qualification establishments and higher education establishments/universities as representatives of formal education and further education establishments, community colleges, multi-generational establishments, senior academies, day care centres for older people and education centres for families representing informal education - being closely linked and co-operation much intensified. The European Qualifications Framework (EQF) is a step in this direction. Within the framework of such a 'change of shape' of the entire education sector, education focused on later life must re-establish itself. Compared to established structures of adult and further learning, it will be easier for this sector of education, having previously been forced to show flexibility and to find niches, to use innovative organisational structures and learning settings in order to offer its experiences – e.g. ways of independent learning and self-organised education – as a model for other systems. The integration of existing networks within the welfare and care sector for older people into a network structure in society as a whole, which requires further development in terms of education, can serve as an equally inspiring model for both sides.

The remodelling of the Welfare State with a new emphasis on individuals taking responsibility for public welfare and a change to a 'society of citizens', which has become a political imperative in the light of economic and financial distortions, will also see the older generation faced with more responsibilities. The general public is increasingly critical of unemployed people or people no longer required to work withdrawing from public life, abstaining from and failing to contribute to both personal learning processes and development processes in society over years or decades. In addition, the experience of various initiatives for older people and government pilot schemes shows that learning and involvement in society in later life do not just have a positive effect on its beneficiaries. Various empirical findings demonstrate that older people who are involved and integrated into groups or 'self-reflexive social milieus' consider their individual lives much more meaningful (cf. Kade 2001). An improvement of the 'subjective state of health' can also be witnessed (cf Staudinger 2008: 88) as well as involvement in society and respective ways of obtaining qualifications as a means of consciously developing one's identity (cf. Braun, Burmeister & Engels 2004; Steinfort 2009). Volunteering by older people and the corresponding 'learning by doing' are also a driving force behind integration and the prevention of exclusion. Research and development projects therefore increasingly focus on educational approaches for older people which are based on people's social surroundings and have a low threshold. Initial findings indicate that low-threshold settings for learning can motivate older people who have previously had little contact with education to continue their learning process and to become involved (cf. Mörchen & Tolksdorf 2009). One success strategy is picking up on personal experiences, rooted in the individual's biography, as well taking up suggestions for improvement regarding the individual's current situation in life and personal surroundings.

Education focused on later life in its practical implementation will have to move away from a supply structure and towards a demand structure, a concept outlined ahead of their times by Dräger, Günther & Thunemeyer, all active in the sector of adult education, as early as 1997. However, the development of a relevant infrastructure facilitating education initiatives by older people is making slow progress, this is despite unanimous agreement on the fact that framework conditions for education focused on later life and active involvement of citizens must be improved on as a prerequisite for older people to be able to show more initiative and to develop their 'sense of self' in the context of people living together, with the needs of all generations met. Overall, the following additional developments seem to be emerging:

- A demand-oriented approach will gain significance as a new concept for (education) establishments – this will include older people who will apply higher standards to education on the basis of their education biography.
- Efforts to improve the quality of life and provision by means of new technologies presuppose certain learning processes in older people – more geragogic research will have to be conducted in this aspect.
- Local and regional governments realise the necessity to include the older population in their educational investments and to create intergenerational education processes, promoting mutual understanding and in turn enabling generations to live together in a constructive way.
- Demand for competent involvement of older people in society, supported by educational measures and co-operative advice, will increase – both on the part of the people involved and on the part of the beneficiaries (cf. Kade 2007:60).
- Education focused on later life must rise to the challenge set by the debate about the future of quality development and the implementation of quality objectives. Processes by which specific, scientifically evaluated quality objectives for education focused on later life have been implemented on a community and local level must be continued on a large-scale level.
- Networks of universities, universities of applied sciences and independent institutes will have to be developed in order to test appropriate access structures to education for specific groups of people in their post-work phase. They must be closely linked to the practical field, that way research on the conditions can be conducted (Bubolz-Lutz et al 2010: 47).

As a consequence, geragogy no longer only represents the theory and practical implementation of education focused on later life but becomes a scientific discipline which puts the scope and limitations of education in an ageing society on the agenda of research and development initiatives. Education becomes an overarching topic which is not only relevant for the older generation at a specific point in time but for all ages. People who were near or in their fifties in 2010 for example, will have an average life expectancy of 90.2 years (men) and 94 years (women). These 'baby boomers' who are slowly 'going grey' are becoming more and more aware that they need to prepare for living a long life and a life in which, due to an ageing society, they will more likely be faced with older people of the same age than with younger ones.

Education and social involvement will be more strongly connected than before and they will not only serve a purpose in terms of preserving the quality of life but also play a role in providing for old age. It is therefore down to politics and society to create conditions enabling education focused on later life; there are clear indications that this would represent an investment in the future which would later pay off in multiple ways. The most powerful argument in this context is the following: people who can grow old leading a satisfied and socially-integrated life consider their quality of life and their state of health to be superior, and are therefore less prone to becoming ill and needing care. Education creates the relevant framework.

References

Baltes, P. B. & Baltes, M. M. (1990). Psychological perspectives on successful aging: The model of selective optimization with compensation. In P. B. Baltes & M. M. Baltes (Hrsg.), *Successful aging. Perspectives from the behavioral sciences* (pp. 1-34). Cambridge: Cambridge University Press.

Barz, Heiner (2006), Bildung – Bemerkungen zur säkularen Wirklichkeit eines humanistischen Leitbegriffs, online-Dokument: http://www.phil-fak.uni-duesseldorf.de/ew/bf/dokumente/tagungen/Antrittsvorlesung.PDF#search=%22Barz%20Bildung%22

Braun, J., Burmeister, J. & Engels, D. (Hrsg) (2004). *SeniorTrainerIn: Neue Verantwortungsrolle und Engagement in Kommunen. Bundesmodellprogramm 'Erfahrungswissen für Initiativen'. Bericht zur ersten Programmphase.* Leipzig: ISAB-Verlag.

Bubolz-Lutz, E. (2000). Bildung und Hochaltrigkeit. In S. Becker, L. Veelken & K.-P. Wallraven (Hrsg.), *Handbuch Altenbildung: Theorien und Konzepte für Gegenwart und Zukunft* (pp. 326-349). Opladen: Leske + Budrich.

Bubolz-Lutz, Elisabeth, Gösken, Eva, Kricheldorff, Cornelia, Schramek, Renate (2010): *Geragogik – Bildung und Lernen im Prozess des Alterns. Das Lehrbuch.* Stuttgart: Kohlhammer

Bundesministerium für Familie, Senioren, Frauen und Jugend (BMFSFJ) (Hrsg.) (2006): Fünfter Bericht zur Lage der älteren Generation in der Bundesrepublik Deutschland:http://www.bmfsfj.de/bmfsfj/generator/ RedaktionBMFSFJ/Abteilung3/Pdf-Anlagen/fuenfter-altenbericht,property=pdf,bereich=bmfsfj,sprache=de,rwb=true.pdf

Deutscher Ausschuss für das Erziehungs- und Bildungswesen (Hrsg.) (1960). *Zur Situation und Aufgabe der deutschen Erwachsenenbildung.* Stuttgart: Klett

Dräger, H., Günther, U. & Thunemeyer, B. (1997). *Autonomie und Infrastruktur. Zur Theorie, Organisation und Praxis differentieller Bildung. Europäische Hochschulschriften.* Frankfurt am Main: Peter Lang Verlag.

Eimeren, B. van & Frees, B. (2005). Nach dem Boom: Größter Zuwachs in internetfernen Gruppen. *Media Perspektiven, 8*, 362-379.

Findsen, B. (2006). Social Institutions as Sites of Learning for Older Adults. *Journal of Transformative Education, 4*, (1). (http://jtd.sagepub.com/cgi/ content)

Gehrke, B. (2008). *Ältere Menschen und Neue Medien. Entwicklungschancen für neue Medienprojekte für Frauen und Männer mit Lebenserfahrung in Nordrhein-Westfalen. Gefördert vom Ministerium für Generationen, Familie, Frauen und Integration des Landes Nordrhein-Westfalen.* Marl: ecmc.

Gukenbiehl, H. L. (1998). Bildung und Bildungssystem. In B. Schäfer & W. Zapf (Hrsg.), *Handwörterbuch zur Gesellschaft Deutschlands* (pp. 85-100). Opladen: Leske + Budrich

Gösken, E., Köster, D. & Kricheldorff, C. (2007). Altersbildung – mehr als die Nutzung von Bildungsangeboten. Profilschärfung und Weiterentwicklung des 5. Altenberichts. *Forum Erwachsenenbildung, (2)*, 39-43.

Kade, S. (2009). *Altern und Bildung: Eine Einführung* (2., aktualisierte und überarbeitete Auflage). Bielefeld: Bertelsmann Verlag.

Kade, S. (2007). *Altern und Bildung. Eine Einführung.* Bielefeld: Bertelsmann Verlag

Kade, S. (2001). *Selbstorganisiertes Alter – Lernen in reflexiven Milieus.* Bielefeld: Bertelsmann Verlag.

Kade, S. (1994). *Altersbildung. Ziele und Konzepte.* (2 volumes). Frankfurt am Main: DIE.

Karl, F. (1992). Beratung und Bildung im Rahmen einer Bring-Struktur. In U. Niederfranke & U. Lehr (Hrsg.), *Altern in unserer Zeit* (S. 164-171). Heidelberg: Quelle & Meyer.

Klehm, W. & Ziebach, P. (1995). Konzepte zugehender Bildungsarbeit: Das Modell „Zwischen Arbeit und Ruhestand". In S. Kühnert (Hrsg.), *Qualifizierung und Professionalisierung in der Altenarbeit* (S. 205-225). Hannover: Vincentz.

Köster, D. & Schramek, R. (2005). Die Autonomie des Alters und ihre Konsequenzen für zivilgesellschaftliches Engagement. Hessische Blätter für Volksbildung. *Zeitschrift für Erwachsenenbildung in Deutschland*, 55, (3), 226–237.

Kolland, F. (2005), *Bildungschancen für ältere Menschen. Ansprüche an ein gelungenes Leben*, Wien.

Kricheldorff, C. (2010): *Bildungsarbeit mit älteren und alten Menschen. In: Aner, K./ Karl,U.: Handbuch Soziale Arbeit und Alter*. Wiesbaden:VS-Verlag, 99-112.

Kricheldorff, C. (2005a). Biografisches Lernen – Neuorientierung durch die Auseinandersetzung mit der eigenen Lebensgeschichte. *BAGSO-Nachrichten*, (1), 14-15.

Kricheldorff, C. (2005b). Biografisches Arbeiten und Lernen. Lebensgeschichtliche Prägungen als Ressourcen. *Pflegemagazin*, (4), 4-12

Laslett, P. (1995). *Das dritte Alter. Historische Soziologie des Alterns*. Weinheim/ München: Juventa.

Lehr, U. & Thomae, H. (1987). *Formen seelischen Alterns*. Stuttgart:Thieme

Mayer, K. U. & Baltes, P. B. (Hrsg.) (1996). *Die Berliner Altersstudie. Ein Projekt der Berlin-Brandenburgischen Akademie der Wissenschaften*. Berlin: Akademie-Verlag.

Mayer, K. U. & Baltes, P. B. (Hrsg.) (1999). *Die Berliner Altersstudie* (2nd edition). Berlin: Akademie-Verlag.

Meder, N. (2002). Nicht informelles Lernen, sondern informelle Bildung ist das gesellschaftliche Problem. *Spektrum Freizeit*, (1), 8-17.

Mörchen, A. & Tolksdorf, M. (Hrsg.) (2009). *Lernort Gemeinde. Ein neues Format der Erwachsenenbildung*. Bielefeld: Bertelsmann Verlag.

Olbrich, E. (1987). Kompetenz im Alter. *Zeitschrift für Gerontologie*, 20, 319-330

Olbertz, J. & Prager, A. (2000). Altenbildung in Ostdeutschland vor und nach der Wende. In S. Becker, L. Veelken & K.-P. Wallraven (Hrsg.), *Handbuch Altenbildung: Theorien und Konzepte für Gegenwart und Zukunft* (pp.125-140). Opladen: Leske + Budrich

Paukens, H. (2002). Quiz-Shows – Bildungsfernsehen des 21. Jahrhunderts? In K. Künzel (Ed.), *Allgemeinbildung zwischen Postmoderne und Bürgergesellschaft. Internationales Jahrbuch für Erwachsenenbildung*, 30 (pp. 141-156). Köln: Böhlau-Verlag.

Petzold, H. & Bubolz, E. (Ed.) (1976a). *Bildungsarbeit mit alten Menschen. Konzepte der Humanwissenschaften*. Stuttgart: Ernst Klett.

Reischmann, J. (2002). Lernen hoch zehn – wer bietet mehr? Vom „Lernen en passant' zu „kompositionellem Lernen' und „lebensbreiter Bildung'. In R. Bergold, P. Dierkes & J. Knoll (Hrsg.), *Vielfalt neu verbinden – Abschlussbericht zum Projekt „Lernen 2000plus – Initiative für eine neue Lernkultur'* (pp. 159-167). Recklinghausen: Bitter.

Sommer, C., Künemund, H. & Kohli, M. (2004). *Zwischen Selbstorganisation und Seniorenakademie. Die Vielfalt der Altersbildung in Deutschland.* Berlin: Weißensee.

Staudinger, U. M. (2008). Was ist das Alter(n) der Persönlichkeit? Eine Antwort aus verhaltenswissenschaftlicher Sicht. In U. M. Staudinger & H. Häfner (Eds.), *Was ist Alter(n)? Neue Antworten auf eine scheinbar einfache Frage* (S. 81-94). Berlin/Heidelberg: Springer.

Steinfort, J. (2009). *Identität und Engagement im Dritten Alter. Eine empirische Untersuchung.* Universität Dortmund: Unveröffentliche Dissertationsschrift.

Tippelt, R., Schmidt, B., Schnurr, S., Sinner, S. & Theisen, C. (2009). *Bildung Älterer. Chancen im demografischen Wandel.* Bielefeld: Bertelsmann Verlag.

Veelken, L. (2003). Reifen und Altern – Geragogik kann man lernen. Oberhausen: Athena.

Veelken, L. (1990). Neues Lernen im Alter. Bildungs- und Kulturarbeit mit „Jungen Alten'. Heidelberg: Sauer-Verlag.

7

Ageing, social policy and changing solidarity in the Netherlands

Jaap Olthof

Have you ever seen an idealist with gray hairs on his head
Or successful men that keep in touch with unsuccessful friends
You only think you did
I could have sworn I saw it too
But as it turns out
It was just a clever ad for cigarettes

Pedro the Lion - Penetration

Introduction: A political perspective on ageing in the Netherlands

Europe is ageing, as statistics point out, at a fast pace. After an era of astonishing growth in the world's population, we witness, even on a global level, a slowing demographic growth (van Nimwegen and van Praag, 2012). Compared to global figures, the Netherlands is inhabited by a relatively young population (van Nimwegen and van Praag, 2012). Nevertheless, Dutch politics claim ageing to be a 'societal disease' and we find their statements often flavoured by a negative approach towards ageing. Doomy interpretations of ageing stress the limits for social security and an inevitable change of social solidarity which is envisaged in a redesign of the social welfare state after decades of economic liberalization (Rose, 2006). Since the 1980s, the Dutch have transformed their universalistic welfare state (Esping-Andersen, 1990) into a neo-liberal welfare state model and zero in on maximum efficiency and cutting down costs (van Dam, 2009). Therefore, the Netherlands face a decreasing and, often, just dissolving safety net (Kwekkeboom, 2010).These days cutting costs is sold under the umbrella of a more positive label 'participation' which is reminiscent of what Alexis de

Tocqueville called a 'Civil Society' (Putnam et al., 1994). Surely, no rational thinking human being would disallow more involvement and solidarity by civilians. Therefore, almost all Dutch political parties point into the same neo-liberal direction: 'Citizen, it's your own responsibility' and they wish to stimulate mainly self-management and self-help of civilians (Baart, 2013). Unfortunately, this heralds great risks for vulnerable groups in the Dutch society such as the ageing population (Carbo and Baart, 2013).

So, in consequence, Dutch social work experiences a significant ideological shift which is forced upon social workers by the decrease of budgets under the ideological umbrella of the 'Social Support Act' (Scholte, 2012). It is as if the Dutch government is declaring; 'Good luck to you social workers with this assignment, we now hand over our responsibilities to your community, to you and to your clients themselves'. In this process ageing is used as a scapegoat, pictured as a burden for the taxpayer, for this 'necessary' political change. Indeed, old people need care and more old people need more care. But this logic does not do justice to the active role of the ageing population in contemporary society (Komp, 2010). In this chapter we examine the position of ageing in Dutch society in order to take the sting out of the one-sided economic way of reasoning; to take issue with global neoliberal ideas. Such ideological changes (Rand 1957; Achterhuis, 2011) - we often tend to forget it is - must be justified with robust evidence, not just by vague assumptions. At the moment the execution of the Social Support Act (*Wet maatschappelijke ontwikkeling*) encompasses a strong focus on participation and own responsibility and is unfortunately based on such vague premises. This ideal of a 'Big Society' is a hidden agenda of the neo-liberal parties, at the very right on the political spectrum, keeping them away from investing in social security and the welfare state. Demanding social participation of the ageing in such a 'Big Society' includes taking a good look at the possibilities for truly participating in society (Eurostat, 2012). Asking for old fashioned 'mechanical solidarity' – in the typology of Durkheim (Durkheim, 1893) - in modern societies where relationships are typed by their 'organic solidarity' seems to be a bridge too far as well. The popular American sociologist Richard Sennett is surprised by the route the Dutch politicians have taken. As Sennett states in an interview (translated from Dutch):

> The idea that everyone can deal with the problems of others, the presence of some sort of general good-heartedness, is a very naïve thought. (Gradener, 2013)

This chapter will initially highlight some of the effects of the ageing population on the expenditures on the welfare state and describes briefly a view on frailty and ageing. Recent social policy reforms focusing on participation such as the 'Social Support Act' and its effects on vulnerable ageing are represented as well as the redesign of Dutch Social Work. Subsequently, we focus on a so-called 'beacon' of this New Style Social Work, respectively: the currently strong emphasis on the individual's own responsibility for self-help and the concept behind the devotion to forms of informal care for ageing. The ample expectations of solidarity, on which recent policy reforms are built and hope for are then analyzed. At the end of this chapter a 'risk society' for the ageing is brought to focus.

The truth about ageing and its effects on the welfare state

Ageing is a universal demographic trend although some parts of the world have more citizens ageing compared to others. Comparison points out that mainly underdeveloped countries will experience a profound rise of the ageing population (United Nations, World Population Prospects, 2010). Europe is by far the most aged part of the world since the decrease of fertility has occurred throughout the last few decades. Especially Germany, Italy, Greece and Sweden have a rather ageing population (Castelijns et al., 2013). In the Netherlands (and throughout other European countries as well) many policy documents use a threshold of the age of 65 for defining the ageing population. The age threshold of those 80+ is often used as well to show the growing number of old people in society. To say it in a brief way; there are more old people than there ever were and they live longer as well. Historically, this is quite a significant change of the population (Castelijns et al., 2013). Logically, the demand for care will rise in this group causing a 'grey pressure' on the financing of welfare state. This means that the number of persons at the age 65 years and older as a percentage of the number of people aged 20–64 years is large. After all, the group of 20-64 year-olds coincides largely with the potential labor force, which has to bear the costs of the ageing population (Duin and Stoeldraijer, 2012).

Measuring Vulnerability

The use of 65 years as a threshold for the ageing population can be questioned. The Netherlands institute for social research (SCP) as well as the recently published Berenschot Report, point at the vulnerability of elderly arguing that this at first is a process of the accumulation of disabilities in physical, mental and social functioning causing an increase of negative health outcomes for elderly (Campen, 2011; Castelijns et al., 2013). When analyzing statistics for these characteristics one finds out that mainly above the age of 75 the risk of disabilities increase rapidly as well as demand for elderly care and the costs cohering with this.

This is expressed by the individual measurement of Disability Adjusted Life Years, the so-called DALYs. A DALY is a summary measure of the burden of disease among populations that combines mortality on the one side and morbidity measures on the other. It is expressed as the number of years lost due to ill-health, disability or early death (Thacker, 2006). DALY figures provide us with some useful insights on the frailty amongst elderly because they combine three important aspects of public health namely; lifespan, quality of life and the number of people experiencing an effect. When expressed in DALY's we can distinguish that the burden of disease is exponentially increasing with age. Therefore, frailty comes with age, especially above the age of 75 years old.

Rising costs due to ageing?

'Frightening findings', some might say. 'This is why we need a transition in our welfare state', others might claim. But is this true? When examining the last Dutch Health Care Performance Report, a publication of the National Institute for Public Health and the Environment (NCIS) one finds conclusions can be drawn rather different (Westert et al., 2010). Only 15 percent of the rise of national costs is related to the ageing population. The rising of prices (35 %) and other related costs (50 %) such as the rise of claims, more patients and technological development and possibilities cause a much more profound impact on the rising of costs. (Westert et al., 2010).

The expansion of technological development and possibilities will stimulate older people to claim new treatments and therapies for their health related problems. This is of course the opposite effect of what was wished for by politicians. As a result the discussion will further economize and focus on the value and role of care in relation to the rise of live expectancy and quality of life (Castelijns et al., 2013).

So, as the figures from the NCIS report indicates (Westert et al., 2010), claiming that transformations in the welfare state are inevitability due to mainly the increase of the ageing population is a rather wrongful conclusion. About ten years ago, even 'left' orientated economists, started pointing towards the rapid ageing of the Dutch population and declared it to be the main ground for a reconstruction of the welfare state (Jacobs et al., 2003). Since then this myth is wide-spread by Dutch politicians. And although we notice total care expenses are rising, it is not right at all to point the finger to ageing as a main factor for this rise. Kathrin Komp and Theo van Tilburg pointed out that this perspective on the role of the ageing is not taking account of their often very active role in society (Komp and van Tilburg, 2010). The activities they employ are often services which otherwise should be supplied by the welfare state. Komp and van Tilburg found as well that ageing is often used as an economically liberal argument for cost reduction in order to bring the welfare state back to smaller proportions (Komp and van Tilburg, 2010). To execute this cost reduction and to start the transition towards more participation of citizens instead of claiming long-term care by the state, a new law was designed, named the 'Social Support Act'.

Changing the Dutch welfare state: The Social Support Act

The Social Support Act (Wmo) came into force in the Netherlands on January the 1st 2007. This Social Support Act holds some strong ideas regarding the transition of the Dutch welfare state. Dependency on the state has to be traded for more personal dependencies between individuals. This is also expressed by the use of popular vocabulary like 'citizens power', 'own responsibility' and 'big society' (Kampen et al., 2013). Since Social Support Act entered into force its underlying ideas are further developed in the form of the projects 'New Style Social Work' (Welzijn Nieuwe Stijl) and the 'New Direction' (*De Kanteling*). The introduction of the Social Support Act gave municipalities responsibility for developing a coherent local policy social support policy. The act requires local authorities to retain and strengthen the existing social capital and to provide support to those people who are in need for it. This consequently led to a switch from a claim and supply-driven approach to a demand and results-led approach. As a result local authorities are responsible for the quality of the support provided by providing institutions.

Ageing in a 'participation state'

What does the Social Support Act imply for the ageing population in the Netherlands? First of all there is the social demand to stay at home longer, more independently. Approximately 780,000 people get long-term care by the state trough the AWBZ (Exceptional Medical Expense Act). Of them, 10% are in the age group of 65 until 74 years old, 23% are in the group of 75 until 84 years and 24% are 85 or older. In total 450,000 ageing use AWBZ care. Of them around 200.000 live in a care institution or nursing home. The other 250,000 ageing receive AWBZ care to make it possible for them to live independently. Regarding to the Social Support Act (Wmo), in total 639,000 people are entitled to aid (CAK, 2012).

Already for some years now Dutch social policy is paying strong attention to advancing self-reliance and independence. The coming years the ageing population will notice the effects of the grand movement in long-term care, regarding the separation of living and care. It is to be expected that institutions delivering care will concentrate more on the wishes of their ageing clients and the elderly themselves should get more freedom of choice. On the other side there will arise an increase of situations for the vulnerable elderly with insufficient care or just only care. This means that for social events elderly will have to rely on family, friends and commercial services and social work since nursing homes will not supply these activities any longer.

The dependence on family, friends, neighbours and other social capital will increase. And as ageing people are expected to live longer 'at home', it is as well expected that they will more and more depend on social welfare organizations and social work (Castelijns et al., 2013). Beside that there will be a stronger dependency on informal care. The rising demand for informal care bears some premises which are put into power in an addition to the Social Support Act, called New-Style Social Work.

New Style Social Work and its premises

The Social Support Act (Wmo) was introduced in order to cut the expenses of the AWBZ (Exceptional Medical Expense Act) and to encourage citizens to take more responsibility for their personal circumstances (Penninx, 2010). This was one of the first concrete initiatives on the part of the government to transform the Dutch welfare state into what now is referred to as a 'participation state'. The fundamental scheme is that people themselves will take more control over their own lives, but also of their neighborhood and community, or even sometimes of society as a whole. As a consequence, not only the municipalities will have to adjust their way of working to this 'new reality', but also social work organizations and professionals have to reform. Though in the last years many municipalities and organizations have made substantial steps forward in the implementation of the Social Support Act, former State Secretary of the Ministry of Health, Welfare and Sport, Jet Bussemaker, appended another incentive in 2009 with the governmental program 'New Style Social Work' (Welzijn Nieuwe Stijl). This New Style Social Work is, so to say, the next step towards further development of the new vision on social work. A blend of eight so-called 'beacons' offers a frame indicating in which way social policy and social work should develop (Scholte, 2010). This skeleton is regarded to be the source for promoted completion of the new professional's achievements and approach (Kluft, 2012). In short, these eight beacons of New Style Social Work are:

1. Demand-oriented methods
2. A pro-active approach towards citizens
3. Focus on the citizens' personal strengths
4. Collective versus individual facilities
5. Informal care versus formal care
6. An Integrated approach of professional organizations
7. A result-oriented focus
8. Space and time for the professional

The beacons were taken from the National Program New Style Social Work titled 'the power of connecting' by the Ministry of Health, welfare and Sport (Ministerie van VWS, 2010).

Self-help and the focus on personal strengths of the ageing

In this section and the next we will center on beacon number 3 and 5 of New Style Social Work, as presented above here. We have chosen these focal points since these beacons are directly connected to the role of informal care as well as to the implications for the self-reliance of the ageing in Dutch society. It must be acknowledged that other beacons will effect quite substantial impact as well but, unfortunately, it is not possible to cover all of them in this chapter. The aim is to analyze some important shortcomings of the Social Support Act and study the latent ideological wishes the act bears in terms of social capital and a change of solidarity.

Focus on the citizens' personal strengths (Beacon 3)

It is said that the new social policy, which focuses in the citizen's potential for co-producing social work, calls for social workers to 'walk with' their clients. In order to realize this, the new social worker is 'present' (beacon 2), meaning visible, to speak with the words of Jos van der Lans pamphlet 'Eropaf! (van der Lans, 2010).

This being present actually means stop operating from consulting rooms but go in people their homes and other community meeting places. The new social worker should be a 'generalist', as Margot Scholte puts it:

> someone who operates in the community, is always on attendance and calls for specialist help when necessary. (Scholte, 2010)

The new professional approaches the vulnerable citizen actively and stimulates him to take personal responsibility for solving his own problems. He takes the time that's needed to respond to questions of citizens, to assist citizens in recognizing and using their personal strengths and to support their initiatives (van Bergen, 2010). Beside that the professional should work increasingly demand-oriented and in this way responds even better to the real questions and needs of the citizen. This all sounds quite terrific but in fact there is little new in this approach and beside that it is mainly started-up to cut costs for long-term care (Pennix, 2010). And, even more dangerous; there are some premises, for example about the own responsibility, self-help and informal care, which put a spanner in the works and enclose quite some serious risks for the vulnerable (ageing population) in society.

Own responsibility: some remarks

Governmental policy is emphasizing the sake of self-help, own responsibility and the freedom of choice in the care for the ageing (VWS, 2012). Increasing the own responsibility, self-help and the possibilities for control by elderly should contribute to a better experienced quality of life and care. Unfortunately, the latter terms are difficult to relate to one another (Zwart-Olde et al., 2013). However, the mantra of self-help is embraced in a tight grip by Dutch political parties at this time. Neo-liberal Prime Minister Mark Rutte as well as the social democratic Minister Diederik Samson are hand in hand in agreement on these themes. As stated before, the core issue here is that vulnerable (old) people and their environment, whether that is family, friends or the neighbourhood, should do more by themselves. In that way, they are themselves responsible for participating. Older people have to live a longer period at home or have pay (more) by themselves when they are in need for professional care. On top of that self-help is not only stimulated, it has become obligated as current forms of formal care are all of a sudden thrown out of the AWBZ financed care with all consequences entailed for vulnerable ageing (Hermans & Evenhuis, 2012). But the term self-help is a strange term, a *contradictio in terminis*, as Evelien Tonkens points out (Tonkens, 2009). In fact, when you are in need for help it is often not possible to help out yourself, otherwise you would not be asking for help in the first place. Beside that it is very hard for vulnerable ageing to pull themselves out of 'the swamp', by themselves.

Many vulnerable people, ageing included, do not ask for help. As a matter of fact, lots of them have been self-helping too long with all the consequences that will entail. As Lillian Linders have pointed out, there is shyness to ask for help as well (Linders, 2010). But not only the vulnerable ageing themselves should contribute more, people in their direct surroundings as well. Former state secretary Veldhuijzen-van Zanten described in her letter of policy on informal care (VWS, 2012) how the neighbour of a chronically ill patient delivered better care than the concerned professional. The message is very clear: rely on your neighbour! But when you cannot help yourself, when no family, friends, neighbours or volunteers are there to support you sufficiently, only then there is the possibility to apply for formal care in your community. Although applying for this does not guarantee civilians professional care will necessarily be supplied to them (De Klerk et al., 2010).

Informal care (versus formal care) for the ageing (Beacon 5)

In the Netherlands there are 3.5 million people active in supplying care in an informal way. At the moment approximately 2.6 million Dutch citizens take long term care for people in their family or neighborhood (Oudijk et al., 2010). In addition, there are 300,000 till 450,000 volunteers active in care. Politics assume there's a potential for growth of these figures. But the question is whether that assumption is correct (VWS, 2012).

In fact, a profound sociological perspective is absent in present social policy. On the short term we will experience a new generation: The Informal Caregivers. This generation was born after the second world war, the so-called 'baby-boomers', grew up in times of individualization, increasing welfare and consequently a strongly developed welfare state. Personal development has always been important to this generation. They not only meet a much heavier and stronger question for care than before, also the willingness of this generation to supply informal care is different. It is not that there are not willing to care for others but they do not want it as a life task like the previous generations had to (Broeze van Groenou, 2012). It's no news to state that in Western societies social relationships and family structures have dramatically changed throughout the twentieth century. Many of us have, for example, moved from a three generation 'extended' family towards a smaller 'nuclear' family nowadays (Laslett, 1972). An effect is that the self-evident responsibility which former generations care takers felt is more lose nowadays. This becomes clear when we take in account the following considerations for supplying informal care.

In the coming years our growing ageing populations will generate a need for much care. This is especially true in respect of the 'oldest ageing' in society. There is a particular increase in the number of people in the age of 80 years and older. This is why the need for care amongst people in this age group, living at home or in an institution, will rise. Besides that, the strong developed medical care keeps the ageing alive longer. That's why we can expect a rising number of people with severe and long-term multiple health problems.

But there is a competition between tasks developing as well (Broeze van Groenou, 2012). In the Netherlands, just as in some other countries, we now will have to work until we are 67 years old. When we arrive to this retiring age, other tasks compete for our attention as well. Mainly there's a rising demand for taking care on different levels, e.g. we have to take care of our grandchildren for the reason that there's a diminishing availability of kindergartens. As Marjolein Broeze van Groenou emphasizes, apart from that we have to participate more in the families of our children due to a larger participation of women on the labour market. Beside that we should not overlook the mounting claim of care for old parents (Broeze van Groenou, 2012). These examples show there is a competition between tasks considering the fact that volunteering caregivers at this age also can experience health problems which might influence their ability. Last but not least, families are often not living in the same village, city or area anymore. Distances between family members have risen due to mobility. As a consequence, physical help is harder to realize over distance. Thus, although ageing might have potential social capital, it is not always possible to find an informal caregiver just up the road.

Defining the informal caregiver

So who is this informal caregiver? Informal care is supplied by informal caregivers and volunteers. Professional care is supplied by those who are employed in the care-sector. The definitions provided down here are the same as the definitions used by the state as formulated in the letter of policy by the Ministry of VWS 'Naast elkaar en met elkaar (VWS, 2009

+ Informal care-giving means long-term care for someone in need of care at home or in an institution by people in ones direct surroundings and which is not provided profession wise. Care is emerging from the existing relationship and is more than just ordinary care; it goes further than the daily emotional and practical support which social relations normally exchange.
+ A care volunteer on the other hand is someone who is supplying care, unpaid, out of an organized cooperation and is non-obligatory committed to other parties. So, in contrary to informal care-giving this help is not coming forth from existing social relationships.
+ A professional is providing their labour from an organization or agency and is receiving a salary for their work. The professional is tied to standardized regulations and stipulations of quality.

When we investigate the care for the ageing we have to acknowledge that roughly 75 percent of all care for older people is supplied by informal care-givers (De Boer et al., 2009). Half of the informal caregivers are in the age group of 50 till 65 years old. Almost 20 percent of all informal caregivers (*mantelzorgers*) give help to a needy older partner. The larger part of the informal caregivers, approximately a 70 percent is combining care-duties with paid labor (De Boer et al., 2009). Just from these figures one can understand that many Dutch already give informal care. Is it possible to rely even more on these informal caregivers?

Some annotations on the capacity of informal caregivers

State secretary of Healthcare Martin van Rijn assumes that children should wash their old mother or cook for her (Volkskrant, 2013). The question is of course whether the vulnerable ageing can refer to an informal network of care. Pressure on the informal care-giver is rising, for many break down is close by (Zwart-Olde et al., 2013). Lillian Linders claims that the State Secretary should just admit the fact that cutting expenses can possibly hurt instead of saying everything will get better when we help out each other (Linders, 2013).

The perceived quality of care by elderly is directly connected to the informal caregivers and the cooperation between formal and informal care in the network (Zwart-Olde et al., 2013). Whether the care offered is contributing to people's experiences of quality of life is mainly dependent on the sense of control by the aged person on his or her own life. Unfortunately, the vulnerable ageing do not have a big social network they can refer to when in need for informal care. (Zwart-Olde et al., 2013). And furthermore, informal care-givers often have to do a lot of work which they cannot share with other informal help because there simply is no one else to help them out. Sometimes they are not able to provide the care needed (for example because of the complexity of it). And as pointed out before, there seems to be a certain 'shyness' to ask for informal care as well (Linders, 2010).

Beside the question whether there is a potential pool for informal caregivers another question stays to be answered. Does an increased commitment of other informal caregivers or volunteers contribute to a better experience of the quality of care? There are some indications that this might be the case (Zwart-Olde et al., 2013) but this strongly depends on the investment which is made in good collaboration by both informal and formal caregivers in such way that in the end the ageing will benefit. Ellen Grootegoed found in her study an unwanted effect of this empowerment and focus on self-help, namely the fact that clients are getting less able to help themselves due to their resistance to ask family for help (Grootegoed, 2012). They say they find it morally unjust having their family functioning as a safety net for the cracks in the present welfare state. Receiving care which is organized and paid by the state does not provoke feelings of guilt but on the other hand asking family is perceived as an unreasonable burden for many (Grootegoed, 2012). It also challenges people's feelings towards independence. Therefore, many keep their care-demands well reserved secretly from family and friends. (Grootegoed, 2012).

Changing solidarity

The call for more informal care by persons in the social network of the ageing client assumes a form of solidarity which is often present in traditional, agricultural societies. As stressed, family structures have changed and vulnerable elderly often do not have extensive social capital. Beside that there is shyness or even unwillingness to ask for help of family and friends. The last decades in the Netherlands, neo-liberal politics started some kind of a war against the vertical solidarity in society (solidarity by paying collectively for risks which might happen to you) and brought to focus a horizontal solidarity. This latter form of solidarity is about insuring yourself individually for the risks you think might happen to you (Komter, 2000). Knowing this, is it right to ask for a more old fashioned mechanical solidarity when financial security moves in another direction? On the other hand, expecting solidarity isn't necessary a bad thing in itself. An ideal society of some sort is inhabited by civilians whom are taking care of each other, triggered by feelings of altruism and humanity (Muehlebach, 2012). But this kind of society is quite far away. So, is it possible to attain a new type of more direct solidarity? Helping each other out implies interdependency and reciprocity between concerned parties. But long-term relationships between those in need and neighbours are often not established because the relationship is not balanced as a whole (Bredewolde and Baars Blom, 2009). Subsequently, the focus should be on this interdependency of social relations and the self-interest has to change to enlightened self-interest in which the added value of social behavior and felt solidarity become more essential. The recently released report of the RMO, *Rondje voor de publieke zaak*, points in the same direction and is striking a blow for the experience of solidarity as a value (RMO, 2013). To expect such solidarity without proper organization is quite naïve, as Richard Sennett indicated (Gradener, 2013) and arguably provokes social exclusion of vulnerable groups in society (Spruyt, 2013), such as the ageing.

A risk society for the ageing

Politicians and policymakers using the term self-help should be explaining much more clear what is expected by helping out oneself and they should point towards where they see potential and possibilities. Nowadays policy reports and neighbourhood programs appeal to positive emotions such as respect, pride and affection (Tonkens and de Wilde, 2013) By throwing in such an emotion management - in the words of Arlie Hochschild (2003), local politicians and policymakers try to create some sort of intuitive social cohesion. This is done by giving civilians a reciprocal sense of unity through the stimulation of positive emotions and interactions between citizens and institutions. In this way communities hope their citizens will develop some sort of identification with other people in their surroundings and feel more attached with the neighbourhood. It is all jolly good fun, confusing as well, but it probably will not make a big difference, at least not the difference which is hoped for. Not as long as wealth is produced and distributed in this way. Ulrich Beck claims that the rise of the production of wealth in our Western societies is systematically going together with the raise of social risks (Beck, 1992). These risks become normal and accepted as part of individualized daily life. A fact is that in an individualized and meritocratic society as the Netherlands, people are increasingly in search for individual recognition of their own identity and own earnings (Tonkens and de Wilde, 2013). The state desires people to find this recognition somewhere else, not by supplied by governmental institutions but by other civilians. Evelien Tonkens entitles this as 'affective citizenship' in the recently published book with the imaginative title: 'When participating hurts' (Tonkens and de Wilde, 2013). We now know the risk which it entails for the ageing.

Let us just take a brief look back, over our shoulders, at the old wrecked welfare state. In the present time there is hardly any attention paid to the added value of a welfare state. We owe to the welfare state we still have a reasonably low poverty and criminality rate (Schinkel, 2013). Schinkel claims that the idea of economic viability as being problematic is just a matter of setting priorities (Schinkel, 2013). Let's talk about priorities a bit then. At the moment almost everyone is getting older (and much older than before) which implies we are all in the need to benefit from collective provisions. When young people want to be ensured a well-groomed future, they themselves will have an interest to keep the services we have established. As long as this pattern of expectations stays the same, the willingness of young people to pay for the raising expenses of ageing will not change (Beer, 2003). Actually it is quite simple; acknowledging the fact that we are getting older, we have to set aside more of our income during our active phase of life to provide us with means for later on in life. It does not make a difference whether we do this collectively controlled by the state or individually through the market. We just have to perceive this mechanism as a priority. Margot Trappenburg is taking a stand for the welfare state as we knew it. Almost emotionally she writes (translated from Dutch):

> If institutions for vulnerable people do not function well enough, we can try to make these institutions better, a bit nicer and more fun, with some more privacy and better facilities? Why is it that everything has to change this radically? Our sweet, not perfect, but reasonably well functioning welfare state is running away from us and what we get in return is a cheaper, do-it-yourself model. (Trappenburg, 2012)

Her words sound like an emotionally loaded lament, maybe even a warning. This chapter brought to focus several points of critique about the strong call for self-help and informal care to solve the problem of rising care expenses. Trusting on the active solidarity of citizens is not a fair solution for the vulnerable ageing in society. Claiming this solution will lead to a better society with better people is, - to speak with the words of Pedro the Lion - just a clever ad (for cigarettes).

References

Achterhuis, H., (2011) *De utopie van de vrije markt*. Rotterdam: Lemniscaat.

Baart, A., (2013) *Kwetsbaarheid mag meer aandacht krijgen*, Available from: http://www.socialevraagstukken.nl/site/2013/05/24/kwetsbaarheid-mag-meer-aandacht-krijgen/ (Accessed: 5-6-2013).

Beck, U., (1992) *Risk society, towards a new modernity*. London: Sage Publications.

Bergen, A. M. van, (2010) *De nieuwe professional*. Utrecht: MOVISIE. Available from: http://www.zilverenkracht.nl/136633/def/home/zelfregie/downloads/de_nieuwe_professional/ (Accessed: 17-5-2013).

Bredewolde, F.M. and Baars-Blom, J.M., (2009) *Kwetsbaar evenwicht*. Zwolle: Centrum voor Samenlevingsvraagstukken. Available from: http://www.surfsharekit.nl:8080/get/smpid:2660/DS5/. (Accessed: 24-5-2013).

Broese van Groenou, M.I. and Boer, A. de, (2009) Uitkomst: ervaren belasting. *In* Boer, A. de Broese van Groenou, M.I. and Timmermans, J.T. ed. *Mantelzorg, een overzicht van de steun van en aan mantelzorgers in 2007*. Den Haag: Sociaal en Cultureel Planbureau.

Broese van Groenou, M.I (2012) Informele zorg 3.0: Schuivende panelen en een krakend fundament Available from: http://www.socialevraagstukken.nl/site/2012/07/02/informele-zorg-3-0-schuivende-panelen-en-een-krakend-fundament/ (Accessed: 1-6-2013).

CAK. (2012) *Zorg zonder verblijf.* Available from: http://www.hetcak.nl/portalserver/portals/cak-portal/pages/k1-2-9-1-zorg-zonder-verblijf.html (Accessed: 3-6-2013)

Duin, C. van. And Stoeldraijer, L. (2012) Bevolkingsprognose voor 2010 – 2060. Den Haag/ Heerlen: Centraal Bureau voor de Statistiek

Campen, C. van. (2011) SCP Kwetsbare Ouderen. Den Haag: Sociaal en Cultureel Planbureau

Carbo, C. and Baart, A. (2013) *De zorgval.* Amsterdam: Thoeris.

Castelijns, E. Kollenburg, A. Van and Meerman, W. te, (2013) *De vergrijzing voorbij.* Nijmegen: Berenschot.

Dam, van, M. (2009) *Niemandsland.* Amsterdam: de bezige bij.

Durkheim, E. (1893) *De la division du travail social.* Paris: Alcan.

Esping-Andersen, G. (1990) *The three worlds of welfare capitalism.* Cambridge: Polity press.

Eurostat. 2012. Active ageing and solidarity between generations. A statistical portrait of the European Union 2012. Luxemburg: Publication Office of the European Union. Available from: http://epp.eurostat.ec.europa.eu/cache/ITY_OFFPUB/KS-EP-11-001/EN/KS-EP-11-001-EN.PDF (Accessed: 15-5-2013).

Gradener, J. (2013) Samenwerking is een ambacht. *Tijdschrift voor Sociale Vraagstukken*, Utrecht: Movisie.

Grootegoed, E. (2012) Tussen zelfredzaamheid en eigen regie: Wmo en de Autonomieparadox. *In* Steyaert, J.and Kwekkeboom, R. *De zorgkracht van sociale netwerken.* Utrecht: Movisie .

Hermans, H. and Evenhuis, H. (2012) *Gezondheid en zelfstandigheid van 50-plussers, geïndiceerd voor ZZP-VG 4*: gegevens op basis van de studie Gezond Ouder met een verstandelijke beperking (GOUD). Available from: http://www.vgn.nl/artikel/15607 (Accessed: 28-5-2013).

Hochschild, A.R. (2003) *The commercialization of intimate life: notes from home and work.* San Francisco: University of California Press.

Jacobs, B. Kalshoven, F. and Tang, P. (2003) Noodzakelijk links. *In Socialisme & Democratie 2003, nr. 10/11.* Den Haag: Wiardi Beckman Stichting. Available from: http://www.wbs.nl/system/files/tang_paul_noodzakelijk_links_sd2003-10-11.pdf (Accessed: 1-6-2013).

Kampen, T. Verhoeven, I. and Verplanke, L. (2013) *De affectieve burger, Hoe de overheid verleidt en verplicht tot zorgzaamheid.* Amsterdam: Van Gennep.

Klerk, M. de, R. Gisling and Timmermans J. (2010) *Op weg met de Wmo. Evaluatie van de Wet maatschappelijk ondersteuning 2007 – 2009*. Den Haag: Sociaal en Cultureel Planbureau.

Kluft , M. (2012) Zeg, bent u misschien de nieuwe professional? De omslag van de visie over welzijn naar het handelen van de nieuwe professional. Utrecht: Movisie/Igitur publications. Available from: http://www.journalsi.org/index. php/si/article/viewFile/295/258 (Accessed: 26-5-2013).

Komp, K. and Tilburg, T. van. (2010) Ageing societies and the welfare state: Where the inter-generational contract is not breached. In *International Journal of Ageing and Later Life*. 5 Available from: http://www.ep.liu.se/ej/ijal/2010/v5/i1/a01/ ijal10v5i1a01.pdf (Accessed: 21-5-2013).

Komter, A.E. Burgers, J. and Engbergsen, G. (2000) *Het cement van de samenleving*. Amsterdam University Press.

Kwekkeboom, R. (2010) *De verantwoordelijkheid van de mensen zelf. De (her)verdeling van de taken rond zorg en ondersteuning tussen overheid en burgers en de betekenis daarvan voor de professionele hulpverlening*. Amsterdam University Press.

Lans, J. van der. (2010) *Er-op-af. De nieuwe start van het sociaal werk*. Amsterdam: Augustus.

Laslett, P. (1972) *Household and Family in Past Time*. London: Cambridge University Press

Linders, L. (2010) *De betekenis van nabijheid. Een onderzoek naar informele zorg in een volksbuurt*. Tilburg: Universiteit van Tilburg.

Linders, L. (2013) *Staatssecretaris Van Rijn moet gewoon zeggen dat bezuinigen pijn doet*. Available from: http://www.socialevraagstukken.nl/site/2013/03/11/ staatssecretaris-van-rijn-moet-gewoon-zeggen-dat-bezuinigen-pijn-doet/ (Accessed: 24-5-2013).

Ministerie van VWS. (2010) *Nationaal programma Welzijn Nieuwe Stijl: de kracht van verbinden*. Den Haag: Ministerie van VWS.

Muehlebach, A. (2012) *The moral neoliberal. Welfare and citizenship in Italy*. Chicago: University of Chicago Press.

Nimwegen, N. van and Praag, van. (2012) *Bevolkingsvraagstukken in Nederland anno 2012. Actief ouder worden in Nederland*. Den Haag: Nederlands Interdisciplinair Demografisch Instituut.

Oudijk, D. Boer, A. de, Woittiez, I. Timmermans, J. and Klerk, M. de. (2010) *Mantelzorg uit de doeken. Een actueel beeld van het aantal mantelzorgers*. Den Haag: Sociaal en Cultureel Planbureau.

Penninx, K. (2010) *Krachtgerichte sociale zorg. Kansen voor sociaal werk in het licht van de stelselherziening AWBZ*. Utrecht: Movisie.

Putnam, R. Leonardi, R. and Nanetti, R.Y. (1994) *Making Democracy Work, Civic Traditions in Modern Italy*, Princeton University Press.

Rand, A. (1957/2005) *Atlas Shruged*. New York: Dutton Books.

RMO, Raad voor Maatschappelijke Ontwikkeling. (2013) *Rondje voor de publieke zaak*. Den Haag: RMO.

Rose, N. (2006) Governing 'advanced' liberal democracies. *In* Sharma, A. En A. Gupta ed. *The Anthropology of the state*. London: Blackwell.

Schinkel, W. (2013) *De Nieuwe Democratie, Naar andere vormen van politiek*. Amsterdam: De Bezige Bij.

Scholte, M. (2010) *Oude waarden in nieuwe tijden. Over de kracht van maatschappelijk werk in de 21ᵉ eeuw*. Haarlem: Hogeschool Inholland.

Scholte, M. and Sprinkhuizen A. (2012) *De sociale kwestie hervat. Consequenties van wet en regelgeving voor sociaal-agogisch werk*. Houten: Bohn Stafleu Van Loghum

Spruyt, B.J. (2013) *Hoe de nieuwe solidariteit uitpakt, zal nog moeten blijken*. Available from: http://www.socialevraagstukken.nl/site/2013/06/08/hoe-de-nieuwe-solidariteit-uitpakt-zal-nog-moeten-blijken/ (Accessed: 26-5-2013).

Thacker, S.B. Stroup D.F. Carande-Kulis V. Marks J.S, Roy K. and Gerberding, J.L. (2006) *Measuring the public's health 121*. Available from: http://www.ncbi.nlm.nih.gov/pmc/articles/PMC1497799/ (Accessed: 2-6-2013).

Tonkens, E. (2009) *Mondige Burgers, Getemde Professionals. Marktwerking en professionaliteit in de publieke sector*. Amsterdam: Uitgeverij van Gennep.

Tonkens, E. and de Wilde, M. (2013) *Als Meedoen pijn doet. actief burgerschap in de wijk*. Amsterdam: Uitgeverij van Gennep.

Trappenburg, M. (2012) *Solidariteit in de 21ˢᵗᵉ eeuw. Blijf bij ons. Ode aan de verzorgingsstaat. In Socialisme & Democratie 2013, nr. 7/8*. Available from: *http://www.margotrappenburg.nl/blijf_bij_ons_-_ode_aan_de_verzorgingsstaat.pdf* (Accessed: 15-5-2013).

Vonk, F. Kromhout, M. Feijten, P. Marangos, A.M. (2013) *Municipal policy in relation to the Social Support Act (Wmo) in 2013*. Sociaal en Cultureel Planbureau.

Volkskrant. 2013. *Langdurige zorg nodig? Heeft u kinderen in de buurt?* Volkskrant, 26-4-2013

VWS, Ministerie van Volksgezondheid, welzijn en Sport. (2012) *Beleidsbrief Mantelzorg*. Den Haag: Ministerie van VWS.

Westert, G.P. Berg, M.J. van den Zwakhals S.LN. Jong, J.D. de and Verkleij, H. (2010) *Dutch Health Care Performance Report 2010*. National Institute for Public Health and the Environment Available from: http://www.gezondheidszorgbalans.nl/object_binary/o10298_dhCPR2010.pdf (Accessed: 4-6-2013).

Zwart- Olde, I. Jacobs, M. Broeze van Groenou, M.I. (2013) *Zorgnetwerken van Kwetsbare Ouderen*, Amsterdam: Vrije Universiteit. Available from: http://www.fsw.vu.nl/nl/Images/Rapportage%20ZKO%20incl%20cover_tcm30-338653.pdf (Accessed: 27-5-2013).

8

'I remember that …' Reminiscence groups with people with dementia:

A valuable site for practice learning[1]

Jonathan Parker

Introduction

This paper describes a small scale group project developing and delivering reminiscence work with people with dementia and undertaken by social work students as part of their practice learning experiences. The potential for enhancing the student learning experience and additional benefits for staff and group participants are explored and the limitations of the study critiqued. Findings indicated that students and staff gain mutual benefits from such projects which also have the potential to create possibilities for the enhancement of service delivery. The project stemmed from a desire and objective to ensure the sustainability of reminiscence work as part of an earlier cross-European comparison of the use of volunteers in working with people with dementia. However, sustainability issues require careful planning and thought. The study highlights the need for the participation of all stakeholders, especially those who are marginalised, in developing and undertaking groupwork.

Reminiscence and life review

The vexed question of terminology pervades literature concerning reminiscence and life review. Whilst often used as synonyms (Butler, 1963), life review is generally assumed to reflect a more systematic and therapeutic approach than reminiscence (Burnside and Haight, 1994; Staudinger, 2001). Bornat (2001) explores the differences and similarities between reminiscence and oral history, suggesting both are intersubjective processes, but oral history has a wider social purpose and represents a critical activity bringing to the fore unseen aspects of the past or changing the locus of control to those who have lived the history whereas reminiscence focuses upon the process of specific memories for those involved. Woods et al. (2005) use the term reminiscence therapy. However, Gibson (2004) takes issue with this description stating that reminiscence is not a therapy, which implies expertise and distance, but is better described as reminiscence work which, she claims, illustrates its participative nature.

In respect of people with dementia, Goldsmith (1996) uses the term 'life story' to refer to the production of a book, an audio or video recording, life review is something less tangible, but often individual, whilst reminiscence refers to shared group memories. Murphy and Moyes (1997), however, understand life story work as a process of life review.

Reminiscence, as a process, is often considered universal; something we all do (Butler, 1963; Gillies and James, 1994). Whilst this view can be challenged on grounds of cultural diversity, personality factors and developmental stage (Merriam 1995; Trueman and Parker, 2006), it is a common activity bound with personal reflection on aspects of experience in the light of the present or future plans. Gibson (2004) suggests that emphasis on the universality of reminiscence has now been replaced by spiritual life review and the search for meaning.

The uses of reminiscence

Reminiscence concerns telling stories of the past, personal histories, individual perceptions of social worlds inhabited and events experienced personally or at a distance (Burnside and Haight, 1994). It can be pleasurable, cathartic or therapeutic. It can be spontaneous or organised and systematic. Bender et al (1999) provide a wide range of twenty possible purposes and benefits that can derive from reminiscence. Using a three-Cs model, these include benefits for clients[2], such as interacting, socialising, learning and engaging in therapeutic activities; benefits for carers to aid communication and improve staff skills, and benefits for the work context or culture of the unit.

Since Butler's paper was published there has been an exponential growth in literature concerning reminiscence and life review and the importance of reminiscence and life review in the caring services is clear (see table 1). Life review has been used in treating older women survivors of childhood sexual abuse (McInnis-Dittrich, 1996) where choice to participate or not is stressed. It has been used to lessen disorientation and to increase social interaction in older people in care (Tabourne, 1995a, 1995b), especially with those who are depressed (Tabourne, 1995b; Arean et al., 1993; Stinson, 2006). Other therapeutic benefits have been observed such as increasing self-acceptance (Magee, 1994); promoting an holistic approach to care (Penn, 1994) and as a counselling tool (Webster and Young, 1988; Malde, 1988). Life review has also proved useful in working with gay and lesbian older people (Galassi, 1991).

Reminiscence is also associated with therapy and change but can be seen as a social and enjoyable activity without being construed as anything more (Bryant, Smart and King, 2005). Hsieh and Wang's (2003) systematic review of nine random control trials using a therapeutic type of reminiscence work with older depressed adults, derived from Erickson's ego-integrity versus despair developmental stage, found varying results ranging from clinical to statistical significance. The methodological differences in the studies used no doubt contributed to the findings, but it did suggest that reminiscence therapy 'should be considered as a viable, valuable and useful intervention to potentially reduce depression in older adults' (p. 344; see also Bachar et al, 1991; Cappeliez, O'Rourke and Chaudhury, 2005; Coleman, 2005). Therapeutic uses are also evident in raising self-esteem (McGowan, 1994); in reconstructing the identities of older people (Buchanan and Middleton, 1995; Burnside and Haight, 1994; Sherman and Peak, 1991) and in stress management for people awaiting surgery (Rybarczyk and Auerbach, 1990) or those in intensive care (Jones, 1995). It has also been used with people with life-threatening illnesses (Cappeliez, et al, 2005; Jonsdottir, et al., 2001; Trueman and Parker, 2004; 2006).

Reminiscence is well-documented for use with older people in care settings (Snell, 1991), psychiatric hospitals (Gwyther, Lowenthal and Morazzo, 1990), nursing homes (Taft and Nehrke, 1990; Brody, 1990; Rattenbury and Stones, 1989; Orton, Allen and Cook, 1989), and for use with people with dementia (Gibson, 1997; Nomazi and Haynes, 1994; Ott, 1993; Martin, 1989; Parker and Penhale, 1998; Penhale and Parker, 1999).

Despite wide usage, scientific evidence of its benefits remains equivocal (George, 1995; Gillies and James, 1994) because of the lack of random-controlled trials of reminiscence work, and despite practice evidence of behavioural and social improvements especially as part of an on-going programme or integrated into daily activities. Woods et al (2005) have up-dated their earlier Cochrane review, the objective being to assess the effectiveness of reminiscence for older people with dementia and their care-givers, searching for data from randomised controlled trials and quasi randomised trials. Five trials were considered but only four had extractable data. Findings indicated that improvements in cognition were evident in comparison with no treatment and social contact groups, mood and general behavioural function improved at follow-up, and care-giver strain showed a significant decrease and staff knowledge of group members' backgrounds improved. No harmful effects were reported. The evidence-base, they conclude, still relies heavily on descriptive and observation studies. Randomised controlled trials are small and of relatively low quality. Reminiscence is, however, popular and training, support and supervision for staff is emphasised. Further research and methodological rigour is needed.

Reminiscence and people with dementia

Gibson (1994) found that large group, generalised reminiscence had a limited role for people with dementia, mainly as an entertainment or diversion. The main benefits came from well-planned, well-structured and specific topic reminiscence and life history usually with individuals. Whilst individual work may take something away from the social benefits of joining in small groups (Bender et al, 1999), there is still an emphasis on interaction and communication between the participant and facilitator. Also, many of the distractions found in groups are not present in individually focussed sessions. Whether undertaken individually or in groups, in a family or care setting, however, Gibson (2004) champions a creative approach that allows participants to express themselves freely whilst recognising the limitations and anxieties that might be raised when people become aware of their cognitive impairment.

Reminiscence work can be useful in a number of ways for people with varying degrees of dementia (Phillips et al, 2006). These include intrapsychic benefits such as maintaining self-esteem, identity and feelings of belonging, reframing the past and planning for the future; and interpersonal and social functions such as dealing with unresolved conflicts, story-telling and passing on traditions (Gibson, 2004). People with dementia can benefit from reminiscence in grounding their present relationships and maintaining warm, caring relationships which may ward off isolation and withdrawal

(Gibson, 2004; Parker, 2003). It may increase participation, socialisation and spontaneity in communication, give rise to behavioural improvements and reduce the distance between care staff and older people (Bender et al, 1999; Gibson, 2004; Parker et al, 1998a, b; Penhale et al, 1998).

Planning for reminiscence and group work

The skills needed to undertake reminiscence work are those which are considered important in any interpersonal human activity (Gibson, 1997), including active listening, empathy, attending to the person, sensitivity and respect. It is important also to note the value base integral to reminiscence work which respects the history, identity and uniqueness of the person. It honours people as social and interactive beings with a great deal to offer from their individual life experiences. In these ways it accords well with an emphasis on personhood and professional values (Kitwood, 1997).

Despite general caveats concerning the limitations of reminiscence work for people with dementia, group work is possible. Parker and Penhale (1998) detail some of the important factors to bear in mind when undertaking reminiscence work in groups with people with dementia which are not dissimilar to those affecting groupwork generally (see Doel, 2006). They include paying attention to planning, preparation and training; finding out about members, inviting and preparing potential members and involving them in the preparations. Practical considerations such as the venue, transport, caregiver issues and personal needs are also important. Matters of recording, revising and evaluating the groups are concerns that also should be shared and determined as a group. With people who have dementia this may raise certain complications but should still be considered. Toseland (1995; 2005) acknowledges that age-related changes and cohort effects must be taken into account but, as Burnside (1994) indicates reminiscence groups are potentially valuable interventions in working with older people with dementia. The central point is that group participants with dementia or otherwise should be as fully involved in the groups as possible (Goldsmith, 1996; Gibson, 2004).

Groups may focus around agreed themes or begin as a more general discussion. It can be helpful to introduce physical objects connected with past events or tasks, play films and music, or even enact role-plays of street parties especially where people may find communication difficult. However the process is planned, it is essential to be sensitive to the needs and concerns of the members' pasts. It is important to keep in mind that, whilst social workers and their agencies can gain benefit from reminiscence work, the sessions are for the benefit of participants not facilitators.

In a cross European study, Penhale et al. (1998) explored the use of volunteers in facilitating reminiscence work with older people with dementia and found that it increased sociability, spontaneity and communication. The research also suggested that it assisted in challenging perceived intergenerational barriers and could foster a sense of self-worth in those running the groups, whilst developing transferable skills. One of the proposed outcomes of this research was to develop sustainability and in the UK part of the project student social workers were recruited to continue the work. The current study details how students and staff experienced the development and implementation of reminiscence work with older people, exploring the impact the experiences had on student learning experiences and its importance for social work practice education.

Methodology

The original study gained ethical approval within the University and from the local research ethics committee, which included plans for its continuation. A sample of ten social work students elected to participate in the groups as part of their practice learning. They were asked if they would complete an anonymous and voluntary questionnaire concerning the process, were assured that this was not part of the practice assessment process and that refusal to participate would have no implications for their learning. All ten participants responded. Staff involved in supporting the reminiscence groups were also asked to evaluate their participation by anonymous questionnaire. This method was chosen rather than an interview approach, which may have gained greater depth, so as to preserve the anonymity of the students who were undertaking practice learning at the time and to protect the sites in which the groups were held. It does, however, limit the study and findings which are further restricted by collecting data only from staff and students and not service users who could contribute in a confirmatory or discomfirmatory way to the responses.

A training module, developed as part of the original study, was provided to student participants and care staff. This was run together to develop rapport between staff and students and included work on dementia, approaches to people, groupwork and reminiscence work.

Three sites were used, two specialised local authority homes and a purpose built NHS Trust unit for older people with dementia. These were chosen to continue the project because of previous associations with the initial project and their provision of student learning experiences. Building on previous relationships was helpful in establishing the groups but may have limited the potential for critical analysis of the project as people wanted it to happen, believed in the work and the method. Five members of staff provided feedback on their perceptions of the benefits of the groups for service users, for themselves as staff, about the learning they thought that students gained. Staff were asked how they might wish to change the reminiscence groups, whether they had used them again, and for any other comments. The students were asked about the learning they thought they had gained, what they valued most, what they would wish to change, the use of the learning, relevance to employment and any other comments they wished to make. The students responded anonymously but were also invited to feedback at an end of practice learning experience plenary session in more general ways to contribute to any revision of the project. The small sample size is recognised as a weakness in the study but the data reflects a particular group of students and staff, providing insights that, whilst by no means generalisable, are usable and testable in similar settings.

Group participants were identified by staff within the care settings, based on their perception of who might benefit. Throughout the project, students became involved in assisting the selection by familiarising themselves with people's history, likes and dislikes. However, the lack of a service user focus is something that limited the study and raises a range of questions for future groups. Participation was, however, voluntary and if a person did not want to attend or left that was accepted.

The questionnaire data were analysed by thematic coding and creating links between identified categories. A conceptual content matrix, adapting Miles and Huberman's (1994) approach, was created to understand how the themes interacted and to identify perceptions and meanings within the data. Staff and student comments were analysed separately and then together to gain perspectives on the data and the focus of respondents' thoughts. The primary analysis of responses considered staff and student responses by the questions asked.

Findings

Gains for group participants, according to staff, included sharing past experiences and stories, participation in social activities and enjoyment as indicated by the following quotation:

> *[they gained] opportunities to discuss their past experiences and to share happy tales. These were very sociable groups. Clients were able to remember many things making use of their long term memory. The clients participated in the reminiscence groups with great enthusiasm. The clients stayed on for longer at times as they appeared to really enjoy reminiscing. (S2)*

Staff gained from the experience of students running these groups by learning more about the service users' pasts, by reciprocal enjoyment and participation in the groups and because group participants interacted and gained pleasure from the groups:

> *I enjoyed the reminiscence groups very much because with only being young it was nice to hear of clients' pasts and stories. (S3)*

> *[I valued the] therapeutic value it held for clients, in terms of increased interaction and pleasure. (S4)*

Staff believed students learnt a range of skills from participating in the groups including instrumental skills of working in groups, facilitation, planning and process, working with individuals, and in particular knowledge of and skills in working with people with dementia.

> *They learnt how to facilitate groups and build a rapport with clients. They learnt about planning a group and how to carry out a systematic process for each group. They also learnt about reviewing and evaluating groups and documented information in clients' individual notes regarding their participation in groups.*
> *I really enjoyed the reminiscence groups the students' facilitated. They worked conscientiously and with zest and enthusiasm. (S2)*

The key themes arising for staff were enjoyment, participation and skills development. For students, the core elements of learning gained from participation included groupwork skills and an acknowledgement of the limitations of groups, interpersonal skills, specific knowledge of a service user group and enjoyment, as shown in the following quotation:

> *There were skills of managing the dynamics of the group – trying to ensure everyone could take part, that the subject matter did not stray to topics which*

could be distressing. I learned the problems of reminiscence work with clients with Alzheimer's related illness. I also learned that reminiscence is far more effective in promoting self-esteem in individual and less structured sessions. I sometimes felt that in group structured sessions clients felt an obligation to remember things – a duty not a choice. (St3)

I believe that I leant a lot about group dynamics and how individual personalities can affect the entire group. The client group seemed to enjoy the reminiscence groups, some may have been more vocal than others, but other people who may not have contributed as much returned to the group voluntarily, which could be indicative of their enjoyment of it. I did initially have qualms about running a group about a subject that I knew very little about but on reflection, this worked to my advantage as I was very interested in the stories that the clients told me and I was even told that my enthusiasm and interest was welcoming, which boosted my confidence at my facilitating role. (St4)

Students also learned about preparation and planning for groups, collecting histories and adapting techniques to ensure communication is effective:

[I gained from] the challenge of communicating with older people with dementia and having the time to begin to understand the character, interests and possible future needs by delving into the files. (St1)

I learned how to choose triggers to memory, and how certain topics would interest women more than men. (St2)

Learning about groupwork, dynamics of groups and ways to deal with any problems arising. Learning about organising work to present an interesting discussion that groups could reminisce about, paying attention to trying to stimulate other senses, touch, taste, smell, hearing. (St9)

Students expressed that they valued being able to undertake groupwork, especially with a marginalised group, people with dementia. Taking part in the groups was found to be a usefully challenging placement experience, one in which they could make a difference and develop self-confidence.

The thing that I value most about running the reminiscence groups is the confidence that I gained from this experience .... because I had to work through my fears. (St5)

[I] enjoyed working with older people in residential care as I believe they often get forgotten once a residential placement takes place. [I] enjoyed the groupwork rather than the one-to-one. (St9)

It was heartening that values and concern for the group participants came to the fore when considering what changes could be made, although of concern that, despite the initial training provided, some respondents felt they had not had any. Changes wanted concerned greater time to observe, develop and plan the groups; more training and to ensure sustainability.

I still wish I had seen it done by a professional before I attempted it myself. I realise that the style would have been different but it would have been helpful to me to have an idea of what I was supposed to be doing before I did it. (St4)

Perhaps an on-going, seamless student involvement identifying the social needs of clients and being able to meet them through reminiscence, one-to-one or small groupwork would be more advantageous to students, clients and staff, than periodic attempts at groupwork covering the same topics. (St1)

There were other perceived problems expressed alongside training issues that need to be highlighted. However, these also appeared to have contributed to the students' learning especially concerning the importance of prior planning:

The original reminiscence groups involved approximately six persons with two students. Group led conversations were virtually nil and reminiscence conversations between clients were non-existent unless heavily promoted. A decision was made to gather a history of each client and to ascertain their interests. This appeared to be a more appropriate approach to meeting the needs. (St1)

Participation in the reminiscence groups was considered by the students to have increased their understanding of work situations and empathy with people with dementia. Students who responded also acknowledged the transferability of the skills they had learned, especially the groupwork and interpersonal skills they developed. Interestingly, participation in the project appeared to impress employers:

I am not working directly with this client group, but do work with people with cancer, often some do have dementia. Reminiscence is a useful tool to use to engage people and develop a rapport. (St10)

[I] gained groupwork skills and joint working skills... and this part of my placement impressed my employers. (St9)

Core themes from students concerned educational and experiential aspects – especially groupwork, interpersonal skills and their transferability - but they also identified values and the social and enjoyable aspects of the work.

The second stage of the analysis of staff and student responses brought to the fore a range of core themes. Staff responses were grouped into three areas, enjoyment (see Bender et al, 1999), participation (Gibson, 2004), and the development or learning of skills (Parker et al, 1999). The emphasis from staff suggested that participation in the reminiscence groups represented a reciprocal socio-facilitative activity; staff, students and service users gained from the interactions. Whilst the questions asked of the students differed slightly to those asked of staff, there was a degree of congruity in the responses. These highlighted skills development; especially skills relating to groupwork, interpersonal relations and specific knowledge of a service user group. The skills were considered by respondents to be transferable. Enjoyment and values-based responses also featured in the comments of students. Figure 1 illustrates the responses and the links between those of staff and students.

To get a greater depth of sophistication in this analysis a variable by case matrix was developed to consider what respondents were saying, to link categories to one another and refine the analysis (de Vaus, 1996). Participation included group participants sharing memories, socialising and raising confidence, and students working with others, undertaking different experiences and developing practice skills. This involvement was associated with enjoyment by students in doing something that was considered to be positive and useful and identified as contributing to their learning about groupwork and organising for reminiscence. This was confirmed by staff who recognised the learning of students:

They learnt how to facilitate groups and build a rapport with clients. They learnt about planning a group and how to carry out a systematic process for each group. They also learnt about reviewing and evaluating groups and documenting information in clients' individual notes regarding their participation in groups. (S2)

Staff appeared more reticent than students in commenting on the value of the groups to them. One staff member indicated that it was the therapeutic value for people with dementia that was most appreciated. This seemed to be associated with remembering past times and participating (S3). Students,

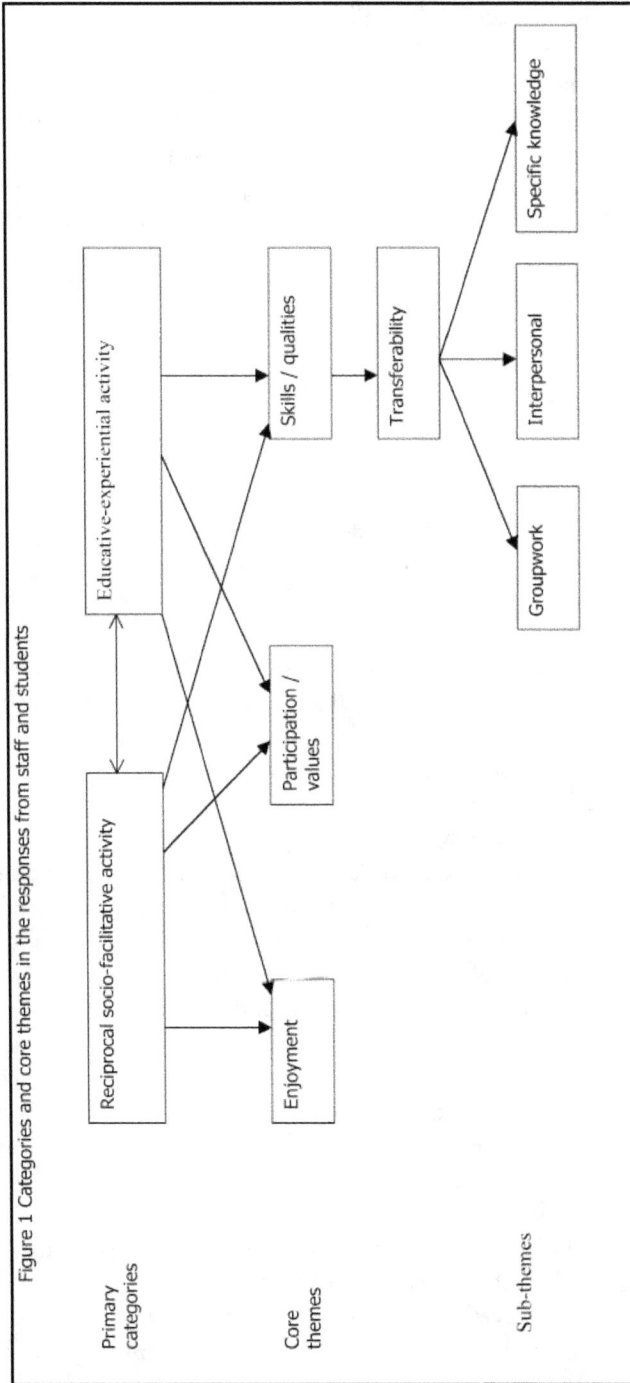

Figure 1 Categories and core themes in the responses from staff and students

Primary categories

Educative-experiential activity

Reciprocal socio-facilitative activity

Core themes

Skills / qualities

Transferability

Participation / values

Enjoyment

Sub-themes

Specific knowledge

Interpersonal

Groupwork

on the other hand, identified the challenges the work made to their own personal stereotypes of older people, of working as colleagues with people from different cultures and understanding different interpretations of reminiscence and old age. They also mentioned the value of developing a person-focused perspective with a group of people generally marginalised within society and within services. These perspectives were important to the students' learning in adapting skills to particular contexts and to the individuals involved.

> *The whole experience gave me the confidence to challenge my own and others' prejudices and to not accept a service that is easy and comfortable but not very beneficial to those it is meant to be for. In short, I would recommend reminiscence work to anyone whatever client group they wish to specialise with. (St7)*

Discussion

The findings concerning the benefits of reminiscence work confirmed earlier studies in emphasising the promotion of social activities, participation, enhanced communication and intergenerational relationships (Bender et al, 1999; Gibson, 2004). The central finding that engagement in the reminiscence groups promoted education, integration between social care staff and students and benefits for group members indicates that this kind of project is important to the types of practice learning opportunity envisaged by the introduction of the new degree in England; enhancing learning by doing and reflecting (see figure 2 overleaf). Positive benefits are reciprocal and this is attractive in developing further practice learning experiences, where benefits for the organisation and service provision can be shown beyond the development of a future skilled workforce. Participation in the groups promoted effective learning for students in skills development, critical reflection, working with others and challenging existing practices. The emphasis on reflective and self critical development as well as enhancing technical skills is important and meets many of the standards set for social work alongside a recognition of continuous learning (Department of Health, 2002; GSCC, 2005). The evaluation of the experience is, in itself, a central component of reflective and deep learning.

Gibson (2004) points out that successful co-leadership is useful but often takes a great deal of preparation to achieve. Whilst training for the groups was undertaken together and co-working between staff and students planned and coordinated, the importance of this was highlighted further

Figure 2 Reminiscence groups as a reciprocal socio-facilitative educational activity

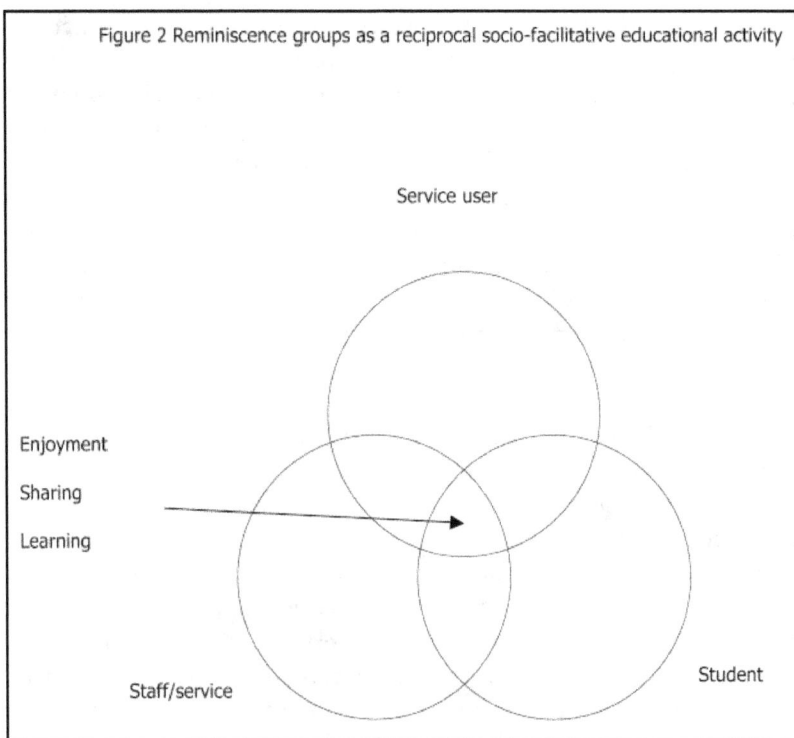

Service user

Enjoyment

Sharing

Learning

Staff/service

Student

in the study. The perceptions of some students that further training was needed needs exploration. It may be that the training was perceived as inadequate, not explicitly related to the work done or it may be that this represented a self-efficacy and confidence issue. A different explanation may suggest the importance of values to the students in providing the best possible service, whilst the discrepancy with the views of practitioners may reflect different standpoints in career or career trajectories. The provision of adequate training is crucial and whatever the reason for the student perception, it emphasises the need for greater attention to planning, training and preparation and for this to be continued and monitored throughout the work.

The work was partly reliant on a reciprocal groupwork model in which themes and processes were discussed and agreed at the outset of each session, but the identification of core themes were set and researched by the facilitators prior to the session. There is a need for greater inclusivity and collecting the views of people with dementia who participated within the groups. Including the views of people with dementia is important and is likely to enhance satisfaction and participation (Killick and Allan, 2001;

Innes et al, 2004). Also, the ethics of inclusion must be promoted. Because of cognitive deficits it was important to ensure that views on the programme and its progression were rehearsed at the beginning of each session and adjustments made in the light of interests and history based on discussion and observation. This flexibility is also central to the process.

Sustainability was part of the original project and integrating the experience with practice learning appeared to be one way of achieving this. However, problems with sustainability occurred within this structure as the organiser moved to other tasks and duties and the practice team could not pick up the project. There are a number of ethical questions that arise from this, including those of setting up specific projects which then require servicing that a university cannot provide, or are left to flounder and not supported. The question of action-research methods that are not fully participative are also questioned in this research. The project stemmed from the objective in the initial research to ensure sustainability and not from a mutually derived, agreed and planned approach. Thus more participative methods would be useful. In future developments, work with employers and user groups is necessary to develop placement initiatives and learning opportunities that provide reciprocal opportunities. Funding issues are important to sustaining these developments but the opportunity is there, in using the daily placement monies that follow social work placements, to ensure the potential for such groups is maximised. It will be important to continue to evaluate the effectiveness of the groups for student learning, service development and group participant enjoyment and partnerships with the universities will help to facilitate this.

The data indicate that reminiscence groups undertaken with people with dementia can generate a number of benefits for people with dementia themselves, for staff and practitioners and for the education and development of social work students. Whilst more robust research is required (Woods et al., 2005) this study adds to the growing literature concerning the value of reminiscence work for people with dementia and indicates that it should be further developed and evaluated.

Groupwork, itself, is explicitly mentioned in the standards for social work education (Topss, 2002) and developing a participative action-research approach to its delivery can help promote learning and transferability to other settings. This confirms earlier research into groupwork education in social work (Birnbaum and Wayne, 2000; Graziano et al., 2002; Wright, 2002).

It will be important to explore further the potential for learning and development. Practice learning opportunities offer different models and partnership arrangements. Qualitative self-reports, whilst valuable, will be enhanced in future research by the collection of hard data and it will be important to ensure that all stakeholders are fully involved at all stages. Partnerships are crucial. As well as the possibilities for learning, the enjoyment and added value for group participants should be core – although it was not the focus of this study, it was central to the original brief and provides an ethical and service rationale for reminiscence groups.

Notes

1. The term 'client' is used to refer to group participants on occasions reflecting the words of respondents in the study.
2. This paper was first published in *Groupwork* 2006, 16 (1), pp. 7-28

References

Arean, P.A., Perri, M.G., Nezu, A.M., and Schein, R.L. (1993) Comparative effectiveness of social problem-solving therapy and reminiscence therapy as treatments for depression in older adults. *Journal of Consulting and Clinical Psychology*, 61, 1, 3-10

Bachar, E., Kindler, S., Schefler, G., and Lerer, B. (1991) Reminiscing as a technique in the group psychotherapy of depression: A comparative study. *British Journal of Clinical Psychology*, 30, 375-377

Bender, M., Bauckham, P., and Norris, A. (1999) *The Therapeutic Purposes of Reminiscence*. London: Sage

Birnbaum, M.L., and Wayne, J. (2000) Group work in foundation generalist education: The necessity for curriculum change. *Journal of Social Work Education*, 36, 2, 347-356

Bornat, J. (2001) Reminiscence and oral history: parallel universes of shared endeavour? *Ageing and Society*, 21, 2, 219-41

Brody, C.M. (1990) Women in a nursing home: Living with hope and meaning. *Psychology of Women Quarterly*, 14, 579-592

Bryant, F., Smart, C., and King, S. (2005) Using the past to enhance the present: boosting happiness through positive reminiscence. *Journal of Happiness Studies*, 6, 3, 227-260

Buchanan, K., and Middleton, D. (1995) Voices of experience: Talk, identity and membership in reminiscence groups. *Ageing and Society*, 15, 4, 457-491

Burnside, I. (1994) Reminiscence group therapy. in I. Burnside and M.G. Schmidt (Eds) *Working with Older Adults: Group process and techniques*. (3rd edition) Boston, Jones and Bartlett (163-178)

Burnside, I., and Haight, B.K. (1994) Reminiscence and Life Review: Therapeutic Intervention for Older People. *Nurse Practitioner*, 19, 4, 55-61

Butler, R.N. (1963) The life review: An interpretation of reminiscence in the aged. *Psychiatry*, 26, 65-76.

Cappeliez, P., O'Rourke, N., and Chaudhury, H. (2005) Functions of reminiscence and mental health in later life. *Aging and Mental Health*, 9, 4, 295-301

Coleman, P. G. (2005) The uses of reminiscence: functions and benefits. *Aging and Mental Health*, 9, 4, 291-294

Department of Health (2002) *Requirements for Social Work Training*. London: DoH

de Vaus, D.A. (1996) *Surveys in Social Research*. London: UCL Press

Doel, M. (2006) *Using Groupwork*. London: Routledge

Galassi, F.S. (1991) A life review workshop for gay and lesbian elders. *Journal of Gerontological Social Work*, 16, 75-86

George, M. (1995) Vital recall. *Community Care*, 9-15 March, 16-17

Gibson, F. (1994) What can reminiscence contribute to people with dementia? in J. Bornat (Ed.) *Reminiscence Reviewed: Perspectives, evaluations, achievements*. Buckingham: Open University Press

Gibson, F. (1997) *Reminiscence and Recall: A guide to good practice*. (2nd edition) London: Age Concern England

Gibson, F. (2004) *The Past in the Present: Using reminiscence in health and social care*. Baltimore, MD: Health Professions Press

Gillies, C. and James, A. (1994) *Reminiscence Work with Old People*. London: Chapman and Hall

Goldsmith, M. (1996) *Hearing the Voice of People with Dementia: Opportunities and obstacles*. London: Jessica Kingsley

Graziano, R., Salmon, R., and Berman, E.S. (2002) Using a group work approach to develop the potential of students in a non-traditional MSW work-study program. *Journal of Teaching in Social Work*, 22, 3/4, 71-88

GSCC (2005) *The Post-Qualifying Framework for Social Work Education and Training*. London: General Social Care Council

Gwyther, L.P., Lowenthal, R.I., and Marazzo, R.A. (1990) Milestoning: Evoking memories for resocialization through group reminiscence. *Gerontologist*, 30, 269-272

Haight, B. K., and Burnside, I. (1993) Reminiscence and life review:Explaining the differences. *Archives in Psychiatric Nursing*, 7, 2, 91-98

Hsieh, H., and Wang, J. (2003) Effect of reminiscence therapy on depression in older adults: A systematic review. *International Journal of Nursing Studies*, 40,

4, 335-345

Innes, A., Archibald, C., and Murphy, C. (Eds.) (2004) *Dementia and Social Inclusion: Marginalised groups and marginalised areas of dementia research, care and practice.* London: Jessica Kingsley

Jones, C. (1995) "Take me away from all this..." Can reminiscence be therapeutic in an intensive care unit? *Intensive and Critical Care Nursing,* 11, 341-343

Jonsdottir, H., Jonsdottir, G., Steingrimsdottir, E., and Tryggvadottir, B. (2001) Group reminiscence among people with end-stage chronic long diseases. *Journal of Advanced Nursing,* 35, 1, 79-87

Killick, J., and Allan, K. (2001) *Communication and the Care of People with Dementia.* Buckingham: Open University Press

Kitwood, T. (1997) *Dementia Reconsidered: The person comes first.* Buckingham: Open University Press

Magee, J.J. (1994) Using themes from mystical traditions to enhance self-acceptance in life review groups. *Journal of Religious Gerontology,* 9, 63-72

Malde, S. (1988) Guided autobiography: A counselling tool for older adults. *Journal of Counseling and Development,* 66, 290-293

Martin, J.M. (1989) Expanding reminiscence therapy with elderly mentally infirm patients. *British Journal of Occupational Therapy,* 52, 432-436

McGowan, T.G. (1994) Mentoring-reminiscence: A conceptual and empirical analysis. *International Journal of Aging and Human Development,* 39, 321-336

McInnis-Dittrich, K. (1996) Adapting life-review therapy for elderly female survivors of childhood sexual abuse. *Families in Society,* 77, 166-173

Merriam, S. (1995) Butler's Life Review: How universal is it? in J. Hendricks (Ed.) *The Meaning of Reminiscence and Life Review.* Amityville, NY: Baywood (7-20)

Miles, M.B., and Huberman, A.M. (1994) *Qualitative Data Analysis.* (2nd edition) Sage: London

Murphy, C., and Moyes, M. (1997) Life story work. in M. Marshall (Ed.) *State of the Art in Dementia Care.* London: Centre for Policy on Ageing

Nomazi, K.H., and Haynes, S.R. (1994) Sensory stimuli reminiscence for patients with Alzheimer's disease: Relevance and implications. *Clinical Gerontologist,* 14, 29-46

Orton, J.D., Allen, M., and Cook, J. (1989) Reminiscence groups with confused nursing center residents: An experimental study. *Social Work in Health Care,* 14, 73-86

Ott, R.L. (1993) Enhancing validation through milestoning with sensory reminiscence. *Journal of Gerontological Social Work,* 20, 147-159

Parker, J. (2003) Positive communication with people who have dementia. in T. Adams and J. Manthorpe (Eds.) *Dementia Care.* London: Arnold (148-163)

Parker, J., and Penhale, B. (1998) *Forgotten People: Positive approaches to dementia care.* Aldershot: Ashgate

Parker, J., Penhale, B., Bradley, G., and Manthorpe, J. (1998a) The EQUAL Project: Action research for the development of practice in dementia care. *Issues in Social Work Education*, 18, 2, 89-96

Parker, J., Penhale, B., Bradley, G., Manthorpe, J., Gynnerstedt, K., and Pierrot, L. (1998b) Training volunteers to run reminiscence groups: The EQUAL Project. *Health Care in Later Life*, 3, 4, 285-298

Penhale, B. and Parker, J. (1999) Developing volunteer skills in reminiscence work with older people with Alzheimer's disease. in J. Bornat, P. Chamberlayne and L. Chant (Eds.) *Reminiscence: Practice, Skills and Settings*. London: Open University/University of East London, Centre for Biography in Social Policy

Penhale, B., Bradley, G., Parker, J. Manthorpe, J., Gynnerstedt, K., Schartua, M-B., Henk-Pierrot, L., Quinio, Y., and Zingraff, J-M. (1998) *EQUAL Project: Enhancing the quality of life of people with Alzheimer's disease, Final Report*. Hull: University of Hull/Växjö College of Health Sciences/IMF, Marseille

Penn, B. (1994) Using patient biography to promote holistic care. *Nursing Times*, 90, 35-36

Phillips, J., Ray, M., and Marshall, M. (2006) *Social Work with Older People*. Basingstoke: Palgrave

Rattenbury, C., and Stones, M.J. (1989) A controlled evaluation of reminiscence and current topics discussion groups in a nursing home context. *Gerontologist*, 29, 768-771

Rybarczyk, B.D., and Auerbach, S.M. (1990) Reminiscence interviews as stress management interventions for older patients undergoing surgery. *Gerontologist*, 30, 522-528

Sherman, E., and Peak, T. (1991) Patterns of reminiscence and assessment of late life adjustment. *Journal of Gerontological Social Work*, 16, 59-74

Snell, J. (1991) Reviving memories. *Nursing Times*, 87, 54-56

Staudinger, U. (2001) Life reflection: a social-cognitive analysis of life review. *Review of General Psychology*, 5, 2, 148-160

Stinson, C. (2006) Structured reminiscence: an intervention to decrease depression and increase self-transcendence in older women. *Journal of Clinical Nursing*, 15, 2, 208-18

Taft, L.B., and Nehrke, M.F. (1990) Reminiscence, life review, and ego integrity in nursing home residents. *International Journal of Aging and Human Development*, 30, 186-196

Tabourne, C. (1995a) The effects of a life review program on disorientation, social interaction and self-esteem of nursing home residents. *International Journal of Aging and Human Development*, 41, 2, 251-266

Tabourne, C. (1995b) The life review program as an intervention for an older adult newly admitted to a nursing home facility: A case study. *Therapeutic Recreation Journal*, 29, 2, 228-236

TOPSS (2002) *National Occupational Standards for Social Work.* London: TOPSS

Toseland, R.W. (1995) *Group Work with the Elderly and Family Caregivers.* New York: Springer

Toseland, R.W. (2005) What's different about working with older people in groups? *Journal of Gerontological Social Work,* 44, 1/2, 5-23

Trueman, I., and Parker, J. (2004) Life review in palliative care. *European Journal of Palliative Care,* 11, 6, 249-53

Trueman, I., and Parker, J. (2006) Exploring community nurses' perceptions of life review in palliative care. *Journal of Clinical Nursing,* 15, 197-207

Webster, J.D., and Young, R.A. (1988) Process variables of the life review: Counseling implications. *International Journal of Aging and Human Development,* 26, 315-323

Woods, B., Spector, A., Jones, C., Orrell, M., and Davies, S. (2005) Reminiscence therapy for dementia. *The Cochrane Database of Systematic Reviews,* Issue 2. Art. No. CD001120.pub2. DOI:10.1002/14651858.CD001120.pub.2

Wright, W. (2002) But I want to do a real group: A personal journey from snubbing to loving to theorizing to demanding activity-based group work. *Social Work with Groups,* 25, 1/2, 107-112

9

Canistherapy as an activation program for seniors in nursing homes and in nursing homes with specific regime

Lenka Maťhová and Zuzana Staffová

Introduction

The ageing population and concomitant care for senior citizens is one of the most serious worldwide problems which European countries amongst others have to cope with. It is very important to provide mental and physical activity for seniors, who are living in their own households and those who are living in nursing homes. Specific activities for encouraging a more active old age include, for example, memory training, music therapy, art therapy, reminiscence therapy, validation, basal stimulation and canistherapy which is a specific form of zootherapy (therapy supported by animals).

Canistherapy is one of the free-time activities that can be undertaken in old age and one of the ways of making seniors more active. Canistherapy contributes to the validation of the capabilities and abilities of seniors and helps seniors to fill their leisure time. Although dogs have been our companions as human beings for at least three thousand years, scientific research relating to the relationship between a human and a dog is relatively new.

First of all, it is necessary to delineate the terminology used in connection with therapeutic interaction between a human and an animal, and especially between a human and a dog. The widely held terms Zootherapy, Animal Assisted Therapy, Animal Assisted Activities, Animal Assisted Education, Animal Assisted Crisis Response and Canistherapy are used in social and therapeutic work in the Czech Republic. This chapter presents the concept of canistherapy as an activation program for seniors in the nursing home and nursing home with specific regime in the region of South Bohemia in the Czech Republic, which is provided by non-profit organization Training Canistherapeutic Association Hafík in Třeboň, located in the region of South Bohemia.

Terminology in zootherapy

Zootherapy

According to Freeman (2007) zootherapy refers to the use of mutual positive influence of both the animal and the human which results in improved memory, motor skills, communication or relieves stress. The animal is always in the role of co-therapist. Types of zootherapy include a wide variety of methods such as Animal Assisted Activities, Animal Assisted Therapy, Animal Assisted Education and Animal Assisted Crisis Response (Freeman, 2007).

Animal Assisted Activities

Animal Assisted Activities (AAA) are activities undertaken with the assistance of animals that provide an opportunity for motivation, education, rest, and/or therapy benefits focused on the improvement of a client's life quality (Eisertová, 2006). According to Eisertová (2006) the aim of AAA is to please the clients, to offer them a new experience, to bring them joy, to improve their quality of life and so on. The results can be expressed only in concepts of joy, satisfaction and happiness.

Animal Assisted Therapy

Animal Assisted Therapy (AAT) is targeted contact between humans and animals, which is focused on improving mental or physical condition – the quality of life or well-being - of the human. The goals of AAT are individually designed to encourage the development of physical, social, emotional or cognitive functions of clients (Freeman, 2007).

Animal Assisted Education

Freeman (2007) describes that Animal Assisted Education (AAE) is an education with the specific assistance of a dog. AAE is a targeted or natural human-animal contact, focused on expanding or improving education and social skills of clients.

Animal Assisted Crisis Response

According to Freeman (2007), Animal Assisted Crisis Response (AACR) is a natural contact between the animal and human when the latter is in a state of crisis, and focuses on the elimination of stress and overall improvement in mental or physical state of clients.

Canistherapy is a therapy using a dog during zootherapy (*canis* is Latin for 'dog'). Eisertová (2007) refers that Jiřina Lacinová from Association of Filia is the author of the term canistherapy in 1993 in the Czech Republic. Canistherapy is one of the models of zootherapy that specifies the type of utilized animal as co-therapists and has been practised since the late 20th century in the Czech Republic. Canistherapy is one of the methods of rehabilitation that serves to support psycho-social health of people of all age categories, in which the relationship between humans and dogs is used (Kalinová, 2003).

Nursing homes and nursing homes with specific regime in the Czech Republic

Nursing home and nursing home with specific regime, a specialist home, in the Czech Republic are residential social services which are established by municipalities and the counties, non-profit organizations, individuals and the Ministry of Labour and Social Affairs. Social service providers must be registered as such and in their activities are governed by the Law of Social Services (Nr. 108/2006 Collection of Laws). According to the Register of Social Services (2013) there are 494 nursing homes and 228 nursing homes established with specific regime, i.e. those providing specialist services for seniors, in the Czech Republic.

Nursing homes

According to s. 49 of the Law of Social Services (Nr. 108/2006 Collection of Laws), nursing homes provide long term social services for people with lower self-sufficiency caused by their old age when their condition requires regular aid from another person. These social services include the following: providing accommodation, providing meals, helping with personal care, providing personal hygiene or providing conditions for hygiene, intermediation of social contacts, social therapeutic activities, activation, help with legal issues and assertion of clients' legal rights, and help with personal matters.

Nursing homes with specific regime

According to s. 50 of the Law of Social Services (Nr. 108/2006 Collection of Laws), nursing homes with specific regime provides long term social services for people who have a lower degree of self-sufficiency caused by their chronic mental illness or dependence on addictive substances, and people with senile dementia, Alzheimer's disease and other types of dementia, who have a lower self-sufficiency when their condition requires regular aid from another physical person. The regime in long term social services is adapted to specific needs of these persons. These social services include the following: providing accommodation, providing meals, helping with personal care, providing personal hygiene or providing conditions for hygiene, intermediation of social contacts, social therapeutic activities, occupational therapy, help with legal issues and assertion of clients' legal rights, and help with personal matters.

Training Canistherapeutic Association Hafík

The Training Canistherapeutic Association Hafík, an NGO (hereinafter Hafík), was founded in January 2001 in Třeboň as a training canistherapeutic association that deals with teaching coaches for training therapeutic dogs, undertaking canistherapeutic teams training, and especially practising canistherapy and felinotherapy. The neeed for professionally conducted canistherapy in the Czech Republic was the impetus for the establishment of that association. Hafík has been an accredited Volunteer Centre in the section of long-term volunteer service since 2008. It follows that Hafík become currently the first organization that is eligible to perform volunteer service in the field of advertising tested volunteers with their therapeutic dogs. The main mission of this long-term accredited volunteer service is to assist persons with disabilities, seniors and to help with the care of young people in the Czech Republic, especially in the southern and central Bohemia.

Hafík cooperates with the National Volunteer Centre Hestia, another NGO, this association is a member of the European Society for Animal Assested Therapy (ESAAT) and Hafík is also training organization in the preparation of volunteers. Volunteers of associations operate in South, Central and West Bohemia. They work essentially in centers for social services, schools and educational facilities, and so forth (Výcvikové canisterapeutické sdružení Hafík, 2012).

Hafík NGO is the only organization in the Czech Republic which is member ESAAT since 2008 and the only organization which received accreditation in the area of training and preparing of canistherapeutic teams in 2010 (which, after completion of education implement activities, education and therapy through dog assistance) (Výcvikové canisterapeutické sdružení Hafík, 2013a).

Objectives of Hafík

The objectives of the Hafík NGO are as follows:

1. to implement canistherapy as one of the methods for support of psychosocial health for people of all ages (canistherapeutic visits to health and social facilities, integration canistherapy camps, psycho-rehabilitation courses, reconditioning stays etc.);
2. to implement of all types of high-quality canistherapy (AAA, AAT, AAE);
3. to train of canistherapeutic teams for canistherapy practicing, teaching instructors for canistherapeutic dog training, training dogs suitable for canistherapy;
4. to perform of educational, consulting activities and providing of expert information to everyone interested in canistherapy (seminars, lectures, etc.);

5. to support and integrate canistherapeutic awareness in society (Výcvikové canisterapeutické sdružení Hafík, 2013b).

Practising of Canistherapy in Seniors: The Training Canistherapy Association Hafik

The nursing home visiting program is one of the programs of the nongovernmental organization Training Canistherapeutic Association Hafik in Třeboň (region of South Bohemia). The canistherapeutic teams (dog-holder teams that have successfully passed the training and examinations for canistherapeutic teams) are the volunteers of canistherapeutic association and usually go to see the clients in the institutions. The team visits of nursing homes or nursing homes with specific regime regularly, usually once a week. The Training Canistherapeutic Association Hafik prefers the visiting program and reflections on the long term practice of canistherapy supports this. The visiting program is gentler to the welfare of the dog as co-therapist, and the volunteer teams are more involved in the planning and preparing of the specific program for each canistherapeutic visit. A high degree of cooperation between volunteers and professionals using the team approach is necessary in the visiting program. The canistherapeutic team, the nursing home or nursing homes with specific regime, the client, and the Training Canistherapeutic Association Hafík, therefore, sign a contract that defines all the rights and responsibilities of all the participants.

In 2012 and in 2013 there were 13 canistherapeutic teams working in nursing homes and in nursing homes in the region of South Bohemia (Table 1 overleaf). The dog-holder teams have implemented the visit program in 6 nursing homes and nursing homes with specific regime in 2013. In this time the need of canistherapy exceeds by a wide margin the number of active canistherapeutic teams in the region of South Bohemia.

Table 1

Canistherapeutic teams and volunteers without a dog in the Training Canistherapeutic Association Hafík

Year	Accredited volunteers after canis-therapeutic examinations (n)	Canistherapeutic teams (human + dog) (n)	Canistherapeutic teams in preparation (n)	Volunteers without a dog (n)
2012	41 - thereof 16 accredited volunteers working with seniors	51 - thereof 17 canistherapeutic teams working with seniors	18	4
2013	41 - thereof 14 accredited volunteers working with seniors	51 - thereof 14 accredited volunteers working with seniors	18	4

Source: Výcvikové canisterapeutické sdružení Hafík (2013).

Canistherapy as an activation program for seniors in the nursing homes and in the nursing home with specific regime in the Czech Republic

Canistherapy as a method of rehabilitation has its own specific place in comprehensive rehabilitation and in comprehensive care. Canistherapy improves physiological, psychological and social conditions of the client and has positive effects on the quality of life and well-being of seniors in residential social services. Professional implementation of canistherapy, careful planning and training program for canistherapeutic teams are the basic requirements for accepting the canistherapy as an effective and successful therapy.

Canistherapy can be provided in an individual form, or a group form and in a visit (temporary) or a resident form. The resident form means that the dog is in the ownership of a nursing home and lives there with clients. The visiting program means that the canistherapeutic teams usually go to see the clients in the institutions.

Canistherapy is used in social services and is most often in the form of visiting programs in the Czech Republic at the present time. The canistherapeutic team regularly go to social services in order to maintain and develop the mental, physical and social condition of the seniors.

Dogs as co-therapist help to create the overall well-being, they are a motivation to the action and movement and have a positive effect on mental state of seniors. Finally, canistherapy helps to develop motor skills, promotes communication and is the topic of the conversation between seniors and social workers in the facilities. Canistherapists cooperate with the staff of the facility to the effective practice of this therapy - it is usually a social worker, physiotherapist, occupational therapist or other professionals.

Benefits of canistherapy during work with seniors

Stančíková and Šabatová, J. (2012) describe benefits of canistherapy during work with seniors in the following ways:

1. canistherapy helps break the barriers during comunication, improves the comunicative enviroment between people and staff of nursing home;
2. the presence of a dog can motivate and encourage cooperation as social rehearsal or to maintain exisiting social skills, education, training of cognitive functions, and so on;
3. it helps to keep seniors active;
4. dogs act as a companion or even as a partner to communicate with;
5. canistherapy can contribute to inclusion into society, to keep social contacts, and to relieve feelings of loneliness;
6. canistherapy eliminates emotional problems and challenging behaviours.

Goals and benefits of the visiting program in the nursing homes and in the nursing homes with specific regime

Long term, high quality canistherapy improves the general health and quality of life of clients in residential social services. Canistherapy is a part of a comprehensive care approach, and it is one of the methods of enhancing activity (animation) of the clients in nursing homes. A dog loves and accepts clients unconditionally and provides them with non-judgmental relationships.

Seniors in nursing homes and nursing homes with specific regime usually have a range of health, social, psychological and personal problems. The admission to a nursing home is accompanied by problems of adaptation, by changes in quality of life, by feelings of loneliness and increased dependence on the help of others. The specific and actual problems of each client, and above all, the positive skills of a client need to be assessed. The particular goals of the canistherapy are set according to the assessment. All contraindications should be noted and examined (e.g. allergy, client's disagreement, fear of dogs, open wounds, danger of aggressive attack by humans on the dog or *vice versa*). It is necessary to use the team approach and cooperate with professionals (e.g. social workers, health care professionals, psychologists, doctors, therapists) and also with family members. Relatives can answer many questions about client's life and about individual, medical and social issues, especially if the client has, for example, Alzheimer's disease, dementia or problems with adaptation after the admission to the nursing home.

Health goals and benefits

Canistherapy meets some of the basic needs of clients, e.g. the need for physical contact, the need for communication and interaction, and the need for activity. Canistherapy, in general, improves physical and psychological welfare of its clients, and therefore it is improving the general health and quality of life of clients in residential social services as well.

Physical goals and benefits

Canistherapy improves people's motor skills and balance. Some specific canistherapeutic activities are specialized in improving fine motor skills (e.g. throwing a ball, hair brushing, fastening on a leash and a collar, touching and holding dog's toys, touching a dog, feeding and praising a dog). The dog is a motivation for walking outside or for walking inside the nursing home. Canistherapy can also be a motivation for physical rehabilitation in general. Some of the canistherapeutic teams are trained to use special method of rehabilitation with a dog – the dog lies besides the client in a special position and improves blood circulation in client's muscles and stimulates muscles and motion in general The method has also a positive impact on an emotional and mental state of the client. The cooperation with a professional is appropriate.

Cognitive and educational goals and benefits, motivation

Canistherapy improves the client's perception and increases ability to pay attention. Specially designed activities with a dog stimulates the mental state of the client, helps to improve concentration and cognitive skills. A therapist can use a dog for training the senses and memory of clients. The quality and benefits of canistherapy, however, depend on the dog handler's and professional's approach and skill.

Psychological and emotional goals and benefits

The canistherapeutic teams that come to a nursing home are usually volunteers. They come to visit clients because they want to help them. They are coming from life outside the nursing home, and they cross the border between the nursing home and the outside world, acting as a bridge. The visits usually occur once a week at a set time. The clients look forward to the canistherapy, and, thanks to the dogs, the day in the nursing home can become very special. The dog is empathetic, and it does not judge the people by their physical handicap, social status or self-sufficiency. Canistherapy can be practised by an individual or in a group form. The group form of canistherapy breaks the isolation of the seniors in their rooms inside the nursing home. There is an opportunity to communicate, to smile and have fun, to show positive skills, and to learn new things. Canistherapy, in general, improves people's self esteem, confidence and mood.

Canistherapy can also be helpful in the process of adaptation after an admission to a nursing home or after hospitalization. It can also help in communication with family members. For the clients, there are a new topics and new experiences to discuss.

Seniors in nursing homes have several personal problems that range from the more to the less serious. Thinking about these problems will occupy the seniors' day if we do not activate the clients with a meaningful program to focus the mind. The important benefits of canistherapy include motivation, positive emotion, acceptable physical contact, meaning of life, and the feeling that somebody else needs the client's attention and looks forward to see the client.

Social goals and benefits

Canistherapy and especially AAT can be provided for a wide spectrum of clients. Canistherapy is provided for clients with Alzheimer's disease, dementia, depression, and other mental illnesses, as well as for immobile clients. The process of socialization is supported by the interaction and communication between a client, a dog, a dog handler, and a therapist. The client of the canistherapy can also be motivated to visit other clients in the nursing home with the dog. The canistherapy can also be organized as a group therapy where the client has the opportunity to meet others. The communication between the staff and clients also improves due to canistherapy. The canistherapeutic team is often stopped by staff members who also feel the positive benefit of the interaction with the dog and at least feel the need to greet the therapeutic dog. The dog changes the general atmosphere in the nursing home. Everyday routine and stereotypes are broken by a canistherapeutic visit. The dog is a motivation, not only for participating in a canistherapy program, but also for everyday activities, e.g. drawing, reading, walking, and meeting other clients in a community room.

Mobile clients can walk the dog outside the nursing home, and they can get a special exercise, e.g. walk the dog to the shop and buy something small, walk the dog to a bus or train station with the therapist, travel by bus in the town, or walk the dog to a family member's house. This brings the client, with a dog as a companion, higher self esteem and the feeling of support and safety.

Conclusion

The aim of canistherapy in residential social facilities is to improve the psychological, physical and social health of senior. Canistherapy is provided individually or in groups based on the individual senior's individually tailored plan in residential social facilities. There is an important in canistherapy to remember that the senior is needed to be able, willing and ready to perform canistherapy activity.

Canistherapy as a method of activation of seniors in residential social services should be practiced professionally (Maťhová, 2012). The right choice of canistherapeutic team is necessary for a good practice of canistherapy. Workers with canistherapeutic dogs have to pass canistherapeutic exams which are essential condition for canistherapy practice (Maťhová, 2012).

According to Maťhová (2012) canistherapy dogs must also pass exams, important are his/her skills and character, good mental and physical condition and regular veterinary care. From the side of residential social facilities is necessary to provide suitable space and the presence of another employee who is assisted during the program and participates in formulating goals for animal assisted therapy (Maťhová, 2012). It is advisable to enter into a written contract on the conditions and method of practising canistherapy with canistherapeutic association with an employee or therapeutic dog (Maťhová, 2012).

Finally, it must be emphasized that it is necessary to work on a professional level to accept canistherapy as an equal therapy of social service, to work on scientific research and publications concerning canistherapeutic approach and benefits.

References

Eisertová J. (2006). *Odborné aktivity v canisterapii.* Diplomová práce. České Budějovice, Česká republika: Jihočeská univerzita v Českých Budějovicích, Zdravotně sociální fakulta.

Eisertová J. (2007). Canisterapie - terminologie. In: M. Velemínský a kol. *Zooterapie ve světle objektivních poznatků (pp 60).* 1st. Ed., České Budějovice, Česká republika: DONA.

Freeman, M. (2007). Terminologie v zooterapii. In: M. Velemínský a kol. *Zooterapie ve světle objektivních poznatků (pp 30-37).* 1st. Ed., České Budějovice, Česká republika: DONA.

Kalinová, V. (2003). *Systém vzdělávání v oblasti canisterapie.* Diplomová práce. České Budějovice, Česká republika: Jihočeská univerzita v Českých Budějovicích, Zdravotně sociální fakulta.

Maťhová, L. (2012). Canisterapie u seniorů s demencí. *Psychiatrie pro praxi.* 13(3): 133-135.

Registr poskytovatelů sociálních služeb (n.d.). Vyhledávání služby. Retrieved January 06, 2013, from http://iregistr.mpsv.cz/sluzba/rozsirenevyhledavanisluzby

Stančíková, M., Šabatová, J. (2012). Canisterapie v teorii a praxi. Sborník her a pomůcek pro praktickou realizaci canisterapie u různých cílových skupin. 1st. ed., Vyškov, Česká republika: Sdružení Piafa ve Vyškově.

Výcvikové canisterapeutické sdružení Hafík (n.d.). Kdo jsme. Retrieved December 29, 2012, from http://www.canisterapie.org/c-39-organizace-a-struktura.html

Výcvikové canisterapeutické sdružení Hafík (n.d.). European Society for Animal Assisted Therapy. Retrieved January 02, 2013a, from http://www.canisterapie.org/c-69-esaat.html

Výcvikové canisterapeutické sdružení Hafík (n.d.). Cíle sdružení. Retrieved January 06, 2013b, from http://www.canisterapie.org/c-40-cile-sdruzeni.html).

Výcvikové canisterapeutické sdružení Hafík (2013). Počet akreditovaných dobrovolníků a canisterapeutických týmů. Interní dokument.

Zákon č. 108/2006 Sb., O sociálních službách, ve znění pozdějších předpisů.

IO

Every medal has two sides:

Opportunities and challenges of active ageing in Flanders

Katrien Meireman and Elke Plovie

Introduction

It's a fact: the population is ageing. The figures speak for themselves. Whereas in 1950 the median age of the global population was 23.6 years, it had risen to 26.4 in the year 2000. It is expected that it will continue to rise and will exceed the milestone of 36 years. In this global context, Europe is the oldest continent. In 1950, the median age of the Europeans was 29.2 years. Half a century later, half of the European population was older than 37.7 years. In 2010 the median age was 40.9 years and it is expected to increase to 47.7 years by 2050. For Belgium, the median age respectively was 38.7 years in 2000 and 40.9 years in 2010 (Eurostat, 2012).

The ageing of our societies is not only noticeable in the rise of the median age, it is also shown in the proportion of seniors. When we take a close look at European societies, we note that this proportion is increasing. In 2060, 30% of the population of the European Union (EU) will be older than 65 years old, what that means is that one out of three persons of the 517 million estimated people in Europe will be 65 years or older. Germany and Italy take the pole position; Ireland closes the ranks (European Commission, 2012; Eurostat, 2012). In 1920 only 10% of the Belgian population was older than 65 years. Today, however, almost one in five of the inhabitants of Belgium is 65 years of age or older. By 2060 this will have risen again to one out of four. In other words: the number of people older than 65 will rise by 80%.

Ageing is one thing. Another issue concerns what we might call *the ageing within the ageing.* Hereby, we point to the increasing proportion of the population older than 80 years. In the EU 4.7% of the citizens is 80 years or older. In Belgium, 4.9% of the people were of that age in 2010 (Eurostat, 2012). This percentage will be estimated to triple between 2010 and 2060 (Federaal Planbureau, 2011: 19).

Table 1
Profile of the population in Belgium %

	2000	2010	2020	2030	2040	2050	2060
0-14 years	17.6	16.9	17.5	17.3	16.7	16.8	16.8
15-64 years	65.6	65.9	63.5	60.7	59.3	58.7	58.4
65 +	16.8	17.2	19.0	22.0	24.0	24.5	24.8

Source: Federaal Planbureau, 2011: 19

Although it is almost a neck-to-neck race with Wallonia, the most ageing region in Belgium is Flanders. In this region the number of people older than 65 will grow by 73% between 2010 and 2060. The population in Brussels is aged the least; nevertheless, the number of individuals of 65 years and older will rise by 77% between 2010 and 2060. The Federaal Planbureau (2011) expects the percentage of persons aged 65 and over in Brussels to rise to approximately 18%.

Table 2
Profile of the population in Flanders (%)

	2000	2010	2020	2030	2040	2050	2060
0-14 years	17.1	16.1	17.0	16.7	16.0	16.3	16.4
15-64 years	66.2	65.7	62.7	59.5	58.1	57.5	57.3
65 en +	16.7	18.2	20.3	23.8	25.9	26.2	26.3

Source: Federaal Planbureau, 2011: 19

The ageing, and the ageing within the ageing, pose several challenges on different domains of life; especially how do we organize social concerns such as housing and care? Which roles can older people take in society and how should we support them in that? How can we manage government spending on pensions and health care? The challenges are addressed by policy makers at local, regional, national and European level. As we all know, in 2012, the issue was placed on the European agenda by the initiative of the European year of active ageing and solidarity between generations. The discourse on active ageing starts from a competence perspective on older people, with an emphasis on enjoying life and living independently.

In fact, the discourse of active ageing is only one of three existing models on the positions of older people in society (De Brauwere, Vanthuyne, & Verschelden, 2008). A first model, the social welfare discourse, describes older people as individuals entitled to rest after years of hard work. This discourse holds a deficit perspective whereby older people are regarded as passive individuals in need of help. An alternative to this social welfare model is the active ageing discourse. A third and last discourse De Brauwere and others (De Brauwere, Vanthuyne, & Verschelden, 2008) distinguish is the model of productive ageing. In this model, older individuals are regarded as competent individuals who can contribute to society. This perspective focuses on empowerment and how social and cultural capital of older people can be increased (De Brauwere, Vanthuyne, & Verschelden, 2008).

In this chapter, we want to concentrate on the active ageing discourse and more specifically on the opportunities and challenges that are connected to this discourse. We will make this exercise within two domains of life, namely long time care and leisure time of older people.

Long time care in the Flanders

We state the obvious perhaps when we say the elderly want to live independently at home as long as possible; they want to postpone residential care as long as possible. However, this is not always possible. The socialization of care includes changes in two ways: on the one hand transformations in the organization of care, on the other hand changes in the content of care.

Concerning the first, we evolve from a society in which individuals with a need for care are helped in total institutions, situated far from society (Goffman, 1961), towards a society which includes people with a need for care. Goffman (1961) defines total institutions as 'a place of residence and work where a large number of like-situated individuals, cut off from the wider society for an appreciable period of time, together lead an enclosed, formally administered round of life'. Living, sleeping, relaxing, working, etc. took place in these institutions. These total institutions were common within many sectors, like those of elderly people, of persons with disabilities or of mental health care. We all remember the movie 'One Flew over the Cuckoo's Nest', directed by Miloš Forman in 1975, based on the book of the same name of Ken Kesey (1962). Since the 1950s, many Western societies are dealing with a reduction of those total institutions (deinstitutionalization) and evolving towards what is called balanced care. Characteristic of balanced care is that care is given in the natural environment of the patient, is focused on his autonomy and need(s), is given by a multidisciplinary team and emphasizes the role of unpaid caregivers. In this paradigm, residential care is reserved mainly for acute problems. This deinstitutionalization started in the USA, in particular within the mental health sector.

Not only the organization of care is switched over the years, our vision of ideal care is changed as well (Thornicroft and Tansella, 1999). The ideal type of care is one that promotes autonomy, is continuous – cross-sectional and longitudinal – effective and efficient, accessible, fair, integral, works coordinated and provides accountability.

In the sector of the care for the elderly, nowadays the socialization of care is generally adopted. While earlier, seniors in Flanders could move to a residential rest home for the elderly without having any disability, and sometimes in their early 60 years, nowadays the average age of moving to an intramural care organization is 82 years. The average age of people, living in a rest home for elderly people is 85.5 years old. This means, people are staying longer at home receiving help in their environment whereas earlier, they were taken care of in total institutions.

During the last decades, the Flemish government has opted for a step-wise approach to care for older people, a kind of socialization into the care sector for elderly persons. The *Woonzorgdecreet*, a decree (2009) that combines homecare facilities and services for elderly people, is based on the idea of stepped care - first self-care, then care by unpaid caregivers from their own environment, then non-specialized professional care and finally specialized professional care. This progression recognizes nine types of homecare services: domestic care, logistic care, sit-in care, home nursing, coordination of services within the National Health Services, local service centers, regional service centers, services of host families and recovery centers. There are no requirements whatsoever to use these services. One of the main goals of these homecare services is that seniors can keep on living in their environment as long as possible and that unpaid caregivers are supported in their task of taking care for the old aged person. A new project is in the pipeline: nightcare. During the night, a volunteer or a paid caregiver stays in the house of the senior, so that the unpaid caregiver can recharge. Another type of night care is that the senior is brought to a residential home for the night and stays at home during the day.

Besides these home care services, this decree recognizes four types of services for seniors: centers for day care, centers for short stay, assistance homes and residential homecare centers. These services for the elderly need to aim at social network building, at the integration in the neighbourhood and organise animation and recreation. The minimum age for seniors to utilise these services is 65 years.

In most Western countries, this kind of 'socialization into care' is warmly welcomed by policymakers, and elderly people and their relatives. Indeed, it has a lot of advantages. We point here to some of them. First, it is demand-driven, is emancipatory and emphasizes the self-reliance of the patient. As said before, seniors want to live as long as possible in their own house, their own environment. The socialization of care can be an answer to this need. By organizing different kinds of extramural assistance, older individuals can choose what they need and therefore, they are encouraged to live as independent as possible. They are not automatically taken care of in a residence that offers them a standard package of care.

Secondly, socialization of care acts against the stigmatization of the older persons in need of care. When these persons are put together in a residential home, far from the society, this is marking them with a stigma. But, when they are included in society, this stigma can diminish and hopefully disappear. Of course, this destigmatization is also positive for the unpaid caregivers. Another advantage for the informal caregiver is that, with the socialization of care, they find themselves less in a position of dependency on the residential home. They feel less patronized and more engaged (Rood, 2008, Van Audenhove, Van Humbeeck en Van Meerbeeck, 2005).

Every medal has its obverse side. Socialization of care confronts us with a number of major challenges. Here we would like to focus on two important challenges, looking from the viewpoint of the older individual in need of care. First there is the risk of social isolation and feelings of loneliness. Although several studies have come to the conclusion that there is no significant higher risk on social isolation and feeling of loneliness within the group of seniors, by defining 'seniors' as older than 55, 60 or 65, they do recognize a significant effect for the oldest age categories, those people who are of interest for the socialization of care approach (Vanden Boer & Pauwels, 2004, Fokkema & Steyaert, 2005). Moreover, they recognize the correlation between social isolation and loneliness on the one hand, and living alone, being a widow(er), being advanced in age, being childless and having bad health on the other hand (Wenger, 1996; Mullins, 1996; Vanden boer & Pauwels, 2004). The elderly are most likely to deal with one of these factors – for example: 31.1% of the seniors in the EU live as a single adult (Eurostat, 2012), so that they have a greater chance of feeling lonely or suffering social isolation. The Eurostat study (2012) shows that in Belgium, slightly more than 15% of the persons aged 65 and over felt left out of society. So it is important that the care for the elderly is taking into account this data.

A second major challenge from the point of view of the elderly at stake that arises from the socialization of care is the need for continuation of care.

Whereas in a total institution continuation of care can be easily guaranteed, it can be more difficult to do so when care is provided by different services and actors.

As the socialization of care starts from the concept of stepped care, it emphasizes the role of the patient and the informal caregiver. Alongside challenges from the viewpoint of the older individual, we can also point to challenges from that of the unpaid caregiver. The informal caregiver pre-eminently is the partner or a child, mostly a daughter, of the aged (European Commission, 2012). Taken into account some demographic and socio-economic evolutions in the Western societies, as there are the decrease in the birth rate, the rising number of divorces, the increase in the level of female economic activity, and the decline of the multi-generational households, the role of the informal caregiver is subjected to great pressure. Will there be enough individuals able to engage themselves to be an informal caregiver? In addition, overburdening and (feelings of) depression may arise. In research to be published, Declercq concludes that one out of four informal caregivers in Flanders is dealing with feelings of depression; 4% suffer a severe depression.

A second concern from the position of the informal caregiver is the fact that nonprofessional caregivers may lack the knowledge of all kinds of available services for the elderly. This might result in situations wherein the aged, not the informal caregiver make use of the most appropriate services.

The socialization of care has also some important consequences for the professional caregiver. Here, we would like to stress one of them: professional caregivers need to switch from 'thinking and acting in the name of the patient' towards 'supporting the patient'. They often tend to *care for* rather than *taking care of*.

Last but not least, there is the reaction of society to socialization of care. It fits perfectly on paper: there seems to be a large public support for the socialization of care. The actual practice is different. Whenever an initiative of care in the society is taken, a flood of criticism appears in the neighbourhood. Examples of this NIMBY (not in my backyard) syndrome show up frequently, as a reaction to the building of a service for elderly in the society, to the fact that psychiatric patients live in a house in the neighbourhood and receive help in the form of assisted living, to the arrival of ex-prisoners, etc. The public support of the socialization of care should rise: the society must be willing to receive and citizens must be prepared to support these people. Of course one should bear in mind the resilience of the neighbourhood when including care in society.

Leisure time of elderly people

'There is a lot to life after 60' it says on the website of the 2012 European Year for Active Ageing and Solidarity Between Generations. Active ageing refers here to the fact that people 'can still play our part in society and enjoy a better quality of life. The challenge is to make the most of the enormous potential that we harbour even at a more advanced age.' (http://europa.eu/ey2012/) Next to employment and independent living, participation in society is put forward as a key area in which active ageing is promoted. This key area is our point of interest in this part of the chapter. We want to investigate what being active in leisure time means for older people. What are the possibilities for older people to engage in later life and which challenges do they experience? We are particularly interested in two areas: lifelong learning and active citizenship.

Lifelong learning

The European Union stipulated that, by 2010, 12.5% of the population should take part in activities in the field of lifelong learning. In the EU2020-strategy, the goal is increased to 15%. The Flemish region in Belgium is certainly not the best student in the EU-class. With 7.5% in 2011, we have scored below the EU average. In general, studies indicate that young, working and higher educated individuals participate most in lifelong learning activities. This is not very promising for learning in later life. This is confirmed by Boeren and Nicaise (Boeren & Nicaise, 2009) who found that only 4% of people aged 65 and above is enrolled in formal adult education.

The European Union has always emphasized the importance of lifelong learning for two reasons: the employability of its citizens and social cohesion. That the first reason is no longer valid for older people is reflected in the significant drops in participation rate at the age of 55 and again at the age of 65 (Vanweddingen, 2008). So then why do they engage in lifelong learning activities? A first motivation is to increase their knowledge and skills to keep up with rapid changes in society (Leirman, 2004; Vanweddingen, 2008). A second motivation is for personal and mental development. Finally, older people also engage for the pleasure of learning itself (Leirman, 2004). When we look at those motivations of older people to learn, we might indeed conclude that we are dealing with active individuals. But the actual figures show a different picture. The vast majority of older people is not engaged in lifelong learning. Why not? We can differentiate between internal obstacles and external obstacles (Oostelaar & Wolfswinkel, 2006). The internal obstacles refer to the personal motivation of older people to learn . 'I am too old to learn' or 'I don't like schools' are common expressions from older people with a lack of motivation. External obstacles relate to the price of lifelong learning activities, the accessibility of those activities in terms of mobility, location and timing.

Social participation

Participation in society was high on the agenda of the 2012 Year of active ageing. Many studies support the positive effect of this participation on the quality of life of individuals and their subjective health (Heylen & Mortelmans, 2009). Also society at large gains from this participation as it increases the level of trust and social cohesion. Here we will focus on what individuals do in later life in terms of volunteering and participation in socio-cultural associations.

Let us start with volunteering. In Flanders, 16,1% of the older population is working on an unpaid basis (Verté, De Witte, & DeDonder, 2007). On average, they spend seven to eight hours a week on their voluntary work. The baby boomer generation (age 55-64) is especially active (Godemont, Goyvaerts, & Marynissen, 2006). After the age of 75, voluntary work decreases substantially. The number one type of activity they undertake is caring for other people, such as visiting ill friends and family, child care, assisting in a home for handicapped or old people.

From the perspective of social work, it is important to know why people engage in voluntary work in later life and what are the obstacles to such engagement. A first motivation of the older generation is based on 'a deep-rooted sense of duty' and altruism (Godemont, Goyvaerts, & Marynissen, 2006)p.79). Social contact is a second motivation and refers to the strength of volunteering to enlarge the social network and prevent individuals from loneliness and exclusion. Personal development as motivation occurred predominantly in the group of young seniors (aged 50 to 64).

Godemont, Goyvaerts and Marynissen (Godemont, Goyvaerts, & Marynissen, 2006) conducted a research on older individuals and voluntary work. They found that experience, in terms of both professional and social competences, is the main strength of older volunteers. Professionals working in the field report that the weaknesses lies in the rigidity of older volunteers with regards to the vision and structure of the organization they are engaged in and their physical condition. To increase the benefits of engaging older people in voluntary work, more efforts must be made to support those volunteers. There is the need for uniform statute for volunteers, a safe environment to carry out their work and for intensive guidance and capacity building.

In Flanders, social participation is also exercised within what is called socio-cultural associations. Such socio-cultural associations are, by law, to fulfill four functions: cultural, educational, social activation, and community development (Cockx, 2005). The associations operate as a network of local chapters. Volunteers are the driving force in planning and organizing activities for the members of these associations. Some of these associations aim at the population at large while others see the older population as their specific target group. 10.5 % of Flemish persons older than 60 participate in a socio-cultural association and nearly 2% are involved as board members in a local branch of such an association (Verté, De Witte, & DeDonder, 2007). This level of participation increases when we look at the senior associations: one out of three seniors is a member of a senior association. Meeting other people and coziness are the main motivations of older people to join such an association. The research of Verté and others (2007) also shows what people do within these senior associations. Recreational social activities such as parties and animated afternoons are the most undertaken activities, followed by meetings with other members, membership magazine, day trips and afternoon debates. Older persons within the senior associations attend activities a few times a year (33.4%), every month (34.8%) or even every week (15%). Problems related to health, mobility, the timing of the activity, lack of interest, and the duty to care for somebody are found to be the main obstacles for participating (more) in socio-cultural associations.

Promoting active ageing within leisure time

A quick look at the recent figures for participation in the field of lifelong learning, voluntary work and socio-cultural organization reveals that there is room for improvement. The question at stake is then: who should take the initiative to bring about this improvement? In this part we will look at the role of national and local policy makers on one hand and the possibilities of organizations within the field on the other hand.

In Flanders, the policy making process with regard to leisure time for elderly is situated at two levels: the Flemish level and the local level of the municipalities. At the Flemish level, it is the Minister for Welfare, Health Care and Family, Jo Vandeurzen, who launched the 2010-2014 Policy Plan for the Elderly. Together with this policy plan, the Flemish government initiated a campaign called 'Generation now: young at heart' (www.generatienu.be). Both the policy plan and the campaign focus on the active involvement of senior citizens within our society. The goal of the policy plan is to create the necessary conditions to secure access of senior citizens to their economic, social and cultural rights, to prevent age-based discrimination and social exclusion, to stimulate the participation of senior citizens in the policy making and evaluating processes and to bring about a inclusive and integrated policy for the elderly (Vandeurzen, 2010). More specific in the domain of leisure time, the policy plan focuses on the recognition of voluntary work of older individuals and the necessary support structures. It also underlines the importance of the socio-cultural associations and the whole field of what is called socio-cultural work for the social integration of the elderly. To promote lifelong learning, Vandeurzen (2010) puts forward a set of objectives which aim to remove the existing obstacles for lifelong learning. Here are some of the specific actions mentioned in the policy plan: price reduction for activities; a programming tailor-mode for seniors; the local library as an accessible first step towards lifelong learning; promoting lifelong learning activities for seniors; and an educational needs analysis.

This Flemish policy plan on elderly is put into practice in each municipality by the means of a local policy plan on elderly. The strengths of those local policy plans lies in the participation of senior citizens in the form of senior citizen councils. Those senior citizen councils are active in 90% of the local municipalities in Flanders. Four out of ten municipalities have attracted a professional civil servant to coordinate this local policy plan on elderly (Vandeurzen, 2010).

Policymakers have certainly pushed the active ageing agenda in the policy plans. It is for organizations and associations within the field to make it happen. They play an important role in removing barriers for participation and in fine-tuning their activities to the needs of all seniors citizens –active, mobile and healthy citizens as well as senior citizens with needs. There is the physical accessibility of activities, the use of communication in announcing activities, the price to participate, as well as more psychological obstacles such as negative learning experiences in the past and unfamiliarity with an organization or the people involved in it (Martens, Meireman, & Raymaekers, 2009). Once older people are enrolled in an activity or program, there is the need to accommodate the educational process to the specific situation of older people and to create a stimulating learning environment (Bertels, Verhoeven, & Messelis, 2005).

As stated at the beginning, the benefits of participation in society are enormous. But the everyday reality in which people live may be completely different. There are many obstacles and the nature of those obstacles varies greatly. The ideal of active ageing is not realistic for each older individual. Therefore Cantillon (Cantillon, Van den Bosch, & Lefebure, 2009) argues to be careful with the (over-)promotion of social participation in later life. 'Accepting the obstacles for social participation will cause less stigmatization for the older individuals who have to deal with these obstacles' (Cantillon, Van den Bosch, & Lefebure, 2009) p. 12).

Conclusion

In this chapter, we started from three views on the position of older people in society: the social welfare discourse, active ageing discourse and productive ageing discourse. Even today, the first discourse is still dominant in the public debate on ageing which is based on a deficit perspective: elderly are seen as a burden to society and have no active role to play anymore. Gradually, a new perspective is emerging, partly as a consequence of the European year on Active Ageing and Solidarity between Generations. In the field of long time care and leisure time, we see indeed that the discourse on active ageing is becoming a reality. This is reflected in the numbers of seniors taking part in voluntary work or lifelong activities as well as in the socialization of care. However, there are also challenges connected to the idea of active ageing in these two areas. These challenges stem from the restricted resilience of the elderly themselves, as well as their relatives and friends. This does not mean that one should stop promoting active ageing, as it is meaningful to many seniors. But we should be sensitive to the actual needs and possibilities of each and every individual senior and take up the challenges.

References

Bertels, E., Verhoeven, S., & Messelis, E. (2005). Lang zullen ze leren! Educatief werken met ouderen. Brussel: Socius.

Boeren, E., & Nicaise, I. (2009). Onderwijs voor volwassenen: wie neemt deel en waarom? . In L. Vanderleyden, M. Callens, & J. Noppe, De sociale staat van Vlaanderen 2009. Brussel: Studiedienst van de Vlaamse Regering.

Cantillon, B., Van den Bosch, K., & Lefebure, S. (2009). Ouderen in Vlaanderen en Europa. Tussen vermogen en afhankelijkheid. Leuven: Acco.

Cockx, F. (2005). De functie (s) van sociaal-cultureel werk. Resultaten van een visieontwikkelingstraject met, door en voor het sociaal-cultureel volwassenenwerk in Vlaanderen . Brussel: Socius.

De Brauwere, G., Vanthuyne, T., & Verschelden, G. (2008). Senioren en niet-formele educatie. Een onderzoek naar de behoeften en interesses van senioren in Zuid-Oost-Vlaanderen. Gent: Hogeschool Gent, Departement sociaal-agogisch werk.

European Commission (2012). The 2012 Ageing Report. Economic and budgetary projections for the27 EU Member States (2010-2060). Brussels: European Union

Eurostat (2012). Active ageing and solidarity between generations 2012 edition. A statistical portrait of the European Union 2012. Luxemburg: European Union.

Godemont, J., Goyvaerts, K., & Marynissen, R. (2006). De vergrijzing verzilverd? Een verkennend onderzoek naar ouderen in het Vlaams vrijwilligerswerk. Antwerpen: Steunpunt Gelijkekansenbeleid. Consortium Universiteit Antwerpen en Universiteit Hasselt.

Goffman, E. (1961). Asylums: essays on the social situation of mental patients and other inmates. New York: Doubleday

Heylen, L., & Mortelmans, D. (2009). Succesvol ouder worden? Sociale participatie in Vlaanderen. In B. Cantillon, K. Van den Bosch, & S. Lefebure, Ouderen in Vlaanderen en Europa. Tussen vermogen en afhankelijkheid. Leuven: Acco.

Leirman, W. (2004). Ouderen bouwen aan levenskwaliteit in de 21ste eeuw. In F. Cockx, & J. De Vriendt, Wisselwerk cahier '04. Sociaal-cultureel werk van, voor en met ouderen. Brussel: Socius.

Martens, M., Meireman, K., & Raymaekers, P. (2009). Seniorenbeleidsonderzoek Leuven met betrekking tot vrije tijd en zelfstandig wonen. Heverlee: KHLeuven

Oostelaar, D., & Wolfswinkel, G. (2006). Ouderen in de samenleving. Basisboek voor hulp- en dienstverleners. Bussum: Coutinho.

Roos, E. (2008). Vermaatschappelijking van de zorg: geluk(t) voor iedereen? Een onderzoek naar de gevolgen van en voorwaarden voor vermaatschappelijking van de zorg. Amersfoort: Bestuur en Management Consultants

Thornicroft G, and Transella M. (1999). The Mental Health Matrix: a manual to improve services. Cambridge: Cambridge University Press.

Van Audenhove, C., e.a. (2005). De vermaatschappelijking van de zorg voor psychiatrische kwetsbare mensen. Leuven: LannooCampus.

Vandeurzen, J. (2010). Ontwerp Vlaams Ouderenbeleidsplan 2010-2014. Brussel: Vlaams Parlement.

Vanweddingen, M. (2008). Leren een leven lang in Vlaanderen. Brussel: Studiedienst van de Vlaamse Regering.

Verté, D., De Witte, N., & DeDonder, L. (2007). Schaakmat of aan zet? Monitor voor lokaal ouderenbeleid in Vlaanderen. Brugge: Vanden Broele.

II

Active Ageing and Dementia:
A Challenge for Social Workers and Professionals in Health Services

Andrea Pilgerstorfer

Introduction

The International Un iversity Week, on which this chapter is based, offers students the possibility for European exchange and can 'light the fire' and generate love for comparative research, which gains more and more importance in the field of social work and social work research in particular.

For the lecture we gave, which formed the foundations for the chapter, our starting point was the *Haus St. Elisabeth*. This is a retirement home run by Caritas St. Pölten in Austria. One specific part of the *Haus* works with the psycho-biographical nursing concept developed by Prof. Dr. Erwin Böhm, which is certified by the Europäisches Netzwerk für psychobiographische Pflegeforschung (European network for psycho biographic nursing research, ENPP, http://www.enpp-boehm.com/de/startseite.htmlhttp://www.enpp-boehm.com/de/startseite.html.)

We presented and discussed the theory and methods employed in psycho-biographical work, especially the impact of such on social work, pointing out its emphasis on useful perspectives for professional relationship building and strategies for communication. It was important to offer students the possibility to try the suggested patterns of communication. This chapter briefly outlines the core aspects of Böhm's approach, and points out the important and helpful principles for social work and health professionals, which can be used postively in providing help for people suffering from dementia.

'Active ageing' is an expression which is increasingly used in society and seen in magazines, but of which, perhaps, there is limited understanding. In fact, there are multiple and varying meanings associated with the term.

The first picture coming into my mind when I consider the term is of a generation of seniors who now travel all over the world, are healthy, nicely dressed and so forth. My grandmother belongs to that group of "young old", or, as we call them in German, *Junge Alte*. They are an interesting target group for business, especially through anti-ageing products. In the labour market the term means seeking for solutions of how to keep human resources working productively in older age. For the health services, research focuses on being active mentally as well as physically. Keeping active and flexible leads to a healthier life and is promoted as being the key to youthfulness.

However, what does it means when we talk about 'active ageing' in the context of dementia? Indeed, we may ask, does it exist for people with dementia? As we know, dementia is one of the most common diseases among the elderly and a major cause of disability (Berr, Wancata, & Ritchie 2005). Does that mean, however, that active ageing stops at that point? My answer would be no, it does not stop, but it has to be adapted to the special needs arising from the emerging illness. Symptoms in dementia vary, and people are affected in different ways by the change in abilities, the loss of memory and changes in personality (Alzheimer's Association Homepage, 10/2012).

The following section provides an overview of some facts and data concerning dementia, and indicates some of the ways in which it may be experienced. In health and social work, the impact of dementia is discussed from a variety of different perspectives: possible perceptions of patients (which are often reflected as an interpretation of others), experiences of relatives and the impressions and meaning of the illness for caregivers. Following this overview, I will present the main points of the Böhm's concept itself. I will then conclude by offering some open questions that will need to be addressed by social work in the future.

When we consider active ageing and decline in cognitive ability (severe enough to interfere with daily life), it presents a contradiction that reflects the challenge between the vision of healthy ageing and capability and an illness with progressive deterioration, increasing needs and dependence. This conundrum presents an overwhelming feeling of loss, but also offers the chance to critique our achievement-and-performance-oriented society that idolises youth and equates it with health! There may be other possibilities for society as promoted by social work.

Facts about dementia

Current estimates indicate that 35.6 million people worldwide are living with dementia. This number is predicted to double by 2030 and more than triple by 2050 (WHO, 2012). Seven million three hundred thousand people in Europe are thought to have Alzheimer's disease, the most common form of dementia (WHO, 2012). In Austria the number is currently suggested to be about 126,000 people (Salzburg, 2012). In Lower Austria, one of the nine governmental regions of Austria, 1,779 persons with dementia were discharged from hospital during the year 2010, comprising 650 men and 1,129 women. Of this number, 1,726 people were aged over 65 years, 610 men and 1,116 women (Statistik Austria, 2011).

Dementia results in a range of harmful disease outcomes, particularly in old-old age (over 80 years), however, with continued developments in medicine prolonging life expectancy, dementia is likely to affect more people in the future. Peter Dal-Bianco, an Austrian expert on Alzheimer's disease from Vienna University, points out that with a package of public health measures the increase of the disease could be retarded. He discusses several aspects such as increased exercise, not smoking, eating more vegetables and fruits and so forth (APA, 2012).

The key symptoms can be described as the four As:

+ Amnesia – losing memory and orientation
+ Aphasia – losing the understanding of language
+ Apraxia – loss of motions and the capacity to recognise objects
+ Agnosia - loss of cognitive abilities (Wittstein, 1991 in Kellenhauser et al., 2004)

People experience mental disturbance. This confusion can show up in different ways: some people cannot remember the place where they are, others cannot understand the time of the day or night, and still others are not able to connect with current settings and events or are not clear about who they are – at times all of these are experienced. For people with dementia, the world around them becomes more and more misunderstood, while carers face the continuous and frequent restriction of social functioning in the daily life of their loved ones (Kellenhauser et al., 2004). Dementia is a chronic disease that progresses over months and years and causes degenerative changes in brain. The course is progressive and leads to the loss of once learned capabilities and eventually death (Pschyrembel, 2002).

Alzheimer's disease is the most common type of dementia, accounting for up to 60% to 80% of cases. The symptoms of Alzheimer's disease result from damage to the brain's nerve cells. The disease gradually gets worse as more cells are damaged and destroyed. Three phases with seven levels of decline are described: the phases include mild or early-stage, mid-stage and late-stage Alzheimer's disease. Symptoms can vary greatly across individuals. Scientists do not yet know why brain cells malfunction and die, but two prime suspects are abnormal microscopic structures called plaques and tangles (Alzheimer's Association, 2009). There are several ideas about the concrete benefit of early-stage diagnosis:

1. Optimising medical management
2. Relief gained from better understanding of symptoms
3. Maximising decision-making autonomy
4. Promoting access to services
5. Risk reduction by care planning
6. Planning for the future
7. Improving clinical outcomes
8. Avoiding or reducing future health and social care costs

Diagnosis may also be considered by some as a human right (Prince et al., 2011). In respect of the increasing dependency that people with dementia are confronted with, it is important to promote understanding and awareness amongst the general population. Speaking about human rights emphasises and promotes the importance of self-esteem for people with dementia in society, and emphasises their citizenship. Earlier diagnosis allows people with dementia to plan ahead while they still have the capacity to make important decisions about their future care. In addition, they and their families can receive timely practical information, advice and support. Only through receiving an early diagnosis can they get access to available drug and non-drug therapies that may improve their cognition and enhance their quality of life. And, they can, if they choose, participate in research for the benefit of future generations (Prince et al., 2011).

To achieve an inclusive understanding and to realise the vision of self-decision-making processes in people, the helping professions also need to be sensitised to needs and concerns resulting from dementia. Close relatives and carers might be one of the first who could suspect a change and request an early diagnose, whilst people with dementia themselves may wish to ignore the changes they experience or maybe sometimes feel ashamed, irritated and confused by them. Helping professionals can assist here. Focussing solely on the symptoms can present only a superficial understanding about the meaning of dementia for patients, relatives and professional caregivers, and awareness of the many meanings possible is important.

The experience of continuous difficulties with memory, decision-making and self-care can cause worry and make people feel anxious about what is happening. Daily life often becomes more and more difficult for them. The on-going process of dementia gradually affects the ways people communicate — both in expressing the thoughts and in understanding what others are saying.

Imagine for one minute that your friend, relative or family member has Alzheimer's disease and reports the following issues:

> *When I go shopping and look at items, most of them never really register in my mind, even though I see them clearly. I have trouble making decisions, because I question whether I am making the right one. I can no longer enjoy my favourite hobbies, because it requires processing skills that I no longer have. I went from being a 'gadget' person, to being threatened by technology that I no longer can use.*
>
> *I go to social functions only to be tortured by the noise and surrounding conversations, because of the loudness that cannot be filtered out. If people try to speak with me in a public setting where there are many other conversations, I just don't understand what they are saying. This is because all of the people speaking come in at the same volume level. All the words run together, and it sounds like a foreign language...*
> *(Michael Ellenbogen)*

For the family and relatives the situation often leads to the point at which someone has to care for the senior with dementia. For Austrian families, a residential home is still the final solution. However, providing help by a home service or a 24 hours nursing service at the person's own home is more likely to be accepted by the individual. Standing at the side and observing the decline of the loved one may confront carers with the arousal of feelings such as denial, anger, anxiety, irritability, and where the dementia is compounded by changing personality and behaviour the situation might be even more complicated.

The behavioural and psychological symptoms of dementia (BPSD) are an integral part of the disease process and present severe problems to patients, their families and caregivers, and, indeed, to society at large. They are grouped in two different symptom clusters:

Behavioural symptoms

These are usually identified on the basis of observation of the patient, and may include physical aggression, screaming, restlessness, agitation, wandering, culturally inappropriate behaviours, sexual dis-inhibition, hoarding, and cursing.

Psychological symptoms

These are mainly assessed on the basis of interviews with patients and relatives using specific protocols and these symptoms can include anxiety, depressive moods, hallucinations and delusions. A psychotic illness within Alzheimer's disease has also been identified (IPA, 2002).

BPSD are treatable to an extent and generally respond better to therapy than other symptoms or syndromes of dementia. There are a number of scales developed to assess BPSD:

- 1986 The Cohen-Mansfield Agitation Inventory (CMAI) focused specifically on behaviours such as hitting, pacing and screaming (Cohen-Mansfield et al., 1989; Cohen-Mansfield, 1996).
- 1987 The Behavioural Pathological Rating Scale for Alzheimer's disease (BEHAVE-AD) focused on specific symptoms in AD, different from those seen in other neuropsychiatric disorders, such as delusions that people are stealing things, fear of being left alone and fragmented sleep (Reisberg et al., 1996).
- 1994 The Neuropsychiatric Inventory (NPI) which has frequency and severity scales for behaviours common to AD, but also includes scales for other dementias (Cummings et al., 1994).
- 1995 The Consortium to Establish a Registry in AD (CERAD) Behavioural Scale focused on both behavioural and psychological symptoms (Tariot et al., 1995; Tariot, 1996) (cit. IPA 2002).

The risk of developing dementia increases with old age (Ziegler & Doblhammer 2009). Figures show that there are more women affected but overall 2-3 % of all people over 65 years are likely to get dementia. At the age of 75 years this figure increases to 7%. The number of cases of dementia for seniors over 80 years rises again to 12% of that group, and for people over 90 years 30% are expected (Theunissen, 2010).

It seems obvious that living with dementia cannot be ignored in society, particularly when the aim for people with dementia is that they can still contribute somehow to our community life. Speaking about dementia and the impact the disease causes, Marshall (2005) draws a picture with multiple perspectives and options to intervene in an empowering way. The different aspects can be seen as both deficits and resources.

1. The starting point must always be the individual experiencing the disease in his or her own unique way, constructing his or her view of the world.
2. The medical approach, which has been used to explain and describe the physical damage and changes to the brain, including all changes in personality and behaviour. Medicine keeps the focus on biochemical reactions and considers 'the rest' - social, psychological and spiritual – as probably important and contributing to healing process and rehabilitation but not their concern. However, rehabilitation is not a term often used in the context of dementia (Marshall, 2005).
3. The social or disability approach reminds us of the centrality of the person, their background and health and on all factors in their environment. The knowledge of relatives and friends as well as professionals is valued (Marshall, 2005).
4. The citizenship model challenges the understandings of professional expertise and received opinions (Marshall, 2005). It presents an inclusive concept which moves towards accepting the idea that service user can be involved in decision-making processes of professionals. People with dementia are themselves assumed to be the experts whilst we professionals have to improve our communication skills to understand what they are saying (Marshall, 2005).

Improving the communication skills of professionals to understand what people are saying was one of the crucial points made by Böhm. He criticised care practice in the 1970s as that of simply keeping patients quiet. Practice at that time concerned keeping patients warm, ensuring they are clean and not hungry. Bohm's ideas were strongly influenced by psychoanalysis and he highlighted a concept of ageing in old-old age or when suffering from dementia which seeks to explain to carers the strange behaviour and conflicts of patients.

Overview of Böhm's Nursing Concept

Prof. Erwin Böhm was born on 16th May 1940 in Austria. He learned car mechanics and completed a nursing diploma in 1963. He worked in mental health care, mainly in gerontological psychiatric care. He created a theory of nursing that aimed to re-activate people with dementia and seniors who displayed unusual behaviour. He was an opponent of the 'warm and well fed' or 'proper' nursing of those days. He was convinced that to know the patient's biography was the best way to understand her/his needs and characteristics (Böhm 1988 in Schneider no date). Böhm developed his nursing model for patients with gerontological psychiatric disorders.

The daily life and normality of the patients is one of the core issues of Böhm's nursing concept. The carer has to know the individual and collective biography and the coping strategies from all persons significant to the person he/she works with. In residential nursing home care, the daily life of the housing service focuses on the habits of the service user, and their daily routines, as well as being attuned to the seasons, and all usual social celebrations (Scheider, no date).

Böhm's approach is based on his understanding of dementia and specific interactions with patients with dementia. Seniors coming into residential care are 'dis – placed' and, therefore, likely to be disoriented. To cope with this situation they use certain strategies which, for carers, may not always be understandable and often not be reasonable (Popp, 2007). See the following example:

> *Mrs. G, 87 years old lives in a nursing home. On her floor there are blankets, towels and plastic accessories. Her idea was to make it obvious to place things on a level to which she believed they belonged. Whenever her blankets are properly put on her bed Mrs G takes them off. Whenever she enters someone else's room, she takes the blue blankets off. One day, Mrs. G went to another room, the room of a new lady who was living there for just a few weeks, a short term resident whilst her family were on holiday. She brought her own blankets with her – all white! Mrs. G was seen looking at those blankets and touching them delightedly. She was seen by a nurse who tried to understand what was happening for her. From that day on she got white blankets. Mrs. G now keeps her white blankets and touches them with joy. But when she manages to go to another room and sees the blue blankets, then she's on her way to take them all off! (Kellnhauser, et al., 2004).*

Ageing can be construed as a regressive process of psyche and soul, when mental deterioration starts people often return to a previous characterising phase of earlier life. The coping mechanisms and behaviours they used then may be reinstated to deal with problems and life events now experienced, and this gives them a degree of security. So it is important to create an atmosphere of those days within residential care settings – beside the personal furniture people can bring with them (in some places). The aim is to maintain independence, self-reliance, self-sufficiency and social competence as long as possible. Reactivating care, however, means to undertake some 'reanimation of the soul of elderly people'. The interpretation of the unique thymo-psychological biography controls the action of carers. (Thymos = vitality; it means the emotional part of psyche (Prell, 2011)).

Seniors should stay self-reliant as long as possible and should keep their social competence where possible. It does not mean that they just stay physically active but also mentally and psychologically – they should think, feel and make decisions on their own for as long as possible (Prell, 2011).

Böhm identifies seven emotional accessibility levels or levels of interaction in a hierarchical order:

1. Socialisation (*Sozialisation*)
   The adult person. Life-long learning is possible. The rules and standards of society can be adapted. Socialisation experiences the individual had are important.

2. Mothers wit/ Mothers humour (*Mutterwitz*)
   In youth and adolescence the focus is on behaviour and feelings, it is assumed that the person can be reached through activating care.

3. Psychological and social basic needs (*Seelische u. soziale Grundbedürfnisse*)

4. Imprints (*Prägungen*)
   Rituals and ongoing attitudes can give security to the older person.

5. Drive (*Triebe*)
   Wishes and daydreams affect people, and demanding and encouraging has to be understood within this context.

6. Intuition (*Intuition*)
   Emotions, fairy tales, superstition and religion are important to people.

7. Basic communication (*Urkommunikation*)
   Emotional access are at the level of a baby, also physical capacities are restricted.

The biographical assessment is very important and is also needed to understand the patient and underpin the interaction between carer and patient (Popp, 2007).

The person's stories are important, they give the information about coping strategies and personality and characteristics of the patient. Helpful questions for Böhm include:

"When and where was the patient born?"
"Were did she/he spend his youth?"
"What can she/he say about the family and numbers, dynamics and atmosphere?"
"What about her/his siblings?"
"What work did the patient undertake?"
"Where did she/he live?"
"Did she/he have hobbies?"
"Emotional experiences and life events – both positive and negative?"
"Partnership, marriage?"
"Children?"
"Destiny or beliefs about the future?" (Prell, 2011)

In respect of BPSD, Böhm is concerned, that the key to 'reading' a person's behaviour is their biography (Schneider, 2006).

The challenge for social work and an inclusive society

Gerontological scientists speak about the life course and about the different duties, resources and difficulties a person faces at different ages. Factors relating to the individual's current life and the ways in which society is constructed, such as changing family structures, emerging new familial or quasi-familial social norms, alternative caregivers, senior housing, changes in health, and the uniqueness of ageing in each cohort, all need to be taken into consideration in our contemporary understanding of gerontological research (Hou, 2012). To address these factors, social policy and practice should be prepared to develop new ideas and work inter-disciplinarily across the different professions entrusted with the work for and with older people, in order to find an inclusive way to treat dependent persons with respect and understanding. It is important that caregivers seek possibilities for the service users to contribute to our (future) society. This contribution given by our seniors reflects the thinking of Ilse Arlt (1876 – 1960), an Austrian pioneer of scientific social work, who stresses that it is important to feel a joy of life. She states that making it possible for people to experience that feeling – this joy of life - is one of the core target for the helping process (Pantucek in Pantucek & Maiss, 2009).

Dementia changes the needs of seniors in an enormous way, which often heralds increased dependency. People experience declining health and loss of independence as well as loss of orientation to the world outside. Social workers, as well as other professionals, interact with people with dementia as service users. To communicate in a relational way, as well as holding knowledge about dementia and noting the importance of symptoms, it is necessary to be trained in person-centred communication methods. Changes in the ability to communicate are unique to each person with dementia: difficulty finding the right word, using familiar words repeatedly, easily losing train of thought. Therefore, sensitive, on-going communication is important, no matter how difficult it may become. While a person may not respond, he or she requires and benefits from continuing communication (Alzheimer's Association, 2012).

The importance of working with biography cannot be overemphasised! Social work manuals also emphasise the need to make the life story visible. One of these tools is the 'biographic time line' (*Biographischer Zeitbalken*). It is a cooperative method to get an overview about the real (time specific) biography of a person in different important life stages. The social worker interviews the service user starting with the date of birth though following topics: Family, Housing, Education, Labour, Delinquency, Health, Help and Treatment (Pantucek, 2005[1]).

The quality of life is an important criterion of success for modern medicine (Radoschewski in Pilgerstorfer, 2009). Different assessments are created and include mostly the evaluation of the following items:

+ health status (including health-associated disabilities)
+ environment (including restrictions, stigma, opportunity for choice)
+ subjective perceptions of mood, physical discomfort and frustration
+ behavioural observation of activity, affect and social involvement
+ caregiver reporting of behaviour and mood (IPA, 2002)

The German association for medicine presents five target points or levels where help should be offered to increase quality of life. The starting point is, of course, the patient him- or herself (see the following figure)

The centre of the diagram is represented by the cognitive capacities, with

Social functioning and relationship	Orientation - adjustment of the environment
	Personal skills of the patient
Help in Daily life	Legal arrangements – decree

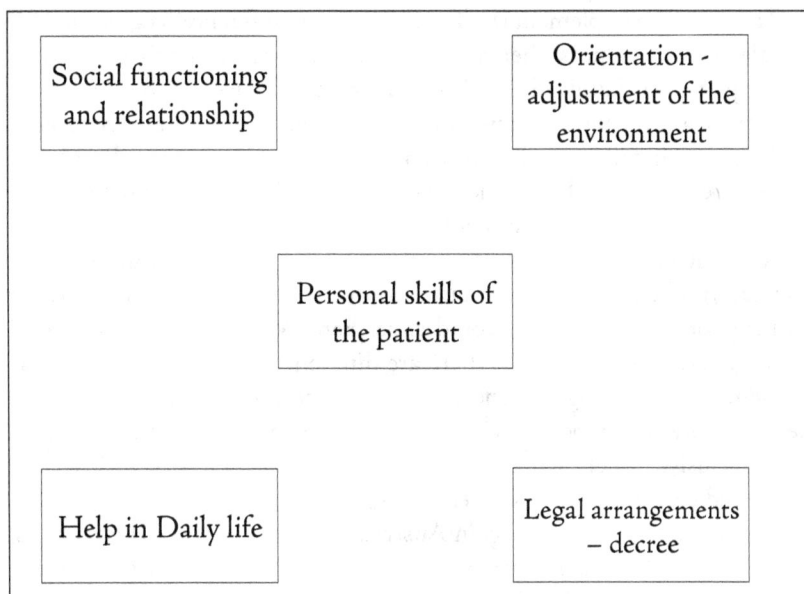

professional help being geared towards keeping the brain active. Crucial points in this are having contact with others, which is further aided by training and sensitising other people in the social network. The environment should be oriented to the needs of the person with dementia and their interests. All features of help in daily life are designed to make it possible to maintain the daily routines and habits (also aided by technical support). The legal arrangements concern the preparations for the moment when the decision-making process is no longer possible for the person and, therefore, arrangements are also made with the caregivers (DEGAM, 2008).

Connecting these five target points and Marshall's (2005) approach can lead to inclusion for the service user as well as a resource-oriented concept for professionals. The starting point, as we have indicated, is the individual: resources, needs, wishes and fears can be understood and joined up with coping strategies and capacities to deal with the disease. The status of physical decline measured by a medical approach links these items to the real circumstances and a specified plan to help achieve individual objectives that can be supported by the social worker. The social or disability approach connects social functioning, data about the environment and ways of coming to terms with the demands of daily life. The experience of the person, their family and other professionals are also seen as important. With their contribution the care plan can be adjusted. The citizenship approach challenges the paradigm of expertise and it promotes self-determination.

The option to implement the 'Family Group Conference' as a method for social work with seniors when several needs increase and have to be tested for future planning. Family Group Conference work focuses on the network of the person at the centre of concern. The solutions coming out of that round table approach will show diversities of opinion and viewpoints. People are empowered, however, by the idea that they are able to decide what they are going to do (Homepage Familienrat, 2012).

A case management approach, according to the US model, which includes advocacy, broker, gatekeeper, linkage, coordination of care, social networking and supportive counselling, could assist here (Wendt, 2001). For social work, it could be shown that there are different options to deal with the challenges of active ageing and dementia respectively, and to handle the helping process with people with dementia diseases. But what of the vision of an inclusive society where seniors can participate and live with several needs and behavioural difficulties among us?

An initiative in Vorarlberg, in Austria, suggests answers. The vision is, that people with dementia can participate in official community life. Seven main topics are considered: dementia-friendly communities and regions, dementia and ethics, culture projects from people with dementia but also for people with dementia, care in hospital, qualifications of professionals and citizens, nutrition and sports/exercises and dementia, technologies and dementia to ensure the inclusion and participation of people with dementia.

The city of Bludenz focuses on being a dementia-friendly town. People with dementia and people without dementia meet every day in different places, in supermarkets, in the neighbourhood, at service centres and in administrative services. There are the crucial starting points to make things change (Homepage: aktion-demenz.at).

Conclusions

This chapter resulting from the Austrian contribution to the international university week in April 2012 in Malaga, and points out the importance of making professionals in social work sensitive to the needs of older people and people with dementia, arguing that there is a need for change in society. The concept of performance and achievement stands against the reality of human needs – to make human rights possible we need to go forward step by step towards creating an inclusive community life.

Note

For further information see www.pantucek.com .

References

Berr, C., Wancata, J. and Ritchie, K. (2005) Prevalence of dementia in the elderly in Europe. *European Neuropsychopharmacology*, 15, 463–471.

Blackman, T., (2000) Defining responsibility for care: approaches to the care of older people in six European countries. *International Journal of Social Welfare* 9, 181–190.

Boughtwood, D., Shanley, C., Adam, J., Santalucia, Y., Kyriazopoulos, H., Rowland, J. and Pond, D. (2011) The role of the bilingual/ bicultural worker in dementia education, support and care. *Dementia* September 13 DOI 10.1177/1471301211416173

Böhm, E. (1999) *Verwirrt nicht die Verwirrten*

Böhm, E. (2001) *Psychobiographisches Pflegemodell nach Böhm*. Grundlagen

Deger-Erlenmaier, H. (1992) Wenn nichts mehr ist, wie es war... Angehörige psychisch kranker Menschen bewältigen ihr Leben

Doyle P.J., de Medeiros, K. and Saunders, P.A. (2011) Nested social groups within the social environment of dementia care assisted living setting. *Dementia* 20.09.2011 DOI 10.1177/1471301211421188

Emilsson, U. M. (2012) The staff's view on dementia and the care in three cultures: A qualitative study in France, Portugal and Sweden. *Dementia* January 2012 vol. 11 no. 1 31-47 DOI 10.1177/1471301211416613

Hähner, U., Niehoff, U., Sack, R.,Walter, H. (1997) Vom Betreuer zum Begleiter. Eine Neuorientierung unter dem Paradigma der Selbstbestimmung

Kellnhauser, E., Schwewoir-Popp, S., Sitzmann, F., Geißner, U., Gümmer, M. and Ullrich, L. (2004) THIEMs Pflege. Professionalität erleben

Kruse, A. (2010) Lebensqualität bei Demenz? Zum gesellschaftlichen und individuellen Umgang mit Grenzsituationen im Alter

Marshall, M. (2005) Perspectives on Rehabilitation and Dementia

Pantucek, P. (2005) Soziale Diagnostik. Verfahren für die Praxis Sozialer Arbeit

Pantucek, P., Maiss, M. et al (2009) Die Aktualität des Denkens von Ilse Arlt

Pantucek P., Vyslouzil, M. et al (1998) Theorie und Praxis Lebenswelt-orientierter Sozialarbeit

Pilgerstorfer, A. (2009) Soziale Unterstützung als Ressource. Eine quantitative Studie über das Beziehungsverhalten Jugendlicher bzw. Junger Erwachsener mit Psychiatrieerfahrung

Popp, I. (2002) Verwirrt nicht die Verwirrten! Was bedeutet Pflege nach Böhm? in Heilberufe 7/2002, 36 – 37

Prince, M., Bryce, R. and Ferri, C. (2011): Alzheimer's Disease International. World Alzheimer Report 2011. The benefits of early diagnosis and intervention

Schneider, C .(2006) Pflege und Betreuung bei psychischen Alterserkrankungen. Eine gerontosoziologische-pflegewissenschaftliche Analyse

Wendt, W. R. (2001) Case Management im Sozial- und Gesundheitswesen

Web resources

Alzheimer's Association http://www.alz.org

Alzheimer's Association (2009) Alzheimer's Disease and Other Dementias http://www.alz.org/national/documents/topicsheet_relateddiseases.pdf

Alzheimer's Association (2012) take care of yourself. 10 ways to be a healthier caregiver http://www.alz.org/national/documents/brochure_caregiverstress.pdf

Alzheimer's Association (2012) Communication http://www.alz.org/national/documents/brochure_communication.pdf

AFI-Kids Homepage http://www.afi-kids.de/about/index.htm

aktion demenz Homepage http://www.aktion-demenz.at/home/aktuelles.html

APA - Austria Presse Agenturam 20.09.2012 http://science.apa.at/site/medizin_und_biotech/detail.htmlkey=SCI_20120920_SCI3945135229513538

Deutsche Gesellschaft für Algemeinmedizin und Familienmedizin (DEGAM) (2008) Demenz. DEGAM Leitlinie 12

Ellenbogen, Michael http://blog.alz.org/the-realities-of-alzheimers-and-overcoming-stigma/

Family Group Conference 29.10.2011 http://www.familienrat-fgc.at/ Land Salzburg (2012) Salzburger Landeskorrespondenz 19.10.2012 Digitales Assistenzsystem für Demenzkanke http://service.salzburg.gv.at/lkorrj/Index?cmd=detail_ind&nachrid=49903

International Psychogeriatric Association (2002) Behavioral and Psychological Symptoms of Dementia (BPSD).Educational Pack

Prell, M. (2011) Psychobiographisches Pflegemodell nach Prof. Böhm. Skript

Pschyrembel (2001) Klinisches Wörterbuch 259. Auflage

Schneider, C. and Wappelshammer, E. (no Year): Eine Interventionsstudie zum personenzentrierten Ansatz von betreuung und Pflege für Menschen mit Demenz. Skript

Statistik Austria (2011) Spitalsentlassugnen 2010

Theunissen, G. (2011) *Geistige Behinderung und Demenz. Situationsbeschreibung und Lösungsansätze aus rehabilitationspädagogischer Sicht* (Power Point Presentation) http://www.aktion-demenz.at/fileadmin/aktionen/2011/17-01-2011_Theunissen.pdf

World Health Organization (WHO) (2012) Dementia: a public health priority. http://whqlibdoc.who.int/publications/2012/9789241564458_eng.pdf

WHO (2010) ICD 10 Online Version http://apps.who.int/classifications/icd10/browse/2010/en

12

Spanish Public policies and practices with seniors:

Active ageing in local and regional public bodies

Maria Luisa Gómez Jiménez

Introduction

The definition of public policies regarding seniors in Spain

Spain is a decentralized Estate[1], which includes the definition of regional social policies regarding seniors. The social and democratic Estate of Spain[2] involves a significant role for public authorities in the definition of Social Rights. Chapter 1 of the Spanish constitution recognizes the charter of fundamental rights, including also rights which are described as being the directing principles of the political and social economy[3]. Theses principles inform public policy and are designed to promote social order among Spanish citizens, without being considered fundamental rights[4].

A reading of the chapter which introduces the socio-economic principles in the Spanish Constitution shows us the significance of the contents included therein. The chapter refers to the right to work, the right to the private property and the right to culture, but also integrates a specific attention to people in need, and dedicates a section to seniors (section 50[5]), another to disabled people (section 49), additional provisions to the family (section 39), to the provision of proper housing policy (section 47), and to the health care system that is needed (section 43).

From this description, we will emphasize the recognition of a seniors' public policy being included as part of the basic socio-economic order. Seniors are accorded fundamental rights as citizens and, in addition, there is recognition of social rights or principles derived directly from the part of the constitution we described above.

In the current chapter, we will pay attention to the description of both the rights of seniors as fundamental rights, and the public policy for seniors as a basic aspect of the Spanish socio-economic system and underpinning legislation.

Distribution of jurisdiction regarding seniors' care

To better understand the main characteristics of the seniors' policy, we need to define the role of public authorities in complying with the target of providing services and care for the group. This implies not just the precise definition of the concept of seniors[6] but also the definition of who is responsible for which part of the seniors' policy. In the case of a decentralized Estate such as Spain, this involves a distribution of jurisdiction among all public authorities with competence and responsibility for such provision. Thus, Regional Governments have assumed, in their respective institutional bodies, the jurisdiction and definition of a specific public policy for seniors. Besides, local authorities provide social services to all citizens in their territorial jurisdiction, including seniors living in the respective local city or municipality. This means that under the word 'seniors', several public bodies with different spheres of jurisdiction can act.

In addition to this, there are interconnected areas which interact with the main issue of seniors policy and which allows a better definition: that is, health care policy and housing policy as well as the pension system as a key example among others.

The significance of these different approaches allows us to draw the realistic picture of the fragmented and sometimes overlapping nature of seniors' policy in contemporary Spain. Thus, we will focus specifically on two components of seniors' policy; the more specific level of attention towards older people as a group, and the general one in terms of fundamental rights for all citizens and how this can be achieved across the different jurisdictions.

National policy for seniors

According to the Spanish Constitution, the national bodies have jurisdiction for health care and external health care provision, the social services system, and specifically the coordination of the health care and economic provisions applied to seniors. The reason for this derives from the inclusion of section 50 in the charter of principles of socio-economic direction, which involves a direct action of public authorities regarding the implementation of these principles locally. This is clearly demonstrated in respect of pensions and retirements care provision. The coordinating jurisdiction at State Level, determine not just the retirement age[7] but also the requirements to enter in the pension system and to afford certain social provisions.

'Moreover, at the national level, a step forward was achieved at the beginning of 2006, with the enacting of national legislation concerning dependency, and to reinforce policies to prevent the lack of autonomy in decision-making of disabled people and seniors[8]. Lately, the National Programme of Reforms of 2012, which have taken place in Spain following the requirements of the European Union, and in response to the economic crisis, demand specific attention and the reduction of expenses and social provisions defined at a national level for the whole country.

Other requirements connected with the idea of active ageing also involve actions from different public bodies, and have created a programme of activities focusing on improvements in the quality of life of seniors citizens at a range of levels.

Again, the institutional bodies able to provide and to set together those policies were not just the territorial bodies but also agencies entitled to do so under the central Spanish legislation. That was the case of 'IMSERSO'[9] Institute of Social Services for Seniors Citizens. This public body was developed after the creation by RDLoi 36/78 , of 16 November, of the management of health care provision in the social security system and unemployment, under the Institute for National Social Services. It was not until RD 1600/2004, July 2nd, however, that the IMSERSO was enacted.

In this framework, in November 2011, the General Department of Social Policy under the Ministry of Health, Social Policy and Equality, presented a White Paper on 'Active Ageing', prepared at the initiative of the government of Spain to serve as a guide for policies aimed at improving the quality of life of older people. Its preparation has involved not only the government but also older people's associations, social partners and numerous experts in the field of the third age.

The White Paper includes more than one hundred proposals that respond to the realities, desires and expectations of older people about their future. To do this, the views of older people about themselves and the general opinion of the public about older people were taken into account. It emphasizes lifelong learning, with particular emphasis on the impact this has on the world of elderly people such as increased personal autonomy and quality of life, improved personal skills, and different areas of development, including older people's use of information technology.

Important as it is as a reference document to guide policymakers and the political decisions they were to make, the document was not legislation but a working paper to encourage accomplishment of European Union requirements at a national level. This means that whilst the direction is set, it will be really implemented when specific sectoral policies adjust their rulemaking to make it possible regionally. It is necessary to have some understanding of the interaction of different sectorial policies affecting seniors life, and their coordinating legal framework at different levels (national, regional and local). This explains why, even if the white papers published in the public authorities were well known, the results were not really the direct translation of their premises into changes unless the political centre or the regional parliament wished to adapt their regulations to make it work. Because of the limitations of this paper to describe all the political interactions and all the sectorial legislation which need to be changed , we will focus, as mentioned above, on a wide description of policies and jurisdiction, paying attention to the legislation enacted in the Andalusian regional government regarding active ageing policies but we will provide a brief description of policies which will be needed to understand the implementation of these policies.

The impact of the economic crisis forces us to reconsider active ageing policy. It also makes us question how these active ageing policies can really make use of resources targeted at seniors needing a specific service or resource, and therefore a specific budget allocation.

Self-governing regions and policy for seniors in Spain: The case of Andalusian region

Each of the self-governing regions in Spain is, now, provided with a wide system of regulations addressing seniors' need. This stemmed from the Spanish Constitution enacted in 1978. According to section 148 and section 149, the State should address certain topics, such as the coordination of health care policies and economic development, public health and the creation of a national social services system.

Nevertheless, the development of these policies were not homogeneous, and each self-governing region enacted their own legislative body of regulations and rules. We will focus on the Andalusian case, since this self-governing region was one of the most concerned for the health care of their citizens. Andalusia provided from the earliest time much needed provision to seniors, and created its own set of rules to differentiate social services for seniors from social services for others citizens with other special needs (such as people with disabilities or those at risk of social exclusion).

The Andalusian self-governing region enacted its main Statutes in 1983[10]. The Andalusian Statute, which works as a basic rule of law in the self-governing region, distributed according to the Spanish Constitutions the duties and rights of Andalusian citizens and public authorities in the region. According to this Statute, Andalusia enacted the Seniors Act, 6/99, of 7 July. In this text, was written that following the directions of section 13.22 of the Statute and the implementation of the Regional Social Services Act, (Act 2/88, of April 4th), the self governing region will develop a specific policy for seniors. The reason for the legislation was to deal with the aging population in the region by improving their quality of life through the provision of health care and social services in the context of the framework of existing national regulations in this area. This legislation to improve care of seniors was significant since it determined the way of giving a voice to those wishing to do something positive in respect of seniors. This was especially important because of the increase of seniors in the region which according to the statistics will overcome the European percentage of senior people (those over 60 years) by six points in 2050. The number of people over 60 years of age is expected to grow by 7 % in the EU and by 16% in Andalusia.

There are a number of day care centres that provide space for promoting active ageing throughout the whole self-governing region. However, in Andalusia the increasing senior population competes for scarce resource.

This is compounded by the significant amount of elderly tourism-cum-migration choosing to retire in the region.

The impact of tourism is positive for the local and regional economy, but the need for the provision of services creates demands because of increased the number of people over 60. The number of German or Anglo-speaking citizens located in the south of Spain create a challenge in the design of policies for seniors in the area, and this is in addition to the impact of the economic crisis in the migration flows towards Spain in general[11].

The policies seek to encourage seniors to take an active role in the society while improving their health care by creating opportunities for them to be more actively involved in the design of their own provision. 'Aging, should be viewed as an opportunity rather than a problem', this statement from the director of Social Services in the Regional Government, points out the main objectives of the policies of active aging that the regional government was passing in order to meet the national direction in this area.

The national White Paper on active ageing introduces criteria that were developed in the regional White Paper, but neither can be implemented without the coordinated effort of public bodies at national and regional levels. According to the extant legislation at regional level regarding seniors, active aging policies introduce a layer of guidance for public bodies which demand the implementation of new services, even where existing ones are still taking place. This is the case in day care centres where many seniors attend and undertake social and cultural activities that aim to promote their autonomy and get older people involved in the cultural life of the community. This means that national policy is renewing the existing infrastructure of Spanish social services in the light of the European Union directions on active ageing.

Challenging questions arise, however, when the lack of economic resources at national or regional levels make it difficult to maintain the existing level of social services resources thus preventing full implementation of these policies[12].

Local Authorities scope regarding seniors services

It was very clear from the beginning of the organizational distribution of tasks among public bodies that local authorities were the ones authorised to deal with local issues and responsibilities, which affected the citizens living in that specific location. But soon, the larger authorities able to provide a wide range of services began to be seen in contrast to those smaller ones which could not afford such high investments in the care of its citizens. This was dealt with through the Spanish constitution by the passing of new legislation detailing local regulations able to set common rules for all in the fulfilment of the requirements established in the Spanish Constitution. The primary act to provide for this tool was the Basis Local Regime Act, (Ley de Bases de Régimen Local, Ley 7/1985, April 2.) This Act, in conjunction with the TRLB (Texto Refundido de Disposiciones Legales Vigente en material de Régimen Local, RD Leg 781/86, April 18th) set the common rules to be applied to all the town halls and local authorities and introduced the definition of the basic social services to be provided by local bodies to their citizens in the coordination with those provided by the state or the regional governments.

The provision of social services seeks to meet the needs and requirements of Spain's senior citizens. This is the same in the provision of health care which, within the national health care framework allowed town halls to complement services with others with the intention of keeping the population healthy. This included such services as water sanitation, the garbage disposal, or the cleaning of streets.

Thus, section 25 and section 26 of the LBRL, stated the list of tasks local authorities could fulfil when they were able to do so. The distinction then concerned the compulsory services the local body needed to provide and those provisions which were not compulsory, or could be linked to the political interest or economic capacity of the local body to assure it. In specifying which services were to be provided, the legislation employed the criteria in a way that bigger villages could afford a better allocation of resources in providing services to the increasing number of citizens living there. This created inefficiencies, however, and in turn this enabled the distinction among villages and services, affecting the quality of life of citizens, when villages were competing for getting better resources with limited incomes. The effect which this system introduced in the local tax systems and local land planning goods meant that it was not difficult to find villages with a higher number of seniors in less populated areas, where the provision of some social services were not even compulsory, and the birth rate was below the Spanish national one. By contrast, the wealthier villages were increasing their resources at the same rate as they could afford new facilities and better infrastructures. This process reached the point of a new reform in the legislation for local bodies, which took place in 2003, by means of Act 57/2003[13], December 16th, of greater municipalities. The objective of the act was to create better organizational bodies able to achieve the goals set by greater municipalities[14].

In the same scenario the definition of tasks that were not explicitly oriented towards municipalities but which were of interest of local bodies created enough room for the development of what it was called the 'improper local jurisdiction' of local authorities. These jurisdictions were involving higher investments and better qualifications but also were generating higher costs to keep running the system.

The situation lurched towards crisis when the economic crunch hit the local economics and prevented the development of supplementary services. Thus allowing localities to lower the level of services they could provide, without any infringement of the law. In response to this situation the new models for regulating local bodies propose the suppression of public entities and a different organization in the provision of services. Thus, the 'legislative project of rationalization and sustainability of local authorities', which was passed by the national government with the idea of setting structural reforms in the local organization introduced a new distribution of tasks affecting the provision of social services by local authorities. This will affect the development of active aging policies for seniors, whereas providing criteria of harmonization in terms of reducing the expenses and facilities, which can be offered to develop these policies.

In conclusion, the map of social services provision for seniors and therefore the development of active aging policies in Spain are connected with the idea of decentralization. The coexistence of different public bodies able to provide the same kind of services initially made possible the definition of active aging policies at national, regional and local levels. However, with the reduction of expenses which are resulting from the economic crisis, seems to be just the opposite model coming into force. The cut-offs will affect not just the reduction of the public sector and public authorities as we know it so far, but the reduction of their power in setting up new services or therefore to provide new active aging policies. In this scenario new imaginative measures need to be taken, seeking synergies among public bodies able to create efficient results for all.

Notes

1   As the Spanish Constitution points out in section one.

2   According to the Spanish Constitution: Section 1. 'Spain is a Social and Democratic Estate'.

3   The charter in the Constitution starts at section 39, with the guiding principles of economic and social Policy, introducing the protection to the 'family' and ends in section 52, with the recognition of the role of professional organizations.

4   The definition of fundamental rights has to do with defenses mechanism existing to protect and guaranty basic institutional rights.

5   Section 50 of the Spanish Constitution declares: 'To citizens in old age, the public authorities shall guarantee economic sufficiency through adequate and periodically updated pensions. Likewise, and independently of the family obligations, they shall promote their welfare through a system of social services which shall take care of their specific problems of health, housing, culture, and leisure'.

6   Interesting as it might be to reflect on the fact of how old do you need to be to be included in this group.

7   As for the debate regarding the retirement age, can be seen the European Parliament questions and the Spanish proposal of enlargement the retirement age gradually to reach the limit of 70 years old.

8   Researchers have addressed the controversial effects of this legislation, in the late years. We are not describing in this chapter the main measures which were introduced in the legislation but the reference which can be read in

9   IMSERSO the Social Security Administration Body responsible for handling Social Services supplementing Social Security System provisions and which deals with older persons and dependent persons.

10   This first rule was changed in the year 2007, to the actual, Andalusia Statute of LO 2/2007, of march 19th

11   http://www.diariosur.es/20090117/local/turismo/costa-mantiene-como-residencia-200901171807.html

12   El impacto de la crisis en las condiciones de vida de las personas mayors, Fundación Primero de Mayo, Madrid. Enero 2013, which can be read in: http://www.1mayo.ccoo.es/nova/files/1018/Informe56.pdf

13   http://www.boe.es/boe/dias/2003/12/17/pdfs/A44771-44791.pdf

14   According to this Act greater municipalities were those over 175.000 inhabitants, making the distinction among those over 175.00 and those over 250.000 inhabitants.

References

Libro Blanco de la Dependencia en España ,

Strategies for promoting active ageing in Andalusia, http://ec.europa.eu/research/innovation-union/pdf/active-healthy-ageing/20120403_easpd.pdf

Junta de Andalucía polices for Active aging: http://www.epractice.eu/files/documents/workshops/13771-1208261390.pdf

El impacto de la crisis en las condiciones de vida de las personas mayores, Fundación Primero de Mayo, Madrid. 2013,

Molero, Carlos: Analisys of the decentralization of public spending in Spain. University of Navarra, 2001.

Aleman Bracho, María del Carmen y García Serrano, Mercedes: Tercer Sector Buscando el equilibrio entre la solidaridad y eficiencia, en http://rua.ua.es/dspace/bitstream/10045/5796/1/ALT_06_02.pdf

Molero, Carlos, *Analysis of decentralization of public spending in Spain, in* http://mpra.ub.uni-muenchen.de/8056/1/MPRA_paper_8056.pdf

Anteproyecto de Ley de Racionalización y sostenibilidad de la Administración local, http://www.minhap.gob.es/es-ES/Prensa/En%20Portada/2013/Documents/ALRASOAL.pdf

13

The discourse of active ageing and Islamic constructions of old age: A bridge too far?

Sara Ashencaen Crabtree and Jonathan Parker

Introduction

For practising Muslims the definitive conceptualisation and understanding of the process of ageing is derived from the uncontested authority of the Holy Qur'an, which refers to old age in various *suras* (Quranic sections or chapters), although arguably by no means as often as death is referred to throughout the sacred script. Such references compose the believer's mind towards recognising that death is a natural and inescapable conclusion to mortal human life. Thereafter, divine resurrection and judgement await when believers will be admitted to Paradise and the unbeliever consigned to hell (Moody, 1990). Close familiarity with the concept and reality of death is encouraged among Muslims to emphasise the transitory nature of human life and the ultimate spiritual goal of the faithful (Raad 1998), something that has also characterised the Abrahamic religions. Old age in Islam therefore marks the decline of physical human life leading to the transition of ultimate transcendence to the afterlife. The portrayal of old age in the Holy Qur'an is entirely unsentimental, where loss and decrepitude is plainly acknowledged as inevitable fates, as shall be shown (Moody, 1990; Sapp, 2008). This is, however, not to overlook the subtle assurance of the position of honour and spiritual wealth that can be accrued by the wise.

The context of reflection on ageing

As this chapter is written it is the middle of a grey and icy January in Southern England. Gustav Holst's The Planet Suite is playing in the background and the writer is suddenly aware that the closing of the mercurial gaiety of Jupiter, the Bringer of Jollity yields to a new melody: an inexorable, slow-marching adagio measured by the tolling of melancholy bells - Saturn, the Bringer of Old Age plays. It is, quite frankly, a somewhat sinister piece of music in places, which rises to a crescendo representing mortal suffering until suddenly some sweet and graceful resolution is achieved towards the end of the piece. Old age, for Holst, the listener may infer, is a state that will be striven against, endured, suffered and deplored - unless the individual can somehow transcend the fear of the extinction.

This view of old age as necessarily one of grim decline is one challenged by positive constructions of ageing as a time of empowerment, individually and collectively, in terms of financial, educational, social and political capital, typified by the privileged position of the so-called Western 'baby-boomer' generation. However, Parker and Ashencaen (in this volume) note the disjunctures created the social devaluing of the ageing process in modern, Western society, which may be denied, for example, through cosmetic surgery and lifestyle choice – and the overt message of social policy that constructs old age and longevity as a costly social problem to be managed with dwindling public resources. To the extent that a commonly conveyed message is that the privileges of the older generations have been bought at the expense of younger cohorts, who face much less secure futures, and will have to work longer and harder to obtain fewer rewards compared to that of their parents' and grandparent's generations. The tensions portrayed between differing approaches to ageing are not, we infer, necessarily countered by the concept of active ageing, which need not deny decline and death.

However, while ageing is considered a demographic and social policy problematic in many industrialised nations, in predominantly Muslim societies this does not appear to be generally the case. We learn, for instance, that in Malaysia while eventually Muslim Malays will eventually be the largest aged sector of society among the various ethnic groups, demographics do not yet indicate that Malaysia can be counted as an ageing nation, (Ong et al., 2009). Nor does Malaysia's neighbour, the tiny, Islamic sultanate of Brunei, appear to voice any serious concerns about the indigenous ageing population, despite the authors stating that ageing will represent a significant socio-economic challenge by the now receding date of 2010 (Cleary, Maricar & Phillips, 2000). Likewise, ageing remains a marginal social policy issue in Indonesia with its majority population of Muslims standing at 88.2% in 2000, where the greatest number of people, and therefore ageing population, live on the islands of Java and Bali. Ageing in the Middle East presents a fragmented picture depending of poverty indictors and potentially civil conflict. Affluent societies like the United Arab Emirates pride themselves being a Welfare State par excellence (Ashencaen Crabtree 2007), where citizens (deemed Nationals solely) may enjoy excellent welfare provision in the form of generous pensions, good social care and cheap domestic labour, if families are unable to provide complete support. By contrast, in Egypt, social welfare resources are very scant, and where poverty and disability are a notable factor among older people, with the curious anomaly of 83.6% of elderly people being male breadwinners with more than two dependents to support but where the feminisation of old age through female longevity is not so clearly apparent as in some other nations (Aboulhassan and Abdel Ghany, 2012).

Although ageing *per se* may not be considered to be an issue in Muslim societies, in industrialised societies globally there is a trend towards increasing the number of working years through later retirement. In Malaysia, for instance, the former pensionable age of 55-years-old has now been moved up 60, being more in line with life-expectancy indicators. In the UK, by contrast, there is no longer a point by which employees may be pensioned off on the grounds of old age. The emphasis placed on economic, as well as social productivity in active ageing (OECD, 1998) is, perhaps, indicative of the global spread of neoliberal market ideologies, although the World Health Organisation also emphasises quality of life issues (WHO, 2002).

Returning to the UK as an example, the move from the dependency discourse created by older people's association with the Welfare State has been important in developing the active ageing discourse. What this means for Muslim elders in Britain is questionable as there is scant research literature available on the specific topic of how this particular group perceives and applies the concept of 'active ageing'; and indeed this reflects a wider, fragmented picture concerning ageing for Muslims in the wider Islamic *ummah* (community of believers) and across minority Muslim communities in Europe and beyond. Our understanding of this complex phenomenon therefore must be gleaned from the scant research literature that does exist pertaining to ageing and its corollaries among Muslims. Naturally such limitations in the scope of such an enterprise are likely to raise more questions than can be answered here. Accordingly, insights will be sought from among the diverse range of literary sources that form the current research-based canon informing our understanding of Islam and ageing.

Faith and spirituality across the lifespan, with a particular focus on ageing, has emerged from the margins to be seen as a phenomenon of rich interdisciplinary, academic interest replete with life experiences, symbolism and metaphor. The so-called 'theology of ageing' is challenged by Barnard (2004) as potentially ageist. However, the author develops a *conceit*[1] playing upon this contested term and the ageing of organised religion (Christianity in this case) in relation to the ageing 'world of thought' (Barnard, 2004: 131), by considering collective ageing and changing perceptions towards once established religious identities, concepts and certainties. One may extend this *conceit* further to reflect that of the three Abrahamic religions, if Judaism is the 'mother' (Sapp, 2008: 20), then Islam is the youngest offspring. Furthermore, while Christianity, the elder child, has long since reached its maturity and is evidently now waning in Europe, judging from the decline of church attendance[2] in the West (Hayes, 2001; Glendinning & Bruce, 2006). Islam, globally the second-largest religion after Christianity, is, by contrast, one of the fastest growing (Al-Krenawi, 2012).

Although such theorisation of ageing, faith and spirituality is largely based on research findings pertaining to Christianity and to a lesser extent, Judaism, in keeping with the tripartite, if sadly often contested and undermined, unity of the Abrahamic religions, certain insights hold great relevance for Islam as well. Yet, whereas for the former two religions, ritual observance of prayer is said to increase in old age (McKinley, 2001) this may not be true of Islam. The well known, seamless holism of Islam where integrating daily prayers of the believer into the ritual fabric of the measured day, may mean such observations relating to other religions may be regarded by some as irrelevant for practising Muslims. Based on her study of British Asian communities Firth (1998: 158) observes that Muslims, Hindus and Sikhs age 'in the context of the whole lifespan'. By which we may understand that there is no conceptualised segment of human life from birth to death that is regarded as distinctive and separate, and specifically so in terms of ageing. This differs from the classical European tradition as depicted in Shakespeare's 'seven ages of man' where man's final age is pathetic in being divested of his sensory and mental faculties (Moody, 1990). To this point in reference to Islam, we shall return.

Shakespeare's rehearsal of man's roles ('parts') upon life's stage as a series of distinct ages, concluding, in all senses with the seventh age, was likely to court audience dismay along with amusement. Today, despite greater longevity and health, the image of the 'second childhood' of decay, remains disturbing. The stereotypic 'cult of youth and hardness' that has pervaded the post-War, global North, as the dominant image of human legitimacy and worth, is revisited by Wilcock (1998: 75) in terms of the inferred contrasting delegitimising of its binary opposite : old age. So too, the associated qualities that old age is meant to confer: experience, wisdom, patience, reminiscence, acceptance - these too become devalued (Wilcock 1998). In this vein, Goodman (1998), following the writings of Rabbi Schachter-Shalomi, considers the acquisition of the status of 'elder' through the virtues of old age well lived. Consciously donning the elder, 'sage' role, and all that is conveyed by that, returns us to the valuing of seniority; and serves to 'heal' the injuries to the ageing process, which are particularly acute in many modern societies.

The renaissance conceptualisation of the stages of man are revised and reflected in Erickson's psychosocial lifespan model, with each 'stage' having its own particular challenges to be resolved. Thus, the older individual, however one defines that, with the prospect of death on the foreseeable horizon, must confront the dilemma of 'integrity versus despair' (Papalia et al., 2003). Satisfaction with the life lived, where time spools to its close, must be gained over the existential dread of mortal extinction if contentment is to be achieved (MacKinlay, 2001). Moreover, Wilcock (1998) argues that although the common assumption is that increasing loss defines old age, on the contrary the consolidation of the individual's identity is strengthened and energised with the passing of the anchoring of the years – demonstrating in part what Erickson would describe as *ego integrity*. We become, in effect, more of what we may regard ourselves as intrinsically to be, which is not dependent upon ephemeral youth and the socially-valorised physical attributes associated with that transitory state. Instead, as Goodman (1998: 66) notes good ageing appears to constitute 'joyful conscious ripening'. While Metropolitan Anthony (1998) employs the analogy of the fiercely burning but extinguishable 'flame' of youth, mellowing to the consoling 'light' of the sage, made radiant by the grace of contemplative wisdom.

Ageing in Islam

To reiterate, there is a paucity of research literature examining the phenomena of ageing among Muslims and capturing their experiences. Perhaps this lack of research creates a statement of integrity across the lifespan and an acknowledgement of natural progress from birth to death over time. However, we have little rigorous research evidence to rely on and must instead acknowledge this to be an area ripe for further inquiry. In reference to Muslim minority communities of the West much of this limited body of knowledge relates to cultural competence issues in medical/

nursing practice primarily but also social work, with a particular focus on effective intervention with elderly Muslims, particularly migrants and refugees (see Parker, 2000; Parker & Ashencaen Crabtree, 2011). Writing from the context of the USA, Van Gorder & Ellor in their study of 'ethnogeriatrics' considers the host of challenges facing the elderly Muslim migrant struggling to relate to a new culture, norms and lifestyle, against the ominous and traumatic backdrop of and public attitudes towards the events of 9/11. The authors explore the tension felt in Muslim families towards the powerful wish to continue to provide complete care for chronically ill elders and their reluctant need for specialist support. Caution is offered to health care providers to avoid alienating elderly Muslim patients through cultural ignorance, who mare potentially already experiencing multiple loss and a significant degree of cultural dislocation resulting in anomie (Van Gorder & Ellor, 2008).

This study resonates with that of Abu-Bader *et al.* (2011) who consider obstacles to successful acculturation of Muslim migrant elders to the USA where failure to make a successful adjustment is likely to result in clinical depression. These authors articulate the two main adjustments expected of such individuals who may be contending with the repercussions of personal trauma and loss. The first adjustment relates to a change in status, effectively a demotion from respected heads of families, to dependents on adult children and grandchildren. Secondly, adjustments must be made to accommodate a very different lifestyle. In each case, as noted by Van Gorder & Ellor (2008) the elder's experience and knowledge of their personal culture and mores may seem irrelevant in the new context.

The issue of Muslim migrant elders from the Middle East is examined in the British context, where both the events of both 9/11 and the later London Islamist bombings of the 7th July 2005, and resultant social attitudes of Islamophobia, generate an uncomfortable sense of vulnerability and exposure among Muslim communities (Fiddian-Qasmiyeh & Qasmiyeh, 2010). Once again, as in the American studies, the theme of disorientation, dispossession, cultural dislocation; and the humiliating belittling of the respected status traditionally accorded to masculinity and age is examined. For the Palestinian and Kurdish participants in this study, State Benefits, necessary for family survival under the condition of unemployment, are seen to usurp the highly respected role of husband and breadwinner.

However, in contrast to these accounts of the perceived diminishment, and even emasculation, of male migrant elders, Dossa's (1999) study of ageing, Ismaili Muslim woman in Canada - forced migrants from Idi Amin's expulsion of Asians from Uganda in 1972 – is enlightening. For such women it would seem that although the cultural norms dictating gender still guide much of daily practice, these are negotiated in parallel to the norms of the new cultural setting. This has enabled some Ismaili women to enjoy professional opportunities not otherwise available to them; and where ageing has enriched and consolidated these women's layered identities successfully to 'a transnational dimension' (Dossa, 1999: 268).

When discussing ageing among Muslims most writers will refer to the pivotal centrality and collective nature of family life (Abu-Bader et al., 2011, Van Gorder & Ellor, 2008; Sheikh, 1998), including whether this is extended beyond the wider family to include the wider community or tribal *hamula* (Al-Krenawi & Graham, 2001). In her study of gender and inter-generational extended and nuclear families in the United Arab Emirates, Ashencaen Crabtree (2007) notes that in keeping with Firth's (1998) observation, old age is regarded as a fluid concept and not particularly dependent on any specific age. Instead it is more connected to role: where, according to some respondents, once her first grandchild is born an Arab woman can no longer regard herself as young, despite the continued early age of marriage and childbearing in the region. The gendered aspects of ageing are something that is, however, pronounced.

The close-knit nature of Muslim families remains a defining feature regardless of the increasing nuclearisation of once extended families (Ashencaen Crabtree et al., 2008). Throughout the Holy Qur'an one may found repeated references urging the promotion of respect to parents, as commanded by Allah, and to a degree comparable only to Confucianism in filial zeal (Sapp, 2008)

'We have enjoined man to show kindness to his parents. With much pain his mother bears him, and with much pain she brings him into the world'. 'Al-Ahqaf', Holy Qur'an: 46.

'Your Lord has enjoined you to worship none but Him, and to show kindness to your parents. If either or both of them attain old age in your dwelling, shown them no sign of impatience, nor rebuke them: but speak to them kind words. Treat them with humility and tenderness and say: 'Lord, be merciful to them. They nursed me when I was an infant.' 'The Night Journey', Holy Qur'an: 17.

In the light of these Islamic precepts further insights can be drawn into the marginalisation of the elderly Muslim migrant struggling to find orientation in jarringly unfamiliar cultures that have apparently forgotten how to value the virtues of survival to old age, something that invokes the concept of respect so often discussed uncritically within Western social work circles.

The Holy Qur'an makes clear the expectation that parents should be cared for by their adult children, as they too were cared for in their infancy. Today, such expectations among many of Muslim descent remain unchanged, and in countries such as Brunei Darussalam, despite its affluence, care of older people is described as grounded in the Malay-Muslim way of life (Cleary *et al.*, 2000). In conversation with one of the authors a middle-aged, cosmopolitan Tunisian woman living in Britain was complacent about the substantial financial support she received from her adult son. In Tunisia, we learned, where ageing parents failed to receive due care and attention from their adult offspring the parents were likely to be held culpable by neighbours for having failed to instruct their children properly in Muslim precepts. In terms of addressing the social issues that population and individual ageing raises, multicultural and multi-faith perspectives have much to offer, and social work is in a primary position to learn from and share such.

Although reaching old age is a token of divine blessing, the portrayal of old age is unappealing in being described as the 'vilest' condition (Moody, 1990). This appears to contradict any notions of grace attached to old age for Muslims; yet, as we learn, this is to misunderstand the ultimate meaning attached to this stage of life in Islam. In order to be able to comprehend what construction the concept of 'active ageing' might hold from an Islamic perspective, it is important to understand that for Muslims the ultimate destination and *goal* of human life is death. This may seem a perversely pessimistic stance that overtly contradicts the 'up-beat' messages that the notion of active ageing normally attempts to promote, with its vision on increased social and civic participation (Parker & Ashencaen, 2013), the universities of the 'Third Age', and the growing social awareness of the financial and political power among the *new* 'old age' in contemporary society. Islam, however, carries an austere message regarding both old age and mortality. Death is referred to throughout the Holy Qur'an, and in a prosaic and unvarnished way, as both natural and inevitable. Believers in the sacred writings are urged to die true Muslims and to dispose of their worldly goods to their next-of-kin as a matter of practical necessity, and as an Islamic good in itself it would seem. There is little sentimentality associated with death but instead the Faithful are encouraged to encounter, witness, reflect on and experience death as both inexorable and closer to the living than may be comfortably appreciated (Raad, 1998). Such teachings begin in early childhood, and visiting the dying and attending graves is encouraged to reinforce the message (Firth, 1998). It is in fact, striking how matter-of-fact even very young Muslims appear to be towards a topic that is considered to be distasteful and even embarrassing – to the extent of being shunned in contemporary Western society (Ashencaen Crabtree and Baba, 2001; Holloway, 2006).

Death for Muslims, as is the case in Judaism and Christianity, is regarded as only the transition from one state of existence to another, where Allah's judgement awaits (Sheikh, 1998). This unavoidable human destiny is therefore viewed with trust and hope, as being the ultimate human goal that will bring the Faithful into the presence of the divine and immutable, by whom the span of each living mortal is decided. Thus death heralds a new, transcendent state of being, through the shedding of mortal remains that of themselves cannot be viewed as an end to human existence as such.

Duties towards the dying and the dead must be observed in Islam, where the former are encouraged to die piously uttering prayers with their last breath (Sheikh, 1998). The body must be ritually prepared for the grave, and must be buried within 24 hours (Ashencaen Crabtree *et al.*, 2008; Raad, 1998). Post-mortems are to be actively avoided for a number of reasons: Kormaromy (2004) claims that this is because it disfigures the body; and because the inherent motive of questioning the cause of death is impious. Sheikh (1998) argues that post-mortems are disliked, but not strictly forbidden, because they will delay burial; and because it has been suggested by the Prophet Muhammed (pbuh) that maybe the dead can still experience physical sensations (Ashencaen Crabtree *et al.*, 2008). Finally, mourning may follow a prescribed path where the bereaved family will be very closely supported for 40 days when public mourning is ritually brought to a close (Raad 1998). However, Abu-Lughod (1992) notes that although Islam prescribes how the form of funeral and mourning rituals, local customs may provide a culturally-informed shape to proceedings, such as the highly demonstrative group lamenting engaged in by some Bedouin Arab women. This is regarded as potentially subversive in appearing to be public defiance or protest against Allah's will, which for piety demands acceptance and, following Kormaromy's (2004) point, 'dampens speculation' about causation and culpability (Abu Lughod, 1992: 193).

How then is the *vile* state of old age to be understood in Islamic terms (Moody, 1990). Furthermore, the question must be raised whether this can be viewed as at all compatible with the new, empowering vision of 'active ageing' or whether such tenuous bridges between two such dissimilar constructs collapse at the first test.

Al-Asr: The late afternoon of old age

The sura 'Al Asr' offers a familiar symbolisation of the length of the human life condensed to a single day. The late afternoon of human life is contemplated as a time of loss, with the physical loss of strength, beauty, fertility, loved ones potentially, and even mental faculties. Thus, the descent into night is to return to Shakespeare's 'second childhood', as Sapp (2008: 22) notes in quoting from the Holy Qur'an: 'whosoever we give long life we turn back to the process of creation'.

Like the Torah, the Qur'an offers no sentimentality or attempts at denial but frankly acknowledges the ravages of time on longevity (Sapp, 2008). Denial of the obvious repercussions of ageing, which is also the denial of mortality, is not a social construction of 'active ageing' that would be considered sensible or pious in the Muslim schema. Furthermore, in Islam, such serious physical compromises do not alter the reverence and respect that the pious Muslim should have towards his ageing parents, which is not dependent upon whether long years lived have resulted in the acquiring of great wisdom or not, as filial respect demands that elderly parents are not contradicted, ridiculed or scolded (Moody, 1999).

For Muslims, learning and education is a lifelong, religious duty open to both males and females (Ashencaen Crabtree *et al.*, 2008). This conforms closely to conventional notions of active ageing. Moreover, age does not dilute the need for daily, ritual, religious observance (Firth, 1998), which as Wilcock (1998: 81) has noted form the 'habit energy' of the disciplined life that retains its integrity through continued adherence to patterns of behaviour and underlying principle laid down over the years. Thus, as Barnard (2004: 182) notes, ageing is simply the way of 'doing living'; and MacKinlay (2001: 135), following Au and Cobb (1995) aptly comments, 'ageing is the process of 'being towards death'. The older person as sage and mentor is a role that is easily compatible with Islamic views of old age, much in keeping with MacKinley's concept of the 'last career' borrowed from Heinz (1994), where the older person may become a conduit of cultural, religious/ritual and symbolic meanings and values passed on to younger generations.

MacKinley (2001), again following Heinz (1994), argues that medical advances may rob or disrupt the aged individual's role of bearing and bestowing cultural and religious meanings within the family/tribal/ community context. So too Parker and Ashencaen (in this volume) refer to how this role may be distorted or denied by social pressures to abandon the traditional role and demeanour of the elder-turned-sage in favour of more socially valorised, youthful behaviours and appearances; an insidious misinterpretation of active ageing that, rather, privileges continued youthfulness. To this extent, Islamic constructions of seniority may seem decidedly out-of-step with modern society's priorities, when old age is valued not in denial of its losses but in the full knowledge of them, which must be embraced and accepted to attain wisdom. The long journey towards death is one rich with transcendent promise.

> 'To see dying as no more than what we call the end of life is to miss life's most intoxicating spiritual ascent' (Wilcock, 1998: 78).

If modern secular society denies suffering any meaning, as Byock (1996) expresses the case, then this contradicts the particular but resonant stance of each one of the Abrahamic religions, which by contrast attach great spiritual significance to human suffering, although the nuances for each faith may differ. The depredations of age carry religious import for Muslims therefore, as signifying most clearly the return to Allah, and where increasing dependency strips away human vanity of its strength and autonomy. The meaning of old age therefore is both to celebrate Allah's power and goodness; but also to emphasise that all creation is completely dependent upon that. The ageing process enables Muslims to engage more fully in meditation upon divine truths that are requisite for wisdom and transcendence. Acceptance of the destiny of mortals in returning to Allah, as revealed with increasing clarity by the ageing process – and is the ultimate manifestation of the meaning of 'Islam': to submit (Sapp, 2008).

Conclusions

The contested concept of 'active ageing' with its notions of emancipation from restrictive ideas of old age as a time of loss and social disengagement; along with its focus on the flexing of renewed empowerment within an ageing society rather than an emphasis on ageing well and healthily but not denying or accepting an inevitable progress towards the end point of life, is not one that appears to sit easily with the doctrines of organised religions such as Islam, which is guided by and derived from antique sacred texts where man's allotted span, in common with Christianity, was placed at no more than seven decades. The banishment of conventional old age, to paraphrase Sapp (2008), in favour of a new model of ageing by contrast sits well with society's socio-economic needs to ensure that the older citizen do not drain resources but remain healthy and economically productive for as long as possible. By contrast, Islam's continued emphasis on old age as a time of material and mortal losses but one that is also elevated by increased spiritual awareness, forms a disjuncture with these contemporary discourses. Creating a bridge between these two apparently incompatible positions is evidently a challenge; and one where any connections may, perhaps, only emerge from the margins of potentially competing discourse.

The position of Muslim elders as intrinsically worthy of respect and care would seem to naturally bestow an automatic advantage for such individuals, as opposed to other groups living in a society that deplores and scorns old age as worthless and a burden. Indeed, adopting such an approach could connect with active ageing in terms of living well and healthily. Nonetheless, the impact of Islamophobia in the prejudicial, psychological equation of the terms 'Muslim' with 'terrorism' is one that weighs heavily upon Muslim minority groups; and where, it would seem, elderly migrants are at greater risk of social isolation, loss of status and depression than their younger counterparts, whose attitudes may eventually be influenced by adopting the host nation's cultural values towards ageing. Yet, the acquisition, consolidation and dissemination of knowledge, along with the mentoring of younger generations are models that accord well with both active ageing discourses and with Islam. This is likely to be one of the most pivotal contributions and bridging paradigms for all older citizen that can be commonly articulated and shared across the divisions of culture, faith, politics and ideology.

Notes

1   This term pertains to the complex but ludic interplay of symbolic meaning, such as can be found in the verses of the 'Metaphysical Poets', such as John Donne, Andrew Marvell and their ilk.

2   MacKinley (2001) argues that ageing Church-goers may prefer to reduce formal observance of religion in Church in preference for more convenient worship at home.

Reference

Aboulhassan, N. and Abdel-Ghany, T. 2012. The impact of urbanization and globalization on social welfare policies in Egypt, in S. Ashencaen Crabtre, J. Parker and A. Azman (eds.) *The Cup, the Gun and the Crescent: Social welfare and civil unrest in Muslim societies*, London: Whiting and Birch.

Abu-Bader, S.H., Tirmazi, M.T. and Ross-Sheriff, F., 2011. The impact of acculturation on depression among older Muslim immigrants in the United States, *Journal of Gerontological Social Work*, 54, 425-448.

Abu-Lughod, L., 1992. Islam and gendered discourses of death, *International Journal of Middle East Studies*, 25, 187-205.

Al-Krenawi, A., 2012. Islam, human rights and social work in a changing world. *In*: Ashencaen Crabtree, S., Parker, J. and Azman, A., eds. *The Cup, the Gun and the Crescent: Social Welfare and civil unrest in Muslim societies*, London: Whiting & Birch, pp. 19-33.

Al-Krenawi, A. and Graham, 2001. The cultural mediator: Bridging the gap between a non-western community and professional social work practice, *British Journal of Social Work*, 43(3), 289-304.

Anthony, Metropolitan of Sourozh, 1998 The spirituality of old age. *In*: A. Jewell, ed., *Ageing, Spirituality & Well-being*. London: Jessica Kingsley Publishers, pp.30-38.

Ashencaen Crabtree, S., 2007. Culture, gender and the influence of social change among Emirati families in the United Arab Emirates, *Journal of Comparative Family Studies*, 38 (4), 575-587.

Ashencaen Crabtree, S. and Baba, I., 2001. The Islamic perspective in social work education. *Social Work Education*, 20 (4), 469-481.

Ashencaen Crabtree, S., Husain, F. & Spalek, B., 2008. *Islam and Social Work: Debating values, transforming practice*. Bristol: Policy Press.

Barnard, K., 2004. Ageist theology: Some Pickwickian prolegomena, *In*: A. Jewell, ed., *Ageing, Spirituality & Well-being*. London: Jessica Kingsley Publishers, pp.180-196.

Byock, I., 1996. The Nature of suffering the nature of opportunity at the end of life, *Clinics in Geriatric Medicine*, 12(2), 237-252

Cleary, M., Maricar, H.A. and Phillips, D.R., 2000. Ageing, Islam and care for older persons in Brunei Darussalam. In: D.R. Phillips, ed., *Ageing in the Asia-Pacific Region*. London: Routledge, pp. 322-333

Dossa, Parin A., 1999. (Re)imagining aging lives: ethnographic narratives of Muslim women in diaspora, *Journal of Cross-Cultural Gerontology*, 14: 245-272.

Fiddian-Qasmiyeh, E. & Qasmiyeh, Y. 2010. Muslim asylum-seekers and refugees:

Negotiating identity, politics and religion in the UK, *Journal of Refugee Studies*, 23(3): 294-314.

Firth, S., 1998. Spirituality and ageing in British Hindus, Sikhs and Muslims In: A. Jewell, ed., *Spirituality & Ageing*. London: Jessica Kingsley Publishers, pp. 158-174.

Fon, S.O., Phillips, D, R., Hamid, T.A. Ageing in Malaysia: progress and prospects. In: FU, T.-H. & Hughes, R., 2009. Ageing in East Asia. London: Routledge, pp. 138-160.

Glendinning, T. and Bruce, S., 2006. New ways to believing or belonging: Is religion giving way to spirituality? *The British Journal of Sociology*, 57(3), 399-413.

Goodman, J. 1998. Harvesting a lifetime. *In*: A. Jewell, ed., *Spirituality & Ageing*. London: Jessica Kingsley Publishers, pp. 65-70.

Hayes, B.C., 2001. Gender differences in religious mobility in Great Britain, *British Journal of Sociology*, 47(4), 643-656.

Holloway, M., 2006. Death the great leveler? Towards a transcultural spirituality of dying and bereavement. *Transcultural spirituality and nursing practice*, doi: 10.1111/j1365-2702.2006.01662.x pp. 833-839

Kormaromy, C., 2004. Cultural diversity in death and dying, *Nursing Management*, 11, 32-35.

MacKinlay, Elizabeth, 2001. *The Spiritual Dimension of Ageing*. London: Jessica Kingsley Publishers.,

Moody, H.R., 1990. The Islamic vision of aging and death, *Generations*, 14(4), p. 15-19.

OECD, 1998. Maintaining Prosperity in and Ageing Society. Paris: OECD.

Ong, F.S., Phillips, D.R. and Hamid, T.A. (2009) Ageing in Malaysia: progress and prospects, in T-H, Fu and R. Hughes (eds.) *Ageing in East Asia: Challenges and policies for the Twenty-first century*. London: Routledge.

Papalia, D.E., Wendkos Olds, S. & Duskin Fieldman, R., 2003. *Human Development*, 9th e1d. Boston: Mcgraw-Hill.

Parker, J., 2000. Social work with refugees and asylum seekers: a rationale for developing practice. *Practice: Social Work in Action*, 12 (3), pp. 61-76.

Parker, J. and Ashencaen Crabtree, S. (2011) Soziale Arbeit mit Migranten in Grossbritannien. *In*: Kunz, T. and Puhl, R., eds. *Arbeitsfeld Interkulturalität: Grundlagen, Methoden und Praxisansätze der Sozialen Arbeit in der Zuwanderungsgesellschaft*. Weinheim: Juventa Verlag.

Parker, J. & Ashencaen Crabtree, S. Problematising active ageing: a theoretical excursus into sociology of ageing for social work practice. *In*: Gómez Jiménez, M.L. and Parker, J. Active Ageing? Perspectives from Europe on a much vaunted topic. London: Whiting & Birch.

Sapp, S., 2008. Mortality and respect: Ageing in the Abrahamic traditions, *Generations*, XXXII(2), pp. 20-24.

Raad, S.A, 1998. Grief, s Muslim perspective. In: K.J. Doka & J.D. Davidson, eds. *Living with Grief: Who We Are, How We Grieve*. Philadelphia: Bruener/ Mazer, pp. 47-56.

Sheikh, A., 1998. Death and dying – a Muslim perspective, *Journal of the Royal Society of Medicine*, 91, 138-140.

Thursby, G.R., 1992. Islamic, Hindu and Buddhist conceptions of aging. In: T.R. Cole, D.D. Van Tassel & R. Kastenbaum., eds. *Handbook of the Humanities and Ageing*. US: Springer Publishing Co, pp. 486-.

Van Gorder, A.C. & Ellor, J.W., 2008. Ethnogeriatrics and comparative religions methods for gerontological research into topics of religion and spirituality, *Journal of Religion, Spirituality and Aging*, 20(3), 206-219

Werth, L., Blevins, D., Toussaint, K.L. & Durham, M.R, 2002, The influence of cultural diversity on end-of-life care and decisions, *American Behavioral Scientist*, 46, 204-219.

WHO, 2002. *Active Ageing: A policy framework*. Geneva: World Health Organization.

Wilcock, P., 1998. Death and the spirituality of ageing. *In*: A. Jewell, ed., *Ageing, Spirituality & Well-being*. London: Jessica Kingsley Publishers, pp.75-85

The Editors and Contributors

Editors

Prof. Dr. María Luisa Gómez Jiménez is Associate Professor of Administrative Law at the University of Málaga (Spain). She is also an associate at the Latin American Program, at Harvard University and Visiting Fellow at the Centre for Social Work, Sociology and Social Policy, at Bournemouth University. Maria Luisa acts as Liason on Public Policy at Higher Education Technology and Learning Association (New York). She has been a visiting fellow at the Virginia Center for Housing Research at Virginia Tech, (Blacksburg), at the Joint Center for Housing Studies in Harvard University, Visiting Scholar at the Center for European Studies and the Institute for Global Law and Policy (Harvard Law). Maria Luisa researches and publishes in the area of Administrative Law and Public Policy, especially concerning land planning and housing law in an international context; social rights, e-health, global administrative law and human rights.

Prof. Dr. Jonathan Parker is Professor of Social Policy & Social Work and Director of the Centre for Social Work, Sociology and Social Policy at Bournemouth University, and Visiting Professor at Universiti Kebangsaan Malaysia. He was one of the founders and director of the Family Assessment and Support Unit, a placement agency attached to the University of Hull, and Head of Department of Social Work. He was Chair of the Association of Teachers in Social Work Education until 2005, Vice Chair of the UK higher education representative body, the Joint University Council for Social Work Education from 2005- 2010, and is an Academician with the Academy of Social Sciences.

Contributors

Dr. Sara Ashencaen Crabtree is Head of Sociology at Bournemouth University and Visiting Professor at Universiti Kebangsaan Malaysia.

She has worked extensively overseas in Southeast Asia, Hong Kong, and the Middle East and is widely published in areas of discrimination and disadvantage, cross-cultural issues and belief. She is the author of the first European book on *Islam and Social Work*. She is currently engaged in research concerning women's relationships with religions.

Prof. Dr. Cornelia Kricheldorff is Vice Rector and Director of the Institute for Applied Research, Development and Training (IAF), Catholic University of Applied Sciences Freiburg, Germany. She is a specialist in gerontology and learning and ageing.

Mgr. Lenka Maťhová graduated from the rehabilitation studies programme in the Faculty of Health and Social Studies, South Bohemia University, Czech Republic, where she now works as a lecturer in the Department of Social Work from 2003. She focuses on social work with seniors, student practice and supervision and issues of occupational therapy, therapies and specific approaches to seniors. She is a member and a volunteer in the nonprofit organization Training Canistherapeutic Association Hafík in Třeboň and a social worker and therapists in the Crisis Center for Children and Families in the South Bohemian Region.

Dr. Katrien Meireman studied sociology at the KU Leuven, Netherlands. She works as a lecturer and researcher at the Leuven University College, Department of Social Work. Her main fields of interests are social policy and social geography.

Dr. Jaap Olthof is a sociologist working in the Academy for Social Sciences at the| Hanzehogeschool, Groningen, Netherlands.

Lina Orlova, is a PhD student at the Department of Social Work, Vilnius University, Lithuania. Her main topics of scientific interest include quality of life, social care services for older people and qualitative methodology in the social sciences.

Mag. (FH) Andrea Katharina Pilgerstorfer lectures on the Bachelor Studies in Social Work at the University of Applied Sciences in St. Pölten, Austria. She also works as a manager of a family care facility "Familienhilfe PLus" (Caritas, St. Pölten).

Elke Plovie studied Educational Sciences at the KU Leuven, Netherlands and is studying for a PhD at the University of Groningen. She is currently working as a lecturer and researcher in the Department of social work of the Leuven University College and as a teaching assistant at KU Leuven. Her research focuses on active citizenship and the body of knowledge of social work.

Assoc. Prof. Dr. Egle Sumskiene of the Social Work Department, Vilnius University, Lithuania, is a social worker, sociologist and expert on disability, mental health and human rights issues and also works in a Lithuanian NGO focusing on mental health and human rights issues.

Prof. Dr. Gabriele Schaefer is an academic in the Social Work Department of the Hochschule/ University of Applied Sciences, Bremen, Germany. She has worked for many years as an academic in New Zealand prior to this and has researched and published widely in psychology for social work.

Mgr. Zuzana Staffová graduated from South Bohemia University, Faculty of Health and Social Studies. She has extensive experience in practising canistherapy and social work with both children with disabilities and seniors. She worked as a special pedagogy teacher in a non-profit organization called "Krteček" in Písek. Currently she is employed at the Municipal Office in Písek at the Social department as head of local administration in the social field. She is a member, a volunteer and a professional consultant of special pedagogy in the non-profit organization Training Canistherapeutic Association Hafík in Třeboň.

Index

www.ingramcontent.com/pod-product-compliance
Lightning Source LLC
Chambersburg PA
CBHW050428280326
41932CB00013BA/2036